September, 2009

To my good friend, Lillian,
With my best wishes,
Love,
Dale

A Duck Looking
for Hunters

Dale N. Amend
LtCol Dale Amend

Copyright 2009

Cover graphics and design by Melanie Amend, Albuquerque, NM

Technical editing by Margo Bouchard, MCP, Albuquerque, NM

Publishing advice and assistance by Donn A. Byrnes, Sage Mesa Publications, Los Lunas, NM

Photos taken from the author's personal collection

Original Map data and information taken from The Perry-Castaneda Map Collection in the University of Texas Library with permission

Map data extraction and adaptation by Melanie Amend, Albuquerque, NM

First Edition - 2009

Library of Congress Control Number: 2009903144

ISBN: 1-4392-3561-9

Table of Contents

Table of Contents (cont.)

To Nancy

My best friend, My lover
My wife of more than five decades
My partner for life

Only the loving providence of our kind and gracious God
could have made you mine.
I am eternally grateful.

Acknowledgments

For many years Dee Amend was alternately my most enthusiastic cheerleader and my harshest slave-driver. "Write the book! Get started!" Eddie Amend gave wise counsel and performed continuous general editing through the entire process of writing the book.

Continuing Education at The University of New Mexico pumped into my previous-century brain the elementary keyboard and computer skills necessary to begin composition. Margo Bouchard patiently instructed me and directed me to a writers' conference full of people who knew a lot about writing books. At the conference I met the person who would become my publisher.

All of my children and their spouses helped on the project. They managed to observe, "Well, you're making progress" rather than "You still don't know much about your computer."

Elaine and Brian Legan set up my first computer in my office. I successfully ignored it until it went away. They later gave continuing computer assistance via the telephone and over sandwiches at lunch time.

Marshall Amend surreptitiously installed my second computer which suffered the same fate as the first candidate. He later managed my acquisition of the excellent new machine which was used in the production of the book. I depended extensively on his computer expertise for the maintenance of back-up disks, the integration of photos into the manuscript and much more.

Bill Hubbard made good suggestions and gave perceptive criticism from his vantage point as a commercially published author.

Donn Byrnes, my publisher, combined insightful sharp criticism with professional praise for the product. As a fellow Air

Force pilot, he understood the FAC business and spoke the pilot's technical language. His company, Sage Mesa Publications, transformed all of my assembled materials into the book you are reading.

My wife, Nancy, proofed everything each time it was re-written. She listened patiently to my complaints when things did not progress well and shared my smiles when something was satisfactorily completed. She cared and supported me.

All of you contributed your capable assistance, your time and your interest. You gave of yourselves. I return my most sincere THANK YOU!

Preface

In 1965 the United States began a large increase in military forces committed to the conflict in Vietnam. I was part of it. This book is the first person, personal experience, true story of my year in Vietnam.

I was a US Air Force pilot, a Forward Air Controller, in South Vietnam. I flew a light unarmed airplane, low and slow. It was my job to locate enemy targets and mark them with smoke rockets or smoke grenades. I then directed the fighter aircraft on air strikes in support of troops on the ground or against other targets.

The story takes place mostly on the 2,400+ foot plateau known as the Central Highlands of South Vietnam. (see maps pages x and xi) The area is distanced from the coastal plains with respect to geography, population, character and weather. My squadron was dispersed around thirteen operating locations. We flew from Pleiku, Ban Me Thuot and the short dirt air strips of eleven other more remote locations. Much of our activity was in conjunction with the Green Berets of the Army Special Forces Camps.

This is a story about war. War is not pretty. War is not nice. Frequently, the requirement is to kill or be killed. This book includes many accounts of the conflicts between the good guys and the bad guys. In war, the good guys don't always win. It hurts when one of your own good guys doesn't make it.

I was not the typical guy involved in the Vietnam War. I wasn't the eighteen or twenty year old slogging along on the ground carrying a rifle and a pack. I was a thirty three year old captain with a wife and four kids at home. My contemporaries were largely pilots who "live in fame or go down in flames..." Our job was different. We had many who came home with well deserved recognition and many who went down in flames.

This story goes well beyond the war itself. It presents varied people, places and events on the periphery of the shooting war proper. The events and places do not fit neatly into a strict chronology. Many subjects are grouped into chapters by type rather than by time. A dateline at the beginning of each chapter helps the reader keep track of time, events and locations. The story over all is presented in roughly chronological form from October 1965 to September 1966.

Everything in this book is completely true. It is the story of what I knew, what I saw and what I did. The times, places and events are presented with their actual names. The actual names of most of the people have been replaced by pseudonyms to protect the privacy of individuals. People who were so widely known as to be public figures are presented under their own actual names. Also, people whose names have been used publicly in other publications are presented under their own actual names.

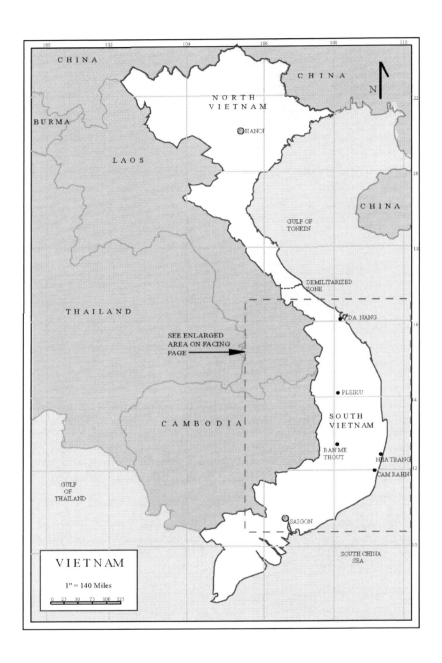

CHINA

NORTH VIETNAM

CHINA

N

BURMA

LAOS

⊙HANOI

GULF OF TONKIN

CHINA

DEMILITARIZED ZONE

THAILAND

DA NANG

SEE ENLARGED AREA ON FACING PAGE →

PLEIKU

CAMBODIA

SOUTH VIETNAM

BAN ME THOUT

NHA TRANG

CAM RAHN

GULF OF THAILAND

⊙SAIGON

SOUTH CHINA SEA

VIETNAM

1" = 140 Miles

0   25   50   75   100   125

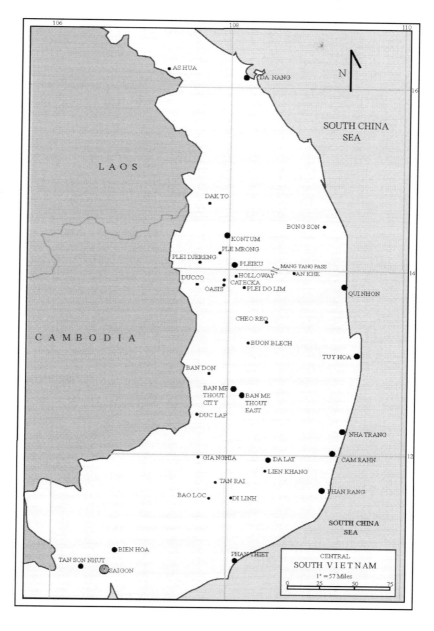

N

106 108 110

• AS HUA

• DA NANG

16

SOUTH CHINA
SEA

L A O S

DAK TO

BONG SON •

• KONTUM
PLE MRONG

PLEI DJERENG

• PLEIKU

MANG YANG PASS

• AN KHE

14

DUCCO

• HOLLOWAY
CATECKA

OASIS

• PLEI DO LIM

QUI NHON •

CHEO REO

• BUON BLECH

TUY HOA •

BAN DON

BAN ME
THOUT
CITY

• BAN ME
THOUT
EAST

• DUC LAP

C A M B O D I A

NHA TRANG •

• GIA NGHIA

• DA LAT

CAM RAHN

12

• LIEN KHANG

• TAN RAI

BAO LOC •

• DI LINH

PHAN RANG •

SOUTH CHINA
SEA

• BIEN HOA

TAN SON NHUT •

SAIGON

PHAN THIET

CENTRAL
SOUTH V I E T N A M
1" = 57 Miles
0   25   50   75

- xi -

Prologue

My radio jarred me alert and wide-eyed. "Any FAC! Any FAC! This is Savoy Two Niner. We're in trouble." The call was spoken in a muted voice, just a whisper, but I could hear it clearly. The call conveyed a message of urgency in a dangerous situation.

I was flying a visual reconnaissance mission in my light, unarmed plane over the Central Highlands of South Vietnam. I was looking for any evidence of enemy activity, but seeing nothing unusual. In five or six seconds my uneventful day became extremely busy. I became the on-scene Forward Air Controller responsible for directing close air support needed by a Special Forces patrol calling for help. No big deal. That was my job as a FAC.

I answered immediately, "Savoy Two Niner, this is Baron One Zero. Where are you and what do you need?"

Fortunately our radio contact was good both ways, limited only by the patrol's need to speak very quietly due to their dangerous nearness to a large enemy force. They described their situation.

"Baron One Zero, Savoy Two Niner. We're a scouting patrol out of Ducco. We are about fifteen klicks west of the camp. We're on the bank of the tributary that flows into the big river on the Cambodian border. A large group of VC are crossing the tributary right under our nose. We need to get the Hell out of here, but they're so damned close we can't move or they'll see us. We need help! Bad! There's a lot of them. If you can put an air strike on them now, you can get a whole bunch of them and save our ass at the same time."

"Two Niner, say your exact location." They gave me their coordinates on the map. I wrote them on my window with grease pencil. "Give me a little time. I'll try to scramble the A-1s from the alert ramp at Pleiku."

Savoy Two Nine was out looking for VC (Viet Cong) activity. Wow! They found it! The patrol had taken up an observation post just over the southeast bank of a secondary river which flowed into the large Ya Krong Po Ko River, the border between South Vietnam and Cambodia. Their situation was dire. They were a patrol of a dozen Green Berets on the edge of an enemy force of many hundreds. If they made a mistake, they were dead. Without help, their survival was questionable.

A rare circumstance had just developed. This was a prime "target of opportunity." If I could successfully direct a surprise air strike on the VC, it could be very effective. It could wipe out a large number of Viet Cong and get the patrol out of trouble.

Chapter 1

Savoy Two Nine in Serious Trouble

May 17, 1966 – Over the Central Highlands of South Vietnam

I called the Pleiku radar control point. "Peacock, this is Baron One Zero." No answer. No surprise. I was too low for radio contact. I started climbing while I located the correct map covering the area where Savoy Two Nine was hiding. That was why I always carried that case full of maps. A little higher now, I tried again. "Peacock, this is Baron One Zero."

This time it worked. "Baron One Zero, this is Peacock."

"Peacock, Baron One Zero, requesting the immediate scramble of the A-1s from the alert ramp. I have friendly troops in close contact with a large enemy force. They need help quick."

1.1 – The A-1 Skyraider, flown by the First Air Commando Squadron in Pleiku

1.2 – A personal greeting from the armament boys

"Roger, Baron One Zero. I'm scrambling a flight of two A-1s right now. Dagger Three One flight is on the way."

"Roger, Peacock. Instruct them to fly west from Pleiku and contact me. I will have further instructions for them as soon as we have radio contact."

The two A-1 pilots ran from the ready room to their waiting airplanes, took off and headed west. So far, everything was working.

The VC were using a large fallen tree as a footbridge to move their unit from the southeast side of the river to the northwest side. The big log also functioned as a bottle-neck, concentrating them into a group. They were vulnerable to air attack, especially if they were hit by surprise.

I stayed far away from the location of Savoy Two Nine to avoid alerting the VC about possible air activity. The success of

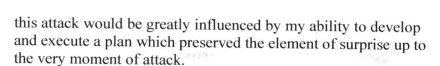

this attack would be greatly influenced by my ability to develop and execute a plan which preserved the element of surprise up to the very moment of attack.

I took the coordinates from my window notes and carefully placed an X in lead pencil at the right place on my 1:50,000 scale topographical map. With the patrol's location defined, I formulated a plan for the attack.

Ball point pen lines previously drawn on my map showed the patrol was on approximately the 210 degree radial of the Pleiku VHF Omni Range (VOR) navigation radio. I needed that information to instruct the A-1s in terms they could understand using their navigation radios.

The O-1E airplane we FACs flew didn't have the VOR navigation radio, but the A-1s used it extensively. The earlier plotting of the Pleiku VOR information onto my maps was what I needed for this strike. It enabled me to talk with the A-1s in terms of their navigation radios. At the same time I could talk to the scouting patrol in terms of the maps both the patrol and I used regularly.

When I talked to the A-1s, I used my UHF radio which the ground troops did not have. When I talked to Savoy Two Nine, I used my FM radio which the A-1s did not have. The fighters and the ground troops could not talk to each other.

The A-1s checked in, "Baron One Zero, Dagger Three One. We are airborne, headed west from Pleiku."

"Dagger Three One, Baron One Zero. Hey, you guys got up pretty fast. I'm glad you're available. I have what may turn out to be a very good target for you. Proceed outbound on the two four zero radial from Pleiku to the Cambodian border. That's the big river. I will rendezvous with you at the intersection of the two four zero radial and the big river. I will be at four thousand feet. (4,000 ft mean sea level on the altimeter was 1,500 ft above the ground.)

"I'm sending you out beyond the target so the VC won't see you or me until we attack them from the back side. After our rendezvous, you will follow me down the big river to the point where a tributary flows into it from the northeast. Make wide S turns as necessary to stay behind me. We will fly up the tributary to the target area. The target is the open area to the northwest of a large fallen tree which reaches across the river. The VC are using the log as a footbridge to cross from the southeast to the northwest side of the river. My smoke will mark the start of the target area.

"You will make your run from the southeast to the northwest. Start your ordnance delivery at my smoke and fan it out to cover the open area. Do not hit short of the river. That's where the friendly patrol is hiding. I have not yet seen the target. I'm working from the map coordinates the patrol gave me. As soon as I can confirm the target visually, I will mark it and clear you in immediately."

"Roger, Baron One Zero. Sounds good. We're heavy with both fuel and ordnance so our minimum loiter speed can't be too slow. Our S turns will have to be pretty wide, but we'll stay behind you. Can't you paddle your canoe a little faster?"

So far everything was going as planned. The VC hadn't seen or heard the A-1s or me. I wanted to keep it that way until we arrived at the target and hit them without warning.

The A-1s reached the intersection of the 240 degree radial of the Pleiku VOR and the Ya Krong Po Ko River only a couple of minutes after I did. They followed me down the river to the confluence where the tributary came into the big river. I turned up the tributary toward Savoy Two Nine's coordinates with Dagger Three One following me. I had briefed Savoy Two Nine on the plan of attack. They were watching for us to arrive.

After we left the large river and started up the tributary, I read my map as carefully as possible. Anyone could have followed the big river. Following the smaller twisting tributary was a lot harder, and I needed to get it right the first time. I still hadn't seen the target. It was the X which I had placed on the map with the coordinates from Savoy Two Nine. I needed to visually pinpoint the target immediately when we got there.

I read the shape of the smaller river and the contours of the adjacent terrain on my topographical map as we neared the target. We were getting close. The plan was excellent and it was working to perfection. The VC would have no clue of the impending attack until they saw me. A few seconds after they saw me, I would have a smoke rocket on the target and the A-1s would commence the attack. Great plan.

We were not quite there yet, less than one klick to go and then, "Hey, Baron, where are you going? You just flew over me."

"Damn!! They're lost. **Lost!"**

They weren't completely lost. They misread their map and gave me coordinates telling me they were about one klick farther up the river than they actually were. They confused one bend in the river and mistook it for another. It was an easy mistake to make. Down on the ground, they really couldn't see the forest for the trees.

I slammed the control stick to one side, stomped on the rudder and jerked the airplane into an extremely abrupt 180 degree turn. Sure enough, with my left wing down, I spotted the log footbridge which crossed the river. I shoved the nose down and put a white phosphorus smoke rocket onto the riverbank at the northwest end of the log.

"Dagger Three One, you're cleared on target."

The A-1s quickly adjusted to my abrupt course reversal without hitting me, and rolled in like we pre-briefed prior to arrival at the target. They made repeated bombing and strafing runs until they expended all of their ordnance.

The map reading error by Savoy Two Nine gave the VC perhaps twenty or thirty seconds to scatter and take cover as best they could, but they were really caught by surprise out in the open. It was an unusually successful air strike.

Savoy Two Nine watched the whole show from front row seats in their close range hiding place and applauded silently. The next time I talked with them, they were anything but quiet.

Two days later, on May 19, 1966, one of our FACs, Capt Leland Yates, banged on my wall and yelled, "Hey, Amend, get your ass over to the club. Savoy Two Nine is here and they want to buy drinks for you."

Savoy Two Nine was a group of a dozen Green Berets from Ducco Special Forces Camp, about forty miles southwest of Pleiku. Capt Finley was the leader of the patrol. He and two of his men had come to Pleiku looking for me. They were at the officers club watching for me to walk up. Finley saw my name tag, "Baron One Zero."

"God Damn, I'm glad to meet you! You can't believe how glad I am to meet you! You really saved our ass! We had to come to Pleiku to find you and buy drinks for you."

"Hey, man, I was just doing my job as a FAC. I'm glad I happened to be in the right place at the right time. It means a lot to me to meet you guys. Otherwise, I'd just remember the call sign "Savoy Two Nine" and the voice on the radio. It's good to know your name and see your face. I sure don't want your job."

We shook hands and slapped backs enthusiastically and talked about everything that had happened two days earlier.

I said, "You guys sounded pretty serious down there. I could tell you were barely whispering, but you came through clearly over the radio."

"Serious! We were scared shitless! There were hundreds of them and a dozen of us. You saved our ass! Your A-1s attacked about two hundred of them that just crossed the river on the foot log. We'd been scouting that place for the last ten days. We counted nearly one thousand VC crossing the log during that period. Are you sure you don't want a beer? I can't believe you're drinking that orange crap."

"No, this is OK, thanks."

"How come you flew past us when you came up the river?"

"You gave me the coordinates for the next bend farther up the river."

"Yeah, I was afraid of that. I thought we might have identified the wrong bend. It's hard to tell when there are so many trees. We could see you coming up the river and then you flew past us. Man, you really turned that little airplane around fast when I told you that you'd flown past us. The lead A-1 came close to hitting you."

"It <u>was</u> kinda close. Could you guys see everything during the attack?"

"Hell, yes, we could see! We had ring side seats just a little above the southeast bank of the little river. We looked down on the area and watched you pound them on the northwest side. They stayed hunkered down all of the time the fighters were there, except when you flew over. Every time you went by, you got a lot of ground fire from them. I do believe that you pissed them off. But you saved us."

It was extremely gratifying to meet Finley and his guys. It made me feel like I had really done something good for real people who were in serious trouble. Their exuberant praise of me personally was so generous it made me somewhat uncomfortable.

"I couldn't hear the ground fire, but that's not surprising. Sometimes we can hear it when they're shooting at us, but lots of times we never hear it. Were you able to get a body count after the attack?"

"No chance! We stayed hidden all the time from our first radio call to you until a few minutes after the fighters finished their bombing and strafing runs. We think the A-1s got quite a few of them. When the airplanes left, twenty or thirty more VC ran across the foot log and then all of them ran off to the northwest. When we thought they were all gone, we took off to the southeast and made it back to camp."

"Were all of your guys OK?"

"Yeah, we didn't even get shot at. They never even saw us. I really want to buy you a beer. Naw, that's wrong. I want to buy you a <u>case</u> of beer. No, that's still wrong. I want to buy you <u>ten</u> cases of beer."

Chapter 2

Don't Send Me to Minot

1958 – Over Oklahoma

We were above the clouds flying smoothly at 15,000 feet in beautiful blue skies when the right engine decided to quit. The airplane quickly lost altitude and descended into the heavy clouds that continued from their tops at 13,000 feet all the way to the ground.

Flying is sometimes described as hours of boredom interrupted by moments of terror. That can indeed be very true.

I was flying the schoolhouse for the Air Force Navigator Training Program at James Connally Air Force Base in Waco, Texas. It was a good job. On that particular day my friend, Cal Thomas, was my co-pilot. We were flying a routine training mission, but the training wasn't for Cal or me. The training took place in the back of the airplane, the schoolhouse. Ten or twelve students were seated at tables to accommodate the use of maps and navigation instruments. Two or three instructors walked around the schoolhouse supervising and teaching the students.

The airplane was the twin reciprocating engine Convair T-29, a rather new airplane sometimes called The Cadillac of the Air Force. It weighed around 43,000 pounds at take off, had good performance, even on one engine, and had a good safety record. Pilots flying it for Navigator Training logged lots of flying time which would later look good on their Air Force flying records. Those records could also serve to open doors into commercial flying with the airlines, an option which quite a few Air Force pilots later pursued.

Sudden engine failure is a startling surprise to a pilot. My first consideration was to determine whether the engine could be kept running to produce partial power. Partial power is a lot better than none, but failure to properly shut down the engine and feather the propeller can sometimes lead to a fire in the engine. There was no squeezing any more power from this engine. It was finished. Although I couldn't tell why at the time, maintenance personnel later found the shaft on the engine oil sump pump had sheared, causing the engine to fail.

The airplane quickly dropped down into the clouds, so I had two serious problems. I had to fly the plane on flight instruments while attending to the failed engine. I shut down the engine and feathered the propeller to reduce aerodynamic drag. While I was determining just how well the airplane was going to fly on one engine, Cal handled the radio calls.

"Oklahoma City Center, this is Jack Tar Two One Three Zero Seven. We have an emergency."

From our "Jack Tar" call sign, the Center already knew our aircraft type, the nature of our mission and that we were flying on an "on top" clearance, remaining clear of clouds. Our "on top" flight clearance required us to visually maintain physical separation from clouds and other air traffic once we had reached our operating altitude above the clouds.

"Jack Tar Zero Seven, this is Oak City Center. What is your emergency?"

"We have a failed engine. We are about thirty miles southwest of Oak City. We are unable to maintain "on top" clearance on one engine. We are in heavy clouds now, descending rapidly, currently passing eleven thousand feet. We must continue to descend until we get down to an altitude the airplane can maintain on one engine. Don't yet know what altitude that will be. Request instructions and clearance for landing at the nearest suitable field."

"Roger, Zero Seven. You are cleared from your present position direct to the Oak City VOR (Oklahoma City Visual Omni Range Navigation Radio) for a VOR approach to Tinker Air Force Base. Expect Tinker GCA (Ground Controlled Approach by radar) pick up as you cross low cone inbound on your VOR approach. Current conditions at Tinker are five hundred feet (cloud ceiling) and one mile (visibility) with intermittent light rain showers. Winds are south at twelve knots. Keep us advised of the altitude you are able to maintain."

While Cal talked with Oak City Center, I studied the let down chart. I was about to execute an instrument approach I had never made to a field where I had never landed. The Center cleared other air traffic out of our way and gave us priority for an approach and landing at Tinker Air Force Base.

The letdown through heavy clouds, the instrument approach, the GCA and the landing all went well. When the airplane touched down on the runway, a few cheers from the back told me those guys thought that I had done a good job. I taxied the plane into the parking area on one engine and shut everything down.

It was interesting to watch as the schoolhouse full of wide-eyed students and instructors filed off the airplane in Oklahoma City. They had expected to land that afternoon at their home base in Waco, Texas. Instead they had just spent the last twenty anxious minutes seated in the crash landing position, leaning forward onto their parachute chest packs against their tables. They looked from side to side out the windows seeing one propeller turning normally and one propeller not moving. They were glad to be on the ground. So was I.

I was finalizing things in the cockpit when I realized the lead navigator instructor hadn't left the plane. He was leaning forward into the cockpit to talk. "Ya know, Dale, that was very interesting. I heard this plane could fly on one engine, but I'd never seen it happen. Quite frankly, you had a bunch of scared people in the back. Some of them were convinced that we were all going to bust our ass together in one big hole in the ground. You did a great job."

"Thanks, Art. I appreciate your comments. Cal helped me and we did what we were supposed to do. It's nice when it works."

He reached forward to shake my hand. We both smiled. It was a good feeling.

Considerably after the Oklahoma City incident, when I had acquired more experience in the plane, I was upgraded to the status of Instructor Pilot. I was assigned to the Instrument Flying Section where my job was to teach ground school and give other pilots their annual instrument flying check rides. It was an even more interesting job with an added touch of prestige.

It was great until Capt Poage's annual instrument flight check. I was assigned to give him his check ride.

Poage had served as a pilot in the Korean War. He was a reserve officer and left active duty after Korea. He had been recalled to active duty against his wishes. When I came to know him, he was a nearly forty year old unhappy "old captain" and didn't like anything, especially young lieutenants. He flew as little as possible, rubbed the other pilots, mostly young lieutenants, the wrong way and was widely disliked.

He wanted me to understand <u>he</u> was fifteen years my senior and out ranked me. We also both knew I was the Instructor Pilot, the Aircraft Commander, and assigned to grade his performance in instrument flying. His proficiency was gravely inadequate. I expect he already knew he had earned a failure before the following incident which topped off his check ride.

We made a practice instrument approach to the Tyler Airport, southeast of Dallas. The last part of the normal procedure was to lower the aircraft landing gear and wing flaps, then adjust engine power settings to execute a landing out of the practice approach. We were allowed to make only practice approaches to that airport, never to land, so Poage knew that we would not be landing.

As we neared the runway, I told him, "You have 'made the field'. Go Around." He took his feet off the rudder pedals and put them flat on the cockpit floor, took his left hand from the control column and his right hand from the throttles, folded his hands in his lap and said, "I can't go around. I'm committed to land."

He seized the dramatic opportunity to "see what the smart-assed young lieutenant will do with this situation." It was a stupid, dangerous stunt.

There were good reasons for having a pilot, a co-pilot and sometimes a flight engineer for the airplane. Particularly at critical times, both a pilot and a co-pilot were required. Depending on the situation, the flight engineer was also valuable. On this occasion, it would have been nice to have a flight engineer in the jump seat. Two more working hands in the cockpit would have been helpful, but we were flying without a flight engineer.

Poage sat with his hands in his lap and watched. I was extremely busy for a short while doing what two crew members should have been doing to execute the go around. The skills of a proficient Instructor Pilot were needed to handle the situation.

My only comment to Capt Poage was, "OK, Sir. We're done with your check. Would you please move to the back and ask Lt Stenerud to come up for his check." When we landed I gave my boss a complete report of the flight.

Word travels fast. A few days later when I walked into the squadron ready room there were several pilots there. I was greeted with smiles, a little applause and some comments, "Yea! You flunked the sour, crotchety, old bastard!"

It put me in an embarrassing position. "Knock it off! That's not true. Don't say it. He failed his instrument flying check. It just happened to be my job to report the facts."

Poage wasn't finished. He wrote a letter to my boss, Capt Duncan, intending to defend himself. Duncan, the head of the Instrument Flying Section, called Poage in to talk.

"Poage, you have put yourself between a rock and a hard spot. You made false statements about Lt Amend in your letter. Amend is a very good Instructor Pilot and a conscientious man who gave you more than every benefit of any doubt. I stand behind him one hundred percent. He didn't fail the check ride. <u>You</u> failed the check ride. And that stupid stunt at the end of the approach to the Tyler airport could have smashed the airplane and the people on it.

"You have two choices with me. You can take the instrument ground school again, have an extra practice flight and another check flight. If you successfully complete all of that, you're passed for this year. If you decline to do any of that or fail any part of it, I'll give this whole report to the wing commander and let him decide what to do with you. How do you wish to proceed?"

Poage wasn't an idiot. He complied with the first option.

By complete coincidence, about three weeks later I pulled out of the parking lot a bit late to go home and happened to see Poage standing by his car. Although the answer to my question was obvious, I rolled down my window and asked anyway, "Sir, do you have a problem?"

"Damned flat tire. No jack."

"I have one in my trunk. I'll get it."

I was wearing a flying suit, a work uniform, and he had on an office uniform with coat and tie. I made the appropriate suggestion, "Let me get it for you, Sir."

Not another word was exchanged between us as I mounted the spare tire on the car and put the flat tire into his trunk. I made a parting wave of my hand as I got into my car. Poage never said a word of thanks and didn't acknowledge my parting gesture.

I didn't hate him. I honestly felt sorry for him. The pilots in the ready room made the correct call. He really was a sour, crotchety, old bastard.

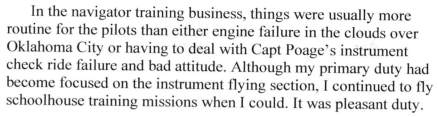

In the navigator training business, things were usually more routine for the pilots than either engine failure in the clouds over Oklahoma City or having to deal with Capt Poage's instrument check ride failure and bad attitude. Although my primary duty had become focused on the instrument flying section, I continued to fly schoolhouse training missions when I could. It was pleasant duty.

On one of those easy days I was flying co-pilot for my old buddy, Cal Thomas. It was a beautiful day and my friend and I were enjoying the leisure of going from point A to point B on auto pilot while the navigators did their thing in the schoolhouse behind us. Cal gazed out the window, waxed philosophical and mused, "I wonder what the poor people are doing today."

It was a well worn comment that alluded to the fact that, at least for the time being, we had it pretty good. I returned the usual cliché, "Yeah, we have it pretty tough, don't we?"

Cal then abandoned philosophy and pursued a practical matter, "You know something else that's tough? Have you tried this burned bony buzzard butt the in-flight kitchen calls fried chicken?" He was gnawing on something brown he'd dug from the lunch box on his lap.

I laughed and said, "Ya know, Cal, I almost got in trouble over one of those flight lunches last week."

"Really? How'd that happen?" He crushed out the last of his cigar. (The cigar was legal when there was no oxygen in use.)

"Well, you know George Doxtater and his wife have a three month old baby. I was flying with George last Tuesday and said to him, 'George, I can tell that you're not helping your wife change any diapers'. He looked puzzled. I pointed at the ugly brownish-yellow mustard he was squeezing from the plastic packet onto his ham sandwich and said, 'If you were changing any diapers, you wouldn't be seriously considering eating that.'"

"Man, that's awful. Did George get mad?"

"I'm not sure, but he looked kinda sick and threw the whole sandwich into the trash can. I quickly changed the subject and started talking about college football. Hey, a new subject for you. What's the latest you've heard from Steve Echols?"

"Steve got his letter of acceptance last week from one of the airlines. He started flying this airplane before you and I did. He's logged over three thousand hours of flying time in three years. Not bad, huh? The airlines like to see that on a resume."

It was an easy flight. It's nice when things are routine.

I came into the house through the back door and edged close to Nancy in the kitchen. Without looking up from her work she said, "You flew with Cal Thomas today, didn't you?"

"You can tell?"

"Sure, I can tell. You stink." She hated Cal's cigars, but she turned and pulled me close anyway and kissed me warmly.

Her affection didn't go unrequited. The kiss I gave her in return registered a couple of notches higher on the passion meter. Life was good on the home front, too.

That was the "flying the schoolhouse" business. It was good. But I haven't told how I got into the business.

I graduated from Colorado State University in 1954 with a BS in General Agriculture and a commission as a Second Lieutenant in the US Air Force. Nancy Garfield, the best woman God ever created, consented and we were married.

Nancy was from a prominent family in Fort Collins, Colorado. It was a small college town with one high school. The high school had one set of Garfield boys and all six of them were Nancy's older brothers. Pop Garfield's old Chevrolet, with its license plate "666666" representing the six boys, was parked near every high school athletic contest. He was on the sidelines and his boys were in the middle of things. They were good athletes and everyone knew them.

Mom Garfield took care of all of them. She nursed their hurts from football in the street, basketball in the driveway and ice hockey on the back grass, even when ice skates clomped into the kitchen. She was tolerant and loving in all they did.

There was a surprise at the end of the production line of Garfield children. It was a girl! She was different. Thank God for the difference! Following the six boys, she stomped through high school in her own way. She was a good student, the prom queen, a cheerleader, a skilled student athlete, Worthy Advisor of Rainbow for Girls and lots more. I didn't know her in high school, but when she hit college, it was more of the same for Nancy. The stage was larger and the young woman was even better. How could I not notice? I grabbed her and held on.

Our lengthy courtship seemed destined for only one conclusion, but I was two years ahead of her. Our schedules didn't quite match, but we worked out a compromise. The Air Force granted my request for a one year delay in reporting for active duty while Nancy finished another year of college. Pop Garfield wasn't happy when he figured out his only little girl was still a few credit hours short and would not graduate. However, all of the Garfields liked me better than the multitude of previous guys who pursued their daughter/sister. We left everyone in the Garfield family happy and launched together for Air Force Pilot Training.

Air Force Pilot Training class 56-S began with "primary" in Moultrie, Georgia. Hawthorne School of Aeronautics taught us to fly in the T-34. It was the fully acrobatic military version of the civilian Beechcraft Bonanza. After the T-34, we flew the T-28 which was roughly the equivalent of World War II fighters.

Those who made it through primary proceeded to "basic" training. Some went to multi-engine training and some went to single engine training. I chose the single engine program and was approved. Basic training was at Webb Air Force Base in Big Spring, Texas. Our class was the first all jet class in Air Force Pilot Training. We flew the T-33, known as the "T-Bird."

Flying the jet was new and exciting. Feeling the G force of acceleration for the first take off was a thrill. There were lots more new experiences coming.

Half way through the program I watched in awe as a visiting jet interceptor F-102 took off. With afterburner blazing, it disappeared out of sight going straight up. The next time I flew solo as a student, I decided to see how long our T-33 jet trainer would fly straight up. The answer was very predictable. Not very long! The airspeed indicator quickly dropped dangerously low. I had unwittingly created a student pilot learning experience.

I executed the "vertical recovery procedure" according to the book. I pulled back on the control stick until the nose came down to where I could see the horizon and then rolled the plane right side up. It was better than falling from the sky tail first. I was glad I remembered the recovery procedure when I needed it. I didn't try the prolonged straight up maneuver again.

Instrument flying was challenging and eliminated many students from flight training. Close formation flying with my wing tip overlapping the wing tip of another jet was a thrill. Shooting solo through canyons of snow white blossoming cumulus clouds, right side up and upside down, rolling and looping, gave understanding to the widely revered poem by John Gillespie Magee, Jr.

High Flight
Oh, I have slipped the surly bonds of earth
And danced the skies on laughter-silvered wings;
Sunward I've climbed, and joined the tumbling mirth
Of sun-split clouds—and done a hundred things
You have not dreamed of—wheeled and soared and swung
High in the sunlit silence. Hov'ring there,
I've chased the shouting wind along, and flung
My eager craft through footless halls of air.
Up, up the long, delirious, burning blue
I've topped the windswept heights with easy grace
Where never lark, or even eagle flew.
And, while with silent, lifting mind I've trod
The high untrespassed sanctity of space,
Put out my hand, and touched the face of God.

I did all of that. I felt privileged to do what Magee spoke of so eloquently. Most folks go through life and never have that experience, but I did. On July 28, 1956, the Air Force pinned wings on my chest and declared me a pilot.

2.1 – US Air Force T-33 Jet Trainer   *2.2 – Pilot Training over West Texas*

*2.3 – 1st Lt Dale Amend – a new US
Air Force Jet Pilot July 1956*

Upon graduation from pilot training it was time to go somewhere and do what we had been trained to do. There were several choices, including jet fighters.

I got my first choice, flying the schoolhouse. Things were going smoothly for me. On October 4, 1957, the Russians launched the world's first satellite. President Kennedy responded boldly, announcing the U.S. goal to have a man on the moon in ten years. The international space race was on -- full throttle. As part of its scramble to improve technological capabilities, the Air Force established a program which included sending officers with non-technical college degrees back to school to get degrees in science and engineering. I happened to fit that category.

With my bachelor's degree in agriculture, I seized upon the opportunity to further my education. I left flying the schoolhouse in January 1960 and went back to school for a degree in Mechanical Engineering from the University of Colorado. In August 1962 I graduated with the engineering degree. The Air

Force assigned me to the Site Activation Task Force in Cheyenne, Wyoming. SATAF had the task of overseeing the construction and activation of Wing V of the Minuteman Intercontinental Ballistic Missile. There were to be two hundred missile silos controlled by twenty launch control facilities spread over Colorado, Wyoming and Nebraska.

In the spring of 1965, the installation of Wing V Minuteman Missile neared completion. My subsequent assignment to Wing VI of the Minuteman looked very likely and reasonable. What an assignment! Yuk! Wing VI was in Minot, North Dakota, one of the last places I'd choose to live and work! There were reputedly only two seasons of the year in Minot, namely winter and the Fourth of July. I was not enthused. Man, Oh Man! Don't send me to Minot! Please, don't send me to Minot!

2.4 – Dale and Nancy Amend family – Cheyenne, Wyoming 1965

Chapter 3

Survival Training en Route to Vietnam

May 1965 – Cheyenne, Wyoming

As the installation of Wing V of the Minuteman neared completion, most of us who worked on that large project wondered what our next assignment would be.

I received my orders, "…to attend Class 66-3 Course 14000, Survival Training, starting 1 July 1965, duration 21 days." That did not sound like preparation for a move to Minot.

Survival training was conducted at Stead Air Force Base, Nevada. The valuable classroom instruction taught or refreshed many important skills and techniques which could enhance a pilot's chances of staying alive if he were to go down unexpectedly in enemy territory.

One concept stood out above all others. In the event of being down, immediately get far away from the airplane and hide. Do not try to fight the war on the ground by yourself. Pilots are expensive. Dead pilots are worthless. Evade contact with the bad guys and do all you can to get back to friendly forces. A downed pilot's most worthless piece of equipment is the M-16 rifle. Don't worry about leaving it in your airplane. The most important item is your survival radio to contact someone trying to find and rescue you. Those few instructions were so important that all else faded into insignificance.

In the field training which followed the classroom, we practiced ground navigation and evasion from the enemy forces chasing us. We learned that while we were on the run, anything we could catch and kill was good to eat if we needed it to stay alive. We ate bugs, crawdads, wild onions and a partially cooked deer we snared with parachute shroud line. Mostly we got tired, hungry and miserable.

After field training we were herded onto the obstacle course. We crawled on our bellies under tangled barbed wire with machine gun fire crackling overhead. We were captured and thrown rudely into the prison camp. I was crammed into an undersized bamboo cage in a cramped painful posture for a long time. When I was finally rolled out on the ground, I couldn't stand.

I was put in a cold dark cubicle. It was so small that I couldn't stretch my aching frame to full length diagonally on the cold concrete floor. The blaring Oriental music screeched so loudly it hurt my ears. At long last, the guard quit pounding on the door, shouting at me and calling me vile names. I removed the cloth bag I was forced to wear over my head. I folded it into a little pillow and lay down in the fetal position.

The door crashed open, "Sit up, you dog! Put the bag back over your head!" A loud string of vulgarities and obscenities followed. I pulled the bag back down over my head and sat against the wall.

After several repetitions of the same sequence, I heard the door open again. There was a pause and the guard quietly closed the door. I remained curled up on the floor and thought, "Thank God! He's finally going to leave me alone." I almost went to sleep.

The door was jerked open and the guard drowned me in a big bucket of cold water.

"Sit up, Yankee Dog! I told you to keep that bag over your head!" followed by twice the nasty cursing. It continued all night. I sat on the cold wet floor shivering in the dark with the wet bag over my head, hating the guard. He did a good job of making me miserable and getting inside my head.

I tried to tell myself, "Get over it, Dale. It's a training class. On day number twenty one it's all over. You'll get a hot shower, a good steak dinner and a certificate of completion. Nancy is going to meet you for the drive home to Cheyenne."

I was impressed how miserable "the prisoner" under artificial bad captive treatment was made to feel. It was good mental preparation for the possibility of such actual confinement. It also enhanced my admiration and appreciation for the American prisoners of war who came through the real thing with their lives and their honor.

Chapter 4

A Duck Looking for Hunters

August 5, 1965 – Hurlburt Field, Florida

Survival training was complete. The words in my next orders "…duty station APO San Francisco, California 96307" didn't mean I would fly around the post office near the little cable cars and the Golden Gate Bridge. I was headed for a place not yet common in the American vocabulary. It was called Vietnam.

Most educated Americans knew where French Indo China was, and that some time ago the French had highly productive rubber and tea plantations there. Most learned folks also remembered the name Dien Bien Phu. In 1953 it was the last great fortress of French domination in what was by then called Vietnam. The Communists already had control of most of the countryside areas and were ready to take Dien Bien Phu. During a fifty five day siege, the Communists pounded the French inside the fortress into pulp. Dien Bien Phu fell on May 17, 1954. That defeat was the final blow that caused the French departure from the region.

Most Americans probably didn't care. They would have been glad to ignore the threat of a Communist take over in Vietnam, although it was becoming a serious issue for the United States. The "Domino Theory" held that the fall of one Southeast Asia country would be followed by the tumbling of others in turn, leading to the fall of the entire region into Communist control. To prevent this from happening, the U.S. was mounting a large force to counter the Communist influence.

After a series of skirmishes off the coast of Vietnam, Congress passed the Gulf of Tonkin Resolution on August 7, 1964. All of this became front page news and a vital concern for all U.S. citizens. The "big buildup" in Vietnam was under way.

When my Permanent Change of Station orders were cut, things were just starting to happen in a large way in Vietnam. My operating squadron hardly existed and its name wasn't even identified on my orders. The orders did say "...attend Combat Crew Training Class 65-11A at Hurlburt Field, Florida."

The composition of the class was interesting. An unusually homogeneous bunch of pilots comprised class number 65-11A. There were seven of us, namely: Rex Jenkins, Herb Youngman, Otis Holmes, Phil Delgado, Ken Murphy, Leonard Jordan and myself. We were all experienced pilots and rather senior captains in the Air Force. The unusual fact was we were all graduate engineers coming from technical assignments where our technical education, rather than our piloting skills, had been employed.

Did it matter that we were all graduate engineers? Not whatsoever. We were all Air Force pilots. We were there to learn to be FACs.

A FAC was a duck looking for hunters.

We were the ducks.

In any large organization, personnel constitute a valuable resource to be optimally utilized. During our previous assignments, the Air Force had needed our engineering skills more than it needed our skills as pilots. However, in general Air Force terms, each of us was primarily a pilot and secondarily an engineer. The "big build up" in Vietnam caused a sudden need for pilots. Non-flying officers could work as engineers. It was back to the cockpit as pilots for the seven of us engineers.

As the crew training began, Rex Jenkins and I quickly became good friends. His wife, Laura, and my Nancy became even closer friends. Rex and I continued crew training while our wives and children waited and played in the sand and the warm water of the Gulf of Mexico. They spent most of their time together.

Nancy told Laura, "As soon as Dale got here, he called and we made arrangements for me to come and join him for these last two weeks of his FAC training. I drove with Steve and Jim from Cheyenne to Oklahoma City. On the way, I left Marshall and Elaine in Colorado with Dale's sister for the time we are here in Florida. Without Edith's gracious help, I might not have been able to come. I hated to leave the two younger ones, but she is so wonderful with children that I have complete confidence in her. Dale hopped a flight from Florida and met us in Oklahoma City. We drove the rest of the way together. Did you fly down here from Seattle?"

"No, it's a long way, but we drove. We left early enough for the kids and me to be here for the whole month of Rex's training. It's a big drive cooped up in the car with three kids, and I have only two more months left before the arrival of number four.

"But, you know, we aren't going to see each other for a whole year, and it gives Rex and me a little more time together before he leaves. I'm so glad you came, Nancy. I wish you had come earlier. You and I have so much in common. I feel like I have known you for a long time. Do you think all of our boys would like to go to that goofy golf place in Destin that you told me about? Should we go tomorrow?"

"Laura, I think that would be a great idea. It's only about a twenty-mile drive and I'm sure they will have fun. Tomorrow would probably be good, too. The hurricane is forecast to hit the coast the following day and might keep us home. Dale said there is concern about the storm. It may cause the evacuation of the airplanes to a base east of here. However, it looks now like the center of the hurricane will come ashore far enough to the west that the training program will stay on schedule."

While the moms and boys waded in the salt water, the other six pilots and I learned about our new assignment as Forward Air Controllers. "Forward" says this was not a "behind the lines" job. It was up front where things were happening. "Air" makes it obvious the job wasn't on the ground. "Controller" recognizes that he was in charge, directing the war planes as they executed their attack missions. The FAC ran the show. The fighters carried the ordnance, but the FAC "told them what they could do with it."

The FAC existed for only one purpose. His job was to insure that ordnance delivered did hit the bad guys and did not hit the good guys, military or civilian. The policy for all of South Vietnam was "the FAC controls the air to ground war." Period!

The reasons for the policy were the FAC had at his disposal the following necessary elements all wrapped into one package: Knowledge of the area, detailed information, visibility, control tools and authority.

Knowledge of the area: The FAC regularly flew visual reconnaissance missions over the local area. He saw and knew more than anyone else about the situation and what was happening. He maintained contact with the US Army Green Berets in the Special Forces Camps with their native Montagnard "strikers" (soldiers). He landed on their short dirt air strips and talked with them over lunch of Spam sandwiches. He knew the Camp Commander personally and occasionally took him for a reconnaissance flight around his camp.

Detailed Information: The FAC always carried an impressive case full of detailed maps. In the Central Highlands, in particular, it was essential to understand and "read" the location of hills, mountains, valleys and ravines from "those funny lines" on topographical maps. The FAC cut up, modified and re-assembled standard "topo" maps to cover particular areas where he operated. Specific points on maps of this type were defined by the two-dimension Cartesian coordinate system. The FAC used that system to plot target locations onto the maps.

The attack aircraft didn't have these maps. They used navigation radios which the FAC didn't have. To bridge this lack of communication, the FAC plotted the location of the navigation radio stations onto his local area topographical map. He then drew the radials and distances from the navigation radio station onto his "topo" map. This enabled him to navigate using his own map and direct the fighter aircraft in terms of the navigation radios which they had. It was difficult, but it worked.

The "Sector FAC" attended regular briefings with local Vietnamese officials regarding what targets should be struck. Much coordination was required to keep everyone happy. The communication and approval system was sometimes so involved that it prevented accomplishing anything. Too often the Province Chief was "out to lunch" and not available to give his approval for a strike. But remember, it was their country, not ours.

Visibility: The FAC flew low and slow so that he could identify the target. Fighters coming from a base a hundred miles away or from an aircraft carrier off shore could not possibly find a target in an unfamiliar area, even if the target was prominent. The FAC could normally see the fighters approaching and direct them to his location. He knew the target area and usually knew the location of friendly and enemy troops. The FAC had to see the target and the fighters had to see the FAC before they could accomplish anything.

Control tools: Usually the first contact between the FAC and the fighters was by radio. Radio contact was followed by visual contact. After visual contact was established, the FAC marked the target with a white phosphorus smoke rocket. The usual instruction to the fighters on their first run was, "Hit my smoke." After their first run, the FAC likely refined the instructions to the fighters for subsequent passes. The FAC might say, "Red Bird leader, on your next pass, hit fifty meters to the north of your first strike." The next fighter might hear, "Red Bird number two, make your drop thirty meters short of your leader's last bomb."

When the FAC ran out of smoke rockets and had yet another target to mark, he reached behind his seat for something that looked like a can of beer. It was a smoke grenade. He held the lever on the side of the grenade with one hand, pulled the pin with his other hand and flew the airplane with his other two hands. Sometimes the FAC needed three or four hands at once. At the right moment he dropped the grenade out the window directly onto the target.

The FAC had three different communication radios. He usually talked to other airplanes on the UHF (Ultra High Frequency) radio. Sometimes he used the VHF (Very High Frequency) radio with other airplanes. He spoke with ground troops on the FM (Frequency Modulation) radio. It was common for the FAC, when supporting ground troops, to simultaneously use two and occasionally three different radios.

Authority: The FAC was not autonomous. He functioned under strict rules and directions. He was, however, the single point of authority on scene for the delivery of ordnance onto a target. Nothing got struck by airpower in South Vietnam without a FAC present and no ordnance was delivered until the FAC cleared the strike aircraft onto the target.

Policy: The FAC established national policy. Whoa! No! No! Just kidding! The FAC did not set any policy! I just attached this last item to the above "laundry list" to create the opportunity for some general comments about national policy in the Vietnam War.

Years earlier, as the end of World War II approached, massive "saturation" bombing raids were conducted on Japan. B-29 Super-Fortresses blanketed entire cities at once. The daily newspapers carried the reports. Movie theaters showed newsreels of two-thirds of the entire city of Tokyo burning. The national reaction of the American people was, "Yea! Kill the dirty Japs!" That was national sentiment at the end of World War II.

Following World War II, cigar chewing and frowning Gen Curt LeMay, as the Commander of Strategic Air Command said, "Bomb the bastards back into the Stone Age." That was his prescription for any enemy of the United States. For the most part, the American people nodded their heads in approval.

In Vietnam, however, there were two large factors which made everything different. First, the Gulf of Tonkin Incident, which precipitated the major U.S. entry into Vietnam, was not at all comparable to the Japanese attack on Pearl Harbor. Second, the age of television had arrived in most homes in America. The ugly images of war were suddenly present at the dinner table all over the land.

The war was conducted by Defense Secretary McNamara and his "Harvard Whiz Kids" as a "war of containment." After all, we didn't want to offend or hurt anyone. The military was never assigned the mission to "Go win the war." The Whiz Kids may have been brilliant regarding business and Wall Street, but they didn't know diddly-squat about conducting a war.

The Whiz Kids and McNamara directed step by step changes in our bombing strategies over North Vietnam. This approach made it easy for the defenders to progressively develop the most intense anti-aircraft environment in the history of modern warfare. Predictably, our losses were extremely high. Meanwhile, in South Vietnam, the incredibly stupid "Rules Of Engagement" hampered our forces into the limited stance of "fighting with one hand tied behind our backs." It's difficult to fight when the other guy has all of the advantages.

Those were the facts. Our military did what it was directed by civilian authority to do. During the course of the conflict, popular support at home gradually deteriorated from un-supportive to negative.

Over all, that was the way it was. My involvement wasn't going to change it. The FAC's job was controlling the air-to-ground war over South Vietnam within the established bounds. I didn't know all of this when I got my orders to go and be a FAC, but understanding came quickly.

The combat crew flying training with the airplane itself was routine and rather uneventful. The first order of business was checking out in a new (old) aircraft. The O-1 was a fixed landing gear "tail dragger," not the tricycle landing gear familiar to most of the pilots. For experienced pilots, learning to fly it was merely something a little bit different.

We soon learned that marking targets with smoke rockets was a very inexact procedure. The O-1 had two rocket tubes under each wing, but no sighting system for aiming the rockets at the target. It was a matter of pointing the airplane properly and firing. Proper alignment was whatever worked for each individual pilot. I found by experience I had to slouch down moderately in the seat and align three points into one point. For me those three points were 1) my eyes while I was in that slouched posture, 2) the second rivet from the bottom in the metal divider in the center of the windscreen and 3) the target itself. When I had those three points merged into one, it was time to fire. There was also quite a bit of guessing to allow for distance from the target, angle of attack of the airplane and other factors.

We also learned marking targets using smoke grenades was even more imprecise and required a dicey flying maneuver to boot. That crude method involved grabbing a smoke grenade from a pouch mounted on the back of the seat, pulling the pin, flying with one hand and dropping the grenade at the right time directly onto the target. It was very important to drop the smoke grenade out the window, not into the cockpit by accident.

(Later in Vietnam, a FAC accidentally dropped an ignited grenade inside the cockpit and paid for the mistake with his life. It was not actually a smoke grenade. It was a magnesium flare which continues to burn until it is consumed, no matter what. The magnesium flare faithfully did what it was designed to do and caused the crash of the plane.)

When the FAC and the fighters had established radio communication and visual contact with each other, the FAC marked the target. Controlling the fighters was a matter of giving them specific instructions regarding what they were to do. That would depend on the mission at hand and the situation at the moment.

Our entire class completed combat crew training on schedule and without incident. Since we were all in crew training in the same small class, we had plenty of common interest and came to know each other rather well. We all went to Vietnam at the same time. I was able to keep track of Jenkins, Youngman and Holmes. The four of us were assigned to the same squadron in Pleiku. Our operating locations were scattered around the Central Highlands.

The other three, who went farther north in I Corp in the vicinity of Da Nang, were Delgado, Murphy and Jordan. I lost contact with them. I knew only that a bomb was placed in Delgado's living quarters in an attempt to "get the FAC." It failed because Phil wasn't there when the bomb exploded. I don't know if the three of them completed their tours of duty as scheduled.

I knew a lot more about the four of us in II Corps. Jenkins, Youngman, Holmes and I respectively flew out of Cheo Reo, Kontum, Gia Nhia and Pleiku. All four locations were part of our squadron based in Pleiku. We had occasional contact with each other in and around Pleiku.

During the year Rex Jenkins flew enough Tiger Hound missions to earn a one month curtailment in the length of his tour of duty. Tiger Hound missions were particularly nasty, dangerous missions over the Ho Chi Minh trail along the border between South Vietnam and Laos. Twenty of those missions earned a FAC a one month curtailment in length of tour. Rex was already somewhat unhappy with the Air Force prior to his assignment to Vietnam. Toward the end of his one year tour of duty, he submitted the resignation of his officer's commission. When his Vietnam tour was completed, he left the Air Force.

Herb Youngman was a West Point man who, upon graduation and commissioning, opted for duty in the Air Force rather than the Army. He flew more Tiger Hound missions than Jenkins and qualified for a two month curtailment of his tour. He went home early, but the FAC business took its toll on Youngman. He spent the last fifty –eight days of his tour in the Cam Ranh Bay hospital suffering from battle fatigue. It was not a glorious conclusion to his tour.

Otis Holmes was killed in the crash of his O-1 on the perimeter wire of the Tan Rai Special Forces Camp. I was appointed Accident Investigation Officer of that incident. The investigation itself became a large and significant task for me. The required completion of the investigation changed the schedule of a future flying assignment for me. The re-scheduling of that flying assignment preserved a few decades of my own life. Those years otherwise would have been subtracted from my own lifespan.

Life in general is uncertain. As human beings, we do not come into this world with expiration dates indelibly stamped on our foreheads. Lacking such labels, we live our lives "seeing through a glass darkly," wondering what that date might be. Even if a FAC did have such a date stamped on his forehead, there might be a question mark after the date.

Among FACs in general, and specifically among the seven in this small group, I may have been the fortunate one. I finished my complete tour in Vietnam. In that year there were more than enough interesting experiences to fill a book. You are reading that book. I had no early curtailment of my tour. I also had no physical injuries and no time spent in the psycho ward. At the end of my twelve months I came home on schedule. I was in one piece and my head was still screwed on straight. I went back to work. Many were not that fortunate. The FAC business was not recommended for health and longevity.

Chapter 5

Pleiku--Central Highlands Military Hub

October 24, 1965 — Pleiku, South Vietnam

It was dark on October 24, 1965 when the C-123 bringing Jenkins, Youngman, Holmes and me from Saigon approached Pleiku. The sky was lighted with flares and tracers as we passed over the Plei Me Special Forces Camp, 25 miles south of Pleiku. The Battle of Plei Me was in full swing. It was the biggest thing so far in the life of the new squadron called the 21st TASS (Tactical Air Support Squadron). The survival of the Plei Me camp was in question, and our FACs were up to their eyeballs in the fight.

Welcome to the war!

The welcoming briefing for the four of us was made by the Squadron Operations Officer, Maj Arch Archuleta. It was short and sweet. "The squadron is extremely busy supporting the battle of Plei Me. There's no way we will be able to take airplanes and pilots away from those missions to check out new FACs. Wander around the compound and find a place to sleep on the floor somewhere. We'll check you out as soon as things cool down."

While we stayed out of the way and waited, the Plei Me Special Forces Camp survived, thanks to the close air support controlled by the FACs of the 21st TASS. The newly created squadron was only three months old and struggling to develop its own identity. It earned a good reputation early in its young life in the Battle of Plei Me.

Three months earlier, this new squadron lacked the people and the airplanes that were to constitute its existence. The two top guys in the squadron were sent to some strange place with only their suit cases and the instructions to "go make a squadron." There were plenty of birth pangs. They had a mess on their hands!

The birth pangs were multiplied by the outside expectations the squadron would be immediately functional. LtCol Rick Oliver, the Commander, and Maj Harry (Arch) Archuleta, the Operations Officer, arrived in Pleiku on July 16, 1965. They *were* the entire squadron; lock, stock and barrel. Arch said when he told a friend where he was going, the friend said, "That's too bad, Arch. Pleiku is the wart on Mother Earth's hemorrhoid." Oliver and Archuleta got busy and created a squadron in Pleiku.

Pleiku was the central location of the Jarai tribe of Montagnard (ethnic minority) people in South Vietnam. In the Jarai language Plei means "village" and Ku means "tail." Thus, the word means "the village of the tail." The French built Pleiku to be an administrative center for the Jarai people, locating it on a plateau 2,400 feet above sea level. In 1947 it was a French village of 170 people. Until the French left in 1954, ethnic Vietnamese were not allowed in Pleiku unless they were employed by the French. After the defeat of the French at Dien Bien Phu and their departure from Southeast Asia, the complexion of Pleiku changed radically. The town became a Vietnamese Provincial Capital.

A subsequent Vietnamese government project to relocate populations from the coastal areas to the highlands caused a rapid increase in Pleiku's size. By 1958 the population was about 5,000. The Montagnard tribes were Jarai, Raday and a few others. Other Pleiku residents included Vietnamese government and military people with their dependents and a few Chinese merchants.

The ethnic Vietnamese considered Pleiku their country's political Siberia for government workers. They were accustomed to the sultry coastal plain or the equally hot Mekong delta. They disliked the colder climate and the epidemic levels of malaria that plagued the town. They also feared the primitive, animistic tribes-people who lived throughout the area. Moreover, few of Pleiku's streets were paved. During the wet monsoon season huge amounts of rain fell and Pleiku became a red mud hole. In the dry monsoon season it was a dust bowl, a red dust bowl.

Probably the only fact of historic note associated with Pleiku was that Ho Chi Minh was born there. "Uncle Ho" had long since gone north where he eventually became the political dictator of North Vietnam .

The establishment of the II Corps U.S. military headquarters about two miles north of Pleiku caused the population to mushroom. When I arrived in the fall of 1965, the population of the "city" and surrounding area was considered to be about 20,000. It seemed to be a much smaller village surrounded by a large number of shacks. Except for a pretty good variety of garden crops, rice was the only agricultural crop of significance. The town was largely dependent on the Vietnamese and American military for its economy.

5.1 – Downtown Pleiku

5.2 – Pleiku, Main street downtown   *5.3 – Pleiku, street-side*
fast food

The Pleiku military compound for U.S. forces was a barbed wire enclosure that encompassed a few poor buildings erected in the 1940s and a few more crude structures hurriedly slapped together in the 1960s. The compound housed supplies, equipment, personnel housing, vehicles, messing facilities, fuel and munitions storage etc.

"Old Pleiku" was a poor temporary runway on what was officially Camp Holloway, named for a US Army Warrant Officer killed in 1962 while flying helicopters from that field. "New Pleiku" was a good 6,000 foot runway being completed when I arrived in the fall of 1965. When it was finished, it was first called Cu Hanh and later was just called Pleiku.

US military activity in all of South Vietnam was broken into four geographical areas. These areas were numbered sequentially from north to south and called I Corps, II Corps, III Corps and IV Corps. II Corps was the largest in area, comprising one half of South Vietnam, with headquarters in Pleiku.

US military involvement was officially called Military Assistance Command Vietnam (MACV) (pronounced mack vee). "US military advisers" under the auspices of MACV had been present since 1960 under President Eisenhower, and their numbers were rapidly increasing. This was the "in country" involvement of US military as contrasted to large American units with their own separate identity. Our FACs in the 21st Tactical Air Support Squadron were part of the "in country" system.

Air Force FAC operations for the "in country" system were under the direction and control of the Air Liaison Officer (ALO). For II Corps that was LtCol Buskirk. Coordination with local Vietnamese authorities for daily operations came through II DASC (II Corps Direct Air Support Center). The system was cumbersome at best and Buskirk regularly rumbled through the middle of it, worsening everything he touched.

Each of the four geographical Corps areas was further broken down into Sectors. It was the Sector FAC's job to coordinate with the Vietnamese and schedule the available pilots and airplanes for the necessary flights each day. Targets were selected from visual reconnaissance reports, intelligence agent reports and several other sources. Approval by the local Province Chief was required before a target could be hit. This was frequently a problem, especially if the target was one of immediate opportunity and the Province Chief wasn't available.

Commonly the decisions and approval through the system were so "wrapped around the axle" that the FAC himself was left to decide what needed to be done. If he could evaluate the situation and had the attack aircraft available, it was his job to seize control and direct the air strike. That was the FAC's job. That's why he was there.

The bad guys also knew why the FAC was there, to direct air strikes. Addressing that fact, the noted correspondent, Bob Considine, writing for the <u>Pacific</u> <u>Stars and Stripes</u> newspaper, on May 22, 1966, wrote, …Some of our hottest pilots have been retrained and put in O-1s. The Cessna-built O-1 has a cruising speed of 90 mph, 75 knots. It's called the Bird Dog and the mission of O-1 pilots is to float over Viet Cong positions and report back on what's cooking. They fly very low, are unarmed, and could be brought down with a well-aimed slingshot.

But, to add to the paradox of the air war in Vietnam, they are shot down less frequently than their immensely faster, sturdier and more menacing aerial comrades. The reason for this is that if the VC shot at the moth-like little planes, the O-1 pilots radio the enemy's position and in a very short time the bigger boys are blasting away at the VC position with cannon and rocket fire.

Bob Considine got some of it right. However, in those two brief paragraphs, he also made one false implication, quoted one false myth and made one false statement. The false implication was that all FACs came from fighter squadrons. That was quickly contradicted by the seven of us who came from technical engineering jobs, and by many others. The false myth was that the VC refrained from shooting at FACs. The VC knew there was a better way for them to avoid an air strike than refraining from shooting at the FAC and disclosing their position. The better way was to simply kill the FAC. The false statement was FACs were shot down less than fighters. Wrong again. Our loss rate was much higher than the loss rate of the fighters we controlled.

The Air Force/Space Digest sent Technical Editor, J.S. Butz Jr., on a reporting mission about Bird Dog FACs in Vietnam. Butz flew eight missions in the back seat of the O-1 with FACs in the Delta, not the Central Highlands. His detailed seven page article in the May 1966 issue of that magazine presented the best reporting I saw about the FACs who controlled the air strikes in South Vietnam.

Butz made two particular points worthy of review. He criticized an April 10, 1966, Washington Post report about "indiscriminant bombings of civilians" by the Air Force. To refute that report, Butz explained the use of FACs to properly identify targets before directing fighters to attack.

He also addressed the difficulty in identifying VC or any other people on the ground when flying by in the O-1. He posed the question, "How can you identify the people on the ground when you fly by?" The FAC's answer, "You can't. It's like flying over Manhattan Island and trying to pick out all of the Italians."

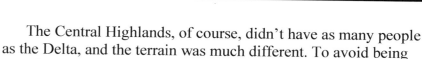

The Central Highlands, of course, didn't have as many people as the Delta, and the terrain was much different. To avoid being seen from the air, it was necessary only to avoid two things, namely color contrast and movement. A person who wore dull colored clothing and remained motionless against a rock, a tree, or a bush probably would not be seen by the FAC.

When I arrived in Pleiku, the 21st TASS was in the process of moving its O-1s and operations from "old Pleiku," Camp Holloway, to "new Pleiku." The runway at Holloway was a temporary construction of PSP, pierced steel planking. The approximately two feet by eight feet planks of PSP were laid on a roughly graded area and attached together by tabs on one slab inserted into slots on the adjacent slab. The PSP had holes about four inches in diameter which allowed the percolation of surface water off the top down through the underlying soil. It also allowed the mud to come back up through the holes.

A PSP runway could be built quickly with limited preparation using equipment of minimal sophistication. It would usually keep aircraft of smaller size from sinking into the mud. The PSP surface, however, quickly developed smaller ripples and larger waves, very undesirable for a runway. With a covering of dust on the surface, the steel planks became slick. When water was added to the dust, the mud on the steel became even slicker.

For helicopters, it was marginally acceptable. For fixed wing aircraft, even small slow ones like the O-1, it was very poor. The operation of larger and heavier aircraft from the PSP at Camp Holloway was out of the question. The PSP runway had sufficed for helicopters. With many bigger fixed wing airplanes arriving, the good runway at Pleiku became mandatory.

Moving our airplanes from Holloway to Pleiku was a simple task. My first flight in the O-1 in Vietnam was to ferry an airplane from Holloway to Pleiku. Major Arch Archuleta, the squadron operations officer, and I went by jeep to Holloway. The two mile return flight was extended, serving as my "dollar ride" around the Pleiku area in general.

As we walked across the Holloway ramp to the airplane, I looked at a bunch of fifteen or twenty shapes the size of large logs in individual fabric containers. They were stacked informally by the operations shack. "What's that?" I asked. Arch casually replied, "Body bags." The occupants of the bags waited quietly for what was presumably their last trip to somewhere. I continued walking.

On every flight after my dollar ride, I carried quite a bit of equipment which was standard for FACs and a little bit of extra stuff of my own. The survival vest I wore over my flying suit or fatigues had a large assortment of pockets filled with a great variety of items. The most important single item in the vest was the survival radio. In the event of ending up on the ground due to unplanned circumstances, the radio was the thing most likely to save the FAC's life. Under the survival vest I wore a flak vest which might possibly deflect a small arms round from penetrating my chest.

Around my waist I wore a pistol belt which carried several rounds of extra ammunition for the 38 caliber pistol in the holster on the belt. Standing in the right front portion of the cockpit, with the strap over a knob, was my M-16 (Browning AR-15) automatic rifle. One magazine of ammunition for the rifle was inserted from the bottom into the chamber. Two more full magazines were taped, upside down, one on either side of the first. This arrangement provided three times the quantity of ammunition and allowed a quick change of magazines.

5.4 – Pistol belt, extra ammunition and 38 caliber pistol

5.5 – M-16 rifle with three magazines taped together

On the floor within easy reach was my case of maps. Flying out of Pleiku, the case always held, at a minimum, one complete map of each of the seven visual reconnaissance areas of the Pleiku Sector. One set of maps represented a very great amount of work. Fifty three topographical maps had to be cut, trimmed and assembled with a mile of scotch tape to make the seven individual maps of visual reconnaissance areas C-1 through C-7.

This allowed me to grab the right map and respond to an immediate need anywhere in Pleiku Sector. The need could be to help a party on the ground or to control an air strike on short notice. Fighters with minimum fuel remaining were commonly diverted to us from farther north where they had been unable to hit their assigned targets because of weather.

5.6 – One FAC with lots of gear to carry

I was always ready with one or more available targets in a nearby area, as defined by a set of coordinates on a map. A finished map consisted of seven or eight of the topographical maps assembled into one sheet large enough to paper the inside of the windows of the cockpit of the O-1. Finding the right map, folding it into manageable dimensions and locating the desired spot on the map required a lot of skill and knowledge of the area. After all of the paper logistics, the FAC had to be good at reading the map. If either the FAC or the ground party committed a significant error in map reading, the result could be serious, quite possibly fatal.

Also on the floor of the cockpit was an optional item I called my "picnic bag." It held a canteen of water, some high energy jellied candy bars and a second survival radio.

The most important thing to do, if down in enemy country, was to quickly get far away from the airplane and hide. I always expected to have with me, upon leaving the airplane, the two vests and the pistol which were attached to my body. I also intended to grab my picnic bag if possible, for the second survival radio and some water and energy bars if needed for a longer time on the ground. My cherished maps would no longer be of use and the M-16 was just a bulky temptation to do something foolish instead of hiding and getting back to friendly forces. I would easily abandon the maps and the rifle in the airplane.

Some pilots had the plan, if worst came to worst, to use all of the available pistol ammunition, except for the last round, on the bad guys. The last round, they intended, was for the pilot himself, rather than to be captured, tortured and then subsequently killed. It did make sense. I guess that I leaned on the crutch of denial that it could ever happen to me. I had no such plan.

The FAC was expected to get the job done and to remain safe while doing it. Such an expectation was nonsense. We were directed to fly at the minimum altitude of 1,500 feet above the ground. The general rule of thumb was that 1,500 feet was mostly safe from rifle fire, 3,000 feet was mostly safe from 30 caliber machine gun fire and 5,000 feet was maybe safe from 50 caliber (12.7 millimeter) fire. If subjected to 12.7 millimeter or larger fire, the O-1 was usually history. For the 30 caliber machine gun or rifle fire, the odds depended on a variety of factors beyond our control.

The common practice was to disregard the 1,500 feet rule and fly at the tree tops whenever necessary to do the job, which was most of the time. Occasionally the 1,500 feet minimum order was re-issued, this time with a firm "stomping of the foot," meaning "this time we're serious." That would last for a while and then we would be back on the tree tops.

A more serious directive was to not try to be a weapons delivery platform instead of being a FAC. The FAC's job was to control air strikes, not to deliver ordnance. Some FACs ignored this directive with varying results. Two of our FACs, Capts Underwood and Mosley, flying out of Dalat, tried to shoot up some

VC from the O-1 with their M-16s. The result was merely two dead FACs and one trashed airplane. Capt Wilbanks, also flying out of Dalat, did essentially the same thing and ended up dead in a trashed airplane. He was, however, credited with saving many lives in the process and was posthumously awarded the Medal of Honor.

Flying the O-1 at the "safe altitude" of 1,500 feet was a good idea, but it frequently imposed such a restriction on the FAC's ability to see what was on the ground that it compromised the effectiveness of the mission. When controlling an air strike, it was hard to accurately mark the target if we could not clearly see the target. Similarly, visual reconnaissance was not accurate if the FAC couldn't report specifically what he saw because he was too far away to see it. But it was nice to know that the big boys sitting in chairs in Saigon wanted us to fly high enough to stay alive. After all, if we didn't make it today, who would fly our missions tomorrow?

It was, therefore, hard to believe that those same guys in those same chairs in Saigon ordered us to fly visual reconnaissance (VR) in the dark. It appeared from our perspective, they had adopted a change of heart. Instead of trying to keep the FACs alive, they had decided to kill us all. Their rationale was that the Viet Cong (VC) (Charlie) moved about and did whatever they did under the cover of darkness. To know what Charlie was doing and where he was doing it, we needed to go see him while he did it, i.e. under the cover of darkness.

Simplistically it sounded reasonable, but there was one enormous obvious flaw in the plan. The purpose of the mission was to see, and in the dark we could not see. On February 20, 1966, I took off at 6:00 AM in the very, very black for a VR flight. It was a scary flight. If I'd had one of the guys who dreamed it up in my back seat, I'd have scared the Hell out of him.

It was not only pointless, it was very dangerous. We couldn't see each other to avoid a mid-air collision and couldn't see which hill or mountain had gotten itself in front of the airplane. Taking

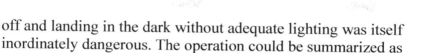

off and landing in the dark without adequate lighting was itself inordinately dangerous. The operation could be summarized as worthless and hazardous. Only a few dramatic failures of VR in the dark were needed for the whole fiasco to be cancelled. Fortunately it all stopped before we killed any FACs in the process.

There was great variety in the FAC business. Flexibility to react to changing circumstances was a common necessity. Missions were cancelled or extended without notice and it was the FAC's job to adjust to the needs of the moment. Sometimes the day could get really long, but probably still quite interesting. On the afternoon of December 9, 1965 II Corps radar kept sending me fighters and I controlled five flights in quick succession. It was exhausting both physically and mentally to work that many. I controlled:

3 F-100s at 3:30 PM

3 F-100s at 4:00 PM

2 F-100s at 4:30 PM

2 A-1s at 5:00PM and

3 F-4Cs which arrived unexpectedly during the middle of the A-1s' strike.

I had a new guy in my back seat observing all of that unscheduled activity. It was a long afternoon and I almost wore him out. The new man was Joe Everitt. He was to become Pleiku Sector FAC, my new immediate boss.

It was unusual to have such an orderly sequence of strikes in such a short time span, but on that day it all went smoothly. The targets were all in the same general area, which made it possible.

Late in the long afternoon, I was directing the two A-1s onto a set of targets just east of the DeBodral tea plantation southeast of Pleiku. II DASC radar control broke in on my radio frequency. "Baron One Zero, this is Peacock. I have a flight of three F-4s diverted from the north. Can you expend their ordnance?"

Call signs were important in radio communication. The call sign "Peacock" told me it was the II DASC radar control point calling me. The person making the call could have been any one of several radar operators who worked there. The call sign "Baron One Zero" was more specific. Every FAC in II Corps was "a Baron FAC" assigned to the 21st TASS. The number "One Zero" identified me personally. Each FAC had his own specific number.

I responded, "Roger, Peacock. Where are the F-4s?"

Peacock came back, "I have them on top of you right now. They have enough fuel for fifteen minutes time on target. Their call sign is Banner Four Three."

I looked up and saw the three F-4s right above me. "Affirmative, Peacock, I can take them."

I instructed the two A-1s, "Dagger One Three, clear the target area and hold to the west while I take care of these F-4s."

Dagger One Three answered very un-enthusiastically, "Roger, Baron One Zero. We're clear."

"Banner Four Three, this is Baron One Zero. Do you have a Tally Ho on me?"

The F-4 flight leader responded, "Affirmative, Baron One Zero. I see you."

"Banner, your target is a large grass hooch (shack). It is two hundred meters north of another grass hooch which is already on fire. Do you see the one on fire and your target two hundred meters north of that?"

"Affirmative. I've got both of them."

"OK, Banner. You're cleared on target. Continue your runs until you have expended everything you have."

I didn't even fire a smoke rocket onto the second hooch which was the target for the F-4s. The first hooch was burning brightly, marking the target for the F-4s better than I could have marked it with a smoke rocket. It was as obvious and easy a target as any attack airplane would have in a year in Vietnam. The three F-4s made their successive bombing runs on the undamaged hooch, expending all of their ordnance. When they were finished, the hooch was still undamaged.

"Thanks, Baron One Zero. That's all we have."

"Roger, Banner Four Three. See ya another day."

Before the F-4s had time to clear the radio frequency (switch to another radio channel for their departure), the A-1 leader quickly came back to me. He wanted to be sure that the F-4s heard him. "OK, Baron, Ya want us to get that other hooch for you?"

The F-4s were new, fast, expensive, high performance airplanes. They were also conservatively directed to pickle (release) their ordnance from a rather high altitude for the safety of that new expensive airplane. That meant their accuracy was greatly degraded. They weren't likely to hit the target. I had just controlled the least effective airplane (the F-4) we had for the purpose of attacking a target on the ground, while the most effective airplane (the A-1) for the same mission waited and watched.

The A-1 was a Korean War vintage single engine propeller driven air plane that carried a heavy ordnance load. It had plenty of fuel for loiter time if needed, usually survived several hits from ground fire and hit the target very accurately. For air to ground attack in South Vietnam, the A-1 was the airplane.

I cleared the A-1s back onto the target. The leader made one pass over the second hooch and dropped a load of CBU (cluster bomb units) in a direct hit. The hooch immediately burned brightly. "OK, Baron, what's next?"

Sometimes the days got really long. On December 14, 1965 I flew Tiger Hound missions on the Ho Chi Minh Trail. We went north from Pleiku to Kontum and staged from there. I flew a total of five sorties and six and a half hours in the air. It was a long day with moderate success. When I got home to Pleiku I was the FAC for an all-nighter on the AC-47 flare ship. At the time, the AC-47s were new "in country" and were required to have a FAC on board to direct their firing. This procedure was later changed when the AC-47 crews acquired more experience.

The days could also be unpredictably long or short. On May 20, 1966, I flew a short fifteen minute flight early, shortened (actually aborted) because the weather was so low that neither I nor the A-1s could work. Later in the afternoon I had an "immediate air strike" west of Plei Djerang. An "immediate" was one called on the spur of the moment for defense reasons or to hit a target of opportunity. A patrol had made contact with Charlie and I brought in two flights of A-1s in their support. Although it wasn't possible to obtain any BDA (bomb damage assessment), it looked like there was a good chance that we did well.

And sometimes we ended up doing the unexpected. June 3, 1966, turned out to be a long day. I was originally scheduled for only one flight of two hours with an observer in the back seat. I ended up flying seven hours and ten minutes on a search mission for the second pilot of an F-4 that was shot down north of Kontum the day before. The first pilot had already been picked up.

Toward the end of the search, we were listening in on another FAC controlling a strike nearby while we watched. The FAC developed engine trouble and had to leave, so I volunteered my services. I covered a heliborne landing operation and then put two F-4s onto a nearby target.

Just before we had to leave we watched friendly artillery respond to some mortars which had just been lobbed by Charlie onto a friendly camp. It was interesting to watch, although I wasn't controlling the artillery.

There were also times we didn't fly, but heard reports about the results of an earlier flight. On June 10, 1966, we got the report that the 101st Airborne had a big fight going on about thirty miles north of Kontum. It was apparently a pretty big thing. They reportedly killed about four hundred North Vietnamese Regulars while losing about forty-five dead. That was the area where I controlled two F-4s a week earlier for the 101st Airborne when their FAC developed engine trouble.

FACs were involved in about everything that happened in the air. That included aerial spraying missions. In many large areas of South Vietnam, extensive vegetative cover made it impossible to see the ground from the air. This allowed the VC to operate essentially unseen by aerial surveillance. On January 25, 1966, my mission was in support of Operation Traildust, a defoliation mission, where C-123s flew low and did a king-sized spraying job to kill vegetation over a large area. On that day one armed Huey (Army chopper), two A-1Es and I covered their operation. The spraying was completed uneventfully. The Huey and the three C-123s went home and I FAC-ed the two A-1Es onto a nearby target.

We also flew defoliation missions in an area around Chu Pong Mountain, near the Cambodian border. It was a hot area for VC activity. Charlie was hanging out there in force and hadn't been bothered except for limited air strikes. C-123s sprayed the area with a contact spray, hoping to kill all the foliage. The intent was to burn off the heavy foliage when it became dry, enabling visual reconnaissance to observe and report any activity on the ground.

A few weeks later, on another defoliation mission, Maj Victor Vasquez was in the front seat for a FAC training ride and I was in the back. I kicked myself for not having my camera in hand. I could have taken some pretty good pictures of two C-123s spraying along the road at Mang Yang Pass. The C-123s were flying as low as possible to let the spray get down with minimum drift. We flew over them to FAC the covering fighters if the C-123s drew ground fire.

The spray made spectacular rainbows behind the planes. It was a wonderful photo opportunity and I had no camera. I'd covered three spraying missions recently and hadn't taken any pictures.

Rats! You probably wouldn't guess, though, what was the most impressive sight on that particular mission. It had nothing to do with defoliation or rainbows. I'd flown over Mang Yang Pass between Pleiku and An Khe several times. Each time I flew there I was impressed and sobered by the sight of thousands of white crosses in neat rows on the hilltops along the pass. The crosses stood silently as evidence of the frustration and failure of the French in their final days in Vietnam.

If FACs weren't working with someone in the air, we might be working with someone on the ground. As an Air Force "Fly Boy," I was greatly impressed by the capabilities of Army artillery. Although I could have done so, I never controlled any artillery missions fired "in anger." On a couple of practice exercises, I did give the fire base a set of coordinates on the map and was amazed to see the resulting explosion occur in the right place. The 175 millimeter guns on Artillery Hill near the Pleiku compound had a range of 30 kilometers (18 miles). It was impressive.

More impressive was what could happen to a FAC if he ignored the admonition, "Don't fly over an artillery fire base. Those guys are going to fire those big guns when they're ready to fire them and you'd better not be in the way." There were serious efforts made toward coordination between air traffic and the artillery boys, but those efforts commonly failed. A FAC (not one of ours) took an artillery round going up through the wing of his O-1. Miraculously, it didn't detonate and didn't hit anything vital. The FAC landed with a super "gee whiz" hole in his wing.

As Pleiku became a larger operational base with more airplanes and equipment, it became a more lucrative target for the enemy. On a quiet night in April 1966 I was sleeping soundly until a few minutes after 2:00 A.M. when the thump-thump-thump began at the flight line. Charlie was doing an accurate job of dropping mortars on the A-1 parking ramp. It was about two miles between that area and our housing. If the alert hadn't sounded, I might have rolled over and gone back to sleep. There was no immediate danger for us in the compound, but on the flight line, it was bad news.

The VC set up the mortars east of the airbase and lobbed several rounds onto the A-1 parking ramp. Before anyone could find them, they had folded up their equipment and faded away into either the vegetation or the local population. Three or four flight line guards were injured by shrapnel, one seriously. Two USAF A-1s and one VNAF A-1 were destroyed and many others damaged to a lesser degree. Our operations building, near the A-1 parking ramp, took some minor hits on the exterior. These marks helped us remember the occasion.

Our O-1 aircraft were parked at the western end of the runway and only a couple of rounds were close to our planes. One of those two rounds hit a C-130 parked close to our O-1s. That round hit perfectly in the wing of the C-130 and penetrated a fuel tank. Most fortunately, the round was a dud and didn't explode. If the round had exploded, the C-130 would probably have exploded, causing a lot of damage to our O-1 aircraft.

Our squadron was always short on pilots. We needed more FACs at just about every one of our operating locations. We got help from an unexpected source. The commander of our sister squadron in Pleiku, the First Air Commando Squadron, flying the A-1, addressed a special meeting.

"Good morning, Gentlemen. You are the most recently arrived twenty-one pilots in this fine squadron and I am glad to have every one of you. However, I am going to lose two-thirds of you. Our sister squadron, the 21st TASS, is seriously short of pilots and we happen to be significantly over our authorized strength. If I were sitting in a chair in Saigon, I would have made the same decision they have made.

"I have been directed to select fourteen of you to transfer to LtCol Rick Oliver's FAC squadron. You will check out in the O-1 and learn how to be FACs. You will then be assigned to one of their thirteen operating locations around II Corps. The other seven of you will remain here in the First Air Commando Squadron and continue to fly the A-1. I will first ask for volunteers to become FACs. If there are fewer than fourteen volunteers, we will draw lots to finish out the requirement of fourteen."

Fewer than fourteen volunteers?! Ha! Who's kidding? How many pilots volunteered to leave the reliable proven workhorse, the A-1, to become FACs and fly the Bird Dog O-1? None. Nada. Zilch. That was zero with a capital Z!

Who wanted to be a FAC? <u>No one!</u>

Well, fourteen of them <u>did</u> become FACs. The twenty-one newest A-1 pilots drew lots and the fortunate seven remained in the First Air Commando Squadron flying the A-1. Our FAC squadron welcomed the other fourteen as our newest FACs.

Chapter 6

Special Forces Camps and Green Berets

1965-1966 – The Central Highlands around Pleiku and Ban Me Thuot

Us Army Special Forces were among the first US troops committed to Vietnam. Beginning in the early 1950s, Special Forces teams deployed from the United States and Okinawa to serve as advisors for the fledgling South Vietnamese Army. Special Forces also trained and advised the Montagnard Civilian Irregular Defense Group (CIDG). In the Central Highlands around Pleiku and Ban Me Thuot, the population was largely Montagnard (Mon-tan-yard) and nearly all of the "Civilian Irregulars" were Montagnards.

In 1961 President John F. Kennedy, in a public address said, "Today I am authorizing the use of the Green Beret headgear exclusively by the US Army Special Forces. The Green Beret will now stand as a symbol of excellence, a badge of courage, a mark of distinction in the fight for freedom." By his statement, JFK increased the public's admiration for the Special Forces. The Men of the Green Beret were the subject of a best selling book called "The Green Berets," a hit record entitled "The Ballad of the Green Berets" and a movie, "The Green Berets," starring John Wayne.

Overall, that was quite a lot of well deserved hype and hoopla. I thought the Special Forces guys needed all the glamour that could be generated, because they had a really bad job. I regularly disagreed with them about our respective jobs. I said their job was worse than mine. They differed and said my job of being a FAC was worse than theirs.

There was a unique factor, not obvious to the casual observer, which made me think the Special Forces job was particularly bad. I was "the FAC in the little airplane." Although we were always good targets, from the ground every FAC looked like every other FAC. That was not true for the Green Beret boys. The American Special Forces men were normally physically larger than all of the ethnic Vietnamese and Montagnards. They were easier targets to locate "in the sights." Furthermore, it was more of an accomplishment to "shoot the American."

The Special Forces established and maintained many camps in the Central Highlands to control the area militarily. Usually about twelve Green Berets advised and provided leadership for a camp. Technically, the camp was commanded and administered by a few ethnic Vietnamese military. About three hundred to six hundred Montagnards, known as "strikers," along with their dependents, comprised most of the population of a camp. In slang terms, the camp personnel consisted of a dozen "Round-eyes" (Americans), about the same number of "Slopes" (Vietnamese) and a few hundred "Yards" (Montagnards). The slang terms were not necessarily complimentary.

6.1 – One cool "Slope" lieutenant and three "Yard"s

There was a nationally serious on-going problem between the ethnic Vietnamese and the native Montagnards. They hated each other. The population of South Vietnam was roughly 17 million. Of those, about 1.2 million were Montagnards. The Vietnamese were clearly in the majority everywhere except in the Central Highlands, the historic homeland of the Montagnards. In the Central Highlands, the Montagnards outnumbered the ethnic Vietnamese.

The Vietnamese were far ahead of the Montagnards socially, culturally, technically, economically and politically. The Vietnamese thought that was how it should be. The Montagnards greatly resented it. The more educated and advanced Montagnards were occasionally the leaders of conflicts referred to as "uprisings" or "rebellions" in the Central Highlands.

There were Christian missionaries in the Central Highlands sponsored by the Christian and Missionary Alliance in the United States. The missionaries found themselves in a precarious position. Their announced purpose in Vietnam was to bring Christianity to the Montagnards, particularly the largest tribe, the Jarai people. Because the missionaries worked with the Jarai, the Vietnamese automatically suspected the missionaries of helping the Jarai against the Vietnamese. In early December 1965, some missionaries in Ban Me Thuot were killed because of their alleged involvement with the Montagnards in a plot to overthrow the Vietnamese government.

A week later, a Montagnard group in Pleiku plotted to assassinate the Premier of Vietnam, Cao Ky, while he was visiting Pleiku. The plot was discovered and the leaders were caught and tried. Some were executed in Pleiku. The Denver Post newspaper reported the event accurately. ...Four Montagnard tribesmen were condemned to death Monday for their part in an unsuccessful revolt...The five man court deliberated 40 minutes...Two days ago a sandbag wall and five firing squad stakes were put up in Pleiku's main public square...The leaders of the rebellion included civil servants, school teachers and an army captain...

The highest paid civilian employee in Pleiku was among those executed. He was a Montagnard who worked for Capt Arnie Teller, the head of Civil Engineering for Pleiku Airbase.

The extreme tension between the Montagnards and the ethnic Vietnamese was a serious on-going concern for all of the Special Forces Camps. Since there were a few hundred Montagnard "strikers" in a camp and only about a dozen Vietnamese "in command" of the camp, the "Yards" could easily take over from the "Slopes" whenever they chose. There was such a takeover at Gia Nhia, where FAC Otis Holmes was stationed. Fortunately, it was peaceful and temporary.

The "Round-eyes," American Advisors, got along well with both the Montagnards and the Vietnamese at most Special Forces Camps. This allowed the American Green Berets to function as keepers of the peace. Nevertheless, the continuing dislike between the Montagnards and the ethnic Vietnamese was a serious problem.

The Special Forces conducted frequent patrols from the camps around their respective areas and often ran into trouble. When they ran into trouble, they called for a FAC. They didn't call an Army unit because there weren't any Army units available to respond. The Special Forces and the Air Force FACs shared a strong common bond of cooperation.

The camps themselves were disasters waiting to happen. The perimeter was a barbed wire structure intended to make entry difficult except through the gate.

Fortification was minimal. Wooden and earthen bunkers provided some protection for machine gun and rifleman emplacements. Punji stakes of sharpened bamboo implanted in the ground and slanted outward toward an attack were also part of the protection. To overcome the wire and punji stakes, attackers carried grass mats to lay over them and walk across on top. In the event of a serious well-mounted attack, a Special Forces Camp was likely to fall unless air power supported the camp. Then it was a whole different ball game.

The living quarters for the Montagnards were little more than dirt floored sheds with two layers of roof made of wooden poles and earthen filler. The upper layer was intended to detonate incoming rounds of mortar fire before the round penetrated the actual living quarters. The strikers cooked on a wood or charcoal fire on the ground using an assortment of pots and pans.

One could observe rather cynically, but also rather accurately, "They've been eating rice and living in the dirt for centuries. So what's the difference?" One difference was that before the war, when they lived in grass huts with dirt floors, they were free to walk many miles on the numerous familiar trails. Now they were confined in Special Forces Camps.

Furthermore, while previously walking barefoot on those trails, a Montagnard probably carried a handcrafted cross bow and looked for something to shoot for supper. Now instead of a breech cloth, he wore a makeshift uniform, probably with shoes, carried a rifle and looked for Viet Cong to shoot before supper.

The Green Beret Special Forces Advisors lived slightly more civilized in a shack of some sort and usually had more than rice to eat. If a visiting FAC came early in the day, he might be fed some Spam and dried scrambled eggs. Around midday he might be treated to a Spam sandwich. In the evening it would probably be Spam and fried dried potatoes. Army "K" rations were also likely to be available and weren't as bad as their reputation.

We FACs worked regularly and closely with the Green Berets. I landed at about twenty Special Forces Camps during my year in Vietnam, sometimes briefly and sometimes for much greater involvement. The camps had many similarities and many individual differences. Most of the camps had poor dirt runways suitable for only helicopters and small fixed wing aircraft.

It was a good common practice to make a pass over the runway at low altitude to check its condition before landing. Commonly the village water buffalo were on the runway and it was necessary to scare them off to the side before landing. If the runway was too muddy or there was too much wind, we couldn't land. Sometimes we had to settle for dropping a burlap bag of mail and some cigarettes onto the camp, much like dropping a smoke grenade out the window to mark a target.

The Green Berets existed in their own isolated world. One day when I dropped in at the Duc Lap camp, the guys were cordial and glad to see me. That was the normal reaction to a FAC's arrival. They were even happier when they found I had brought them a case of pop and a case of beer.

Occasionally we ran a taxi service for someone who was stuck at a camp after some sort of business. On June 6, 1966, I flew Capt Warren Dodson, the Senior Advisor, around Plei Mrong Special Forces Camp to check on some of his troops. When I returned Dodson to his camp, a photographer was waiting for me. He had finished his business there and been stuck for four more days. He was grateful for a ride back to Pleiku.

The Montagnards who lived inside a camp or in an adjacent village made rice wine. They stored it in bottles, hollowed sections of bamboo, salvaged cans, dried gourds, earthenware crockery etc. If it held liquid, it was probably filled with rice wine for a special occasion. Strangely, there was an unexpected parallel that could be drawn between those Montagnard special occasions and certain practices back home.

We've all known folks referred to as "Hatch, Match and Dispatch Christians." They seldom darken the doorway of the church, but do want to avail themselves of the services of the church on three special occasions during their lifetimes. They want the minister to baptize the newly "hatched" baby for a good start in life. They want a nice aisle for their daughter to walk for the "matching" ceremony, the wedding. And when it's time to go, they want to be properly "dispatched" with a respectable funeral. Sounds proper.

The parallel between the Montagnards and the Hatch, Match and Dispatch Christians back home centered on those same three special events. The Montagnards celebrated births, weddings and deaths with generous amounts of rice wine. No matter which of the three occasions, there was plenty of rice wine.

With Julio Diaz, a new Army FAC along for the ride, I landed at the Plei Do Lim Special Forces Camp. A Vietnamese Lieutenant took us around to visit the camp and the people. The Lieutenant's main interest seemed to be the opportunity to pose for photos of himself with the Americans, but he was very helpful.

It was the chance of a lifetime for picture taking. A National Geographic magazine photographer would have gone bananas taking wonderful pictures. Three hundred native Montagnards were there for a celebration complete with rice wine and all. It was quite a strange spectacle. We went from group to group and the people were extremely hospitable and receptive to our presence at the gathering. Initially, I tried to have the Vietnamese Lieutenant explain that I was very appreciative of their repeated generous offers, but could not drink because I had to fly the airplane home. That didn't work at all.

Every little gathering of people held rice wine up to my mouth, insisting that I join in the drinking. I held many second, third and fourth hand containers to my mouth and pretended to drink. Each time I smiled and tried to let them know how good it was and how grateful I was for their sharing. Occasionally I tried my entire French vocabulary and said, "Merci beau coup," not knowing if they understood my feeble effort to say, "Thank you."

We left the gathering not knowing if the event being celebrated was a birth, a wedding or a death. Two things were certain, 1) It was a happy occasion with an abundance of rice wine and 2) All people do indeed smile in the same language.

6.2 – Rice wine celebration at the village adjacent to Plei Do Lim Special Forces Camp. Birth? Wedding? Death?

6.3 – Everything that would hold liquid was filled with rice wine.

6.4 – Please tell them thank you very much, but, I can't drink. I have to fly the airplane.

6.5 – Capt Julio Diaz samples the special local brew.

My first view of Plei Me Special Forces Camp was from the C-123 that initially brought me to Pleiku from Saigon. The Battle of Plei Me was in full swing on the October evening. Much later, on a quiet day when not much was happening, I took Capt Bill Fritsch to Plei Me. I asked the Senior Advisor, Capt David Yeater, to show him around the camp. Fritsch was an F-4C pilot from Cam Ranh, visiting in Pleiku for a week's orientation. He said they had about twice as many pilots as they needed. They got half the flying time they should, and had rather low morale. They did things like the Pleiku field trip to try to keep busy. I was glad to help and enjoyed talking with him.

On another occasion, I was back at Plei Me on business. Lt Mel Orwig and I landed there to study their defenses to be more knowledgeable in the event the camp came under attack and we needed to provide air support. Capt David Yeater was again our contact. Yeater fed us lunch while we discussed their defenses. He offered, "Would you guys like to do some practice firing of your weapons while you're here?"

I said, "I sure would, Dave. I've been carrying these guns for nearly nine months and I've practiced with the M-16 only one time. I've never fired this particular 38."

The practice was good. We fired about forty rounds with the M-16 and about twenty rounds with the pistol. Having carried the guns for several months, hoping that they were OK, it was nice to know they fired properly and were close to being accurately sighted.

While we were on the other side of the camp firing, an Army ground crewman drove a tank trailer across the dirt runway and parked it about twenty yards from our airplane. That was of no concern until we heard the whop-whop-whop-whop of the rotor blades on a Chinook helicopter approaching the tank trailer. Orwig recognized the danger before I did and took off running toward our airplane. He was too late.

By the time he got there, the Chinook had already applied full power and was lifting the tank trailer for transport to another location. Orwig couldn't get to the chopper pilot, so he took it out on the truck driver who was watching the chopper and tanker successfully depart. "You dumb son of a bitch, what the Hell do you think you're doing!?"

"Sir, we had to move that tanker."

"Well, you stupid shit bird, you just filled our airplane with dirt and almost flipped it over. What the Hell do you have in your empty head for brains? You had the whole field available and you came and parked that big truck right next to our airplane. You damned near put it on its back."

I almost felt a little bit sorry for the dumb gravel-scratching grunt that Orwig chewed up and spit out. He really didn't appear to be very bright. What I wanted was the opportunity to eat on the chopper pilot, but he was out of reach. He should have known better. It was a stupid stunt for both the ground crewman and the Chinook pilot.

After we finished calling the departed chopper pilot all of the bad names we could think of, Capt Yeater told us about an incident on their patrol last week. "We were about four miles northwest of camp when we ran into a fire fight. It wasn't much of a fight and no one was hurt. It appeared that all of the VC took off when the north side of our patrol surprised them and took three VC prisoners.

"The contact with the other VC was apparently over, but we couldn't be sure. It was getting late in the afternoon and we needed to get back to camp. No one could tell if the remaining VC of that fire fight or other VC were setting an ambush for us before we got back. The prisoners were a liability to guard and transport to camp."

I asked the obvious question, "What did you do with them?"

"I didn't want to lose the intelligence information we had captured, but it was too dangerous to try to get all three of them and all of my men safely back to camp. I had our best Montagnard question all three for a while and then asked him which one of them seemed to be least valuable for intelligence. He pointed one out for me and I had one of my guys shoot him in front of the other two."

"Did you keep the other two?"

"No, we did the same thing again and I asked my Montagnard which one seemed more valuable for intelligence. He told me and we shot the other one. By then prisoner number three was very cooperative and caused no trouble as we hurried back to camp."

Some people might say, "Capt Yeater was guilty of murder for killing those prisoners. That was a crime! He should be charged with murder and put on trial." Others would say, "Yeater and his patrol were in a very dangerous situation where their own survival was in great question. This is war! It's no damned Sunday school picnic! Yeater's prime responsibility was for the safety of the men under his command. He acted judiciously and wisely." You may decide for yourself.

FACs frequently helped the Green Beret boys. Sometimes they were in a position to return the favor. Occasionally some quick aviation gasoline at a remote location was valuable. On July 18, 1966, it was the end of a long dull afternoon of flying visual reconnaissance. I was near Buon Ea Yang Special Forces Camp headed home to Ban Me Thuot. My radio suddenly came to life."Baron Four Two, this is Hardwood." It was the radar control point for Darlac Sector calling me.

"Hardwood, this is Baron Four Two."

"Baron Four Two, I have some fighters diverted from the north that need a target. Can you take them?"

"Hardwood, I have a target, but I'm almost out of fuel. Do I have time to get to Ban Me Thuot for fuel and return to the target?"

"Probably not. There are three F-4s and I'll have them on top of your present location in twenty five minutes. They will have fifteen minutes of fuel on target when they get there."

"Roger, Hardwood. Bring them in. I'll try to get some fuel at Buon Ea Yang. Maybe I can make it in time."

Then using my FM radio, "Buon Ea Yang, this is Baron Four Two."

"Hey, Baron Four Two, this is Buon Ea Yang. How're ya doing today?"

"Boun Ea Yang, I have some fighters coming in from the north on short notice. They're low on fuel and so am I. There isn't time for me to get to Ban Me Thuot for fuel. Can you meet me at the end of your runway and give me a few gallons in each tank from your gas barrel? It'll have to be really fast. I can be at your tank in five minutes."

"Hell, yes, Baron. I'll be there by the time you are."

"Boun Ea Yang, I'll stay strapped in and keep it running. Give me a little in each tank and be sure you get the caps on tight. Hurry. And stay clear of the prop. Thanks buddy. I owe you one."

They had a seldom used 55 gallon steel barrel of aviation gasoline sitting at the end of their dirt runway for just such a need. It had a hand cranked pump and enough hose to reach my tanks. So far, everything looked good. I pulled up by the gas barrel as two of their sergeants slid their jeep to a stop in a cloud of dust. They cranked some fuel into each tank in record time. I waved my thanks and took off in the opposite direction.

"Hardwood, this is Baron Four Two. I got fuel and I'm back in the air headed for the target ten miles south of Buon Ea Yang. Where are your fighters?"

"They're five minutes out, Baron. They should be there at the same time you are."

With no warning, my engine quit abruptly and then sputtered back to partial power. I switched to the other fuel tank with the same result. Damn! Did I get some bad fuel?

"May Day! May Day! (It was the one and only time in a career of flying airplanes for the US Air Force I ever used this universal distress call.) Hardwood, this is Baron Four Two. I'm headed back to Ban Me Thuot with an engine that's failing. I don't think I'm going to get there. Tell the rescue chopper I'm following the road from Buon Ea Yang to Ban Me Thuot. When it quits, I'll try to put it on the road or somewhere close."

I was the unsuspecting victim of an interesting phenomenon. An incompletely sealed barrel sitting in the sun will "breathe." In the heat of daytime, the contents of the barrel become warm and expand, causing the barrel to "exhale." In the cooler night time temperature, the contents of the barrel contract, creating lower pressure and the barrel "inhales" the moist outside air. The vapor in the moist air cools and condenses into water, which is heavier than gasoline, and settles to the bottom of the barrel.

This cycle, repeated each day, eventually creates a pool of water in the bottom of the barrel of gasoline. The pump, being designed to empty all of the contents from the barrel, has its intake at the bottom of the barrel. When a FAC in a hurry begs for gasoline, the pump faithfully extracts whatever is on the bottom of the barrel and puts it into the tanks of the FAC's airplane, both gasoline and water.

The O-1's gasoline engine does not run on water.

I continued to switch from one tank to the other, trying to coax some power from the engine. It would run a little, then quit, then maybe run a little more, then quit again. I continued to lose altitude. The sight of the rescue chopper had never been so welcome. They got there quickly and followed me as I kept switching from one tank to the other and flying lower and lower.

I barely got it on the ground at Ban Me Thuot and the engine quit completely before I could taxi off the runway. Later the flight mechanic drained a nearly full pop bottle of water from each wing tank.

The boys at Boun Ea Yang had done their best to help me. I appreciated their quick response when I was in a big hurry. Unfortunately, it didn't work.

6.6 – It was a fuel barrel like these that "breathed" and gathered condensate in the bottom. A pump like this put the resulting water into my fuel tanks.

6.7 – These Boun Ea Yang Special Forces Green Berets unknowingly pumped the water (condensate) into my fuel tanks.

Page 71

Poor facilities and equipment at Special Forces Camps often led to problems for airplanes. Five days after the water in the fuel incident at Buon Ea Yang, we had an airplane problem related to the runway at Ban Don Special Forces Camp. With plenty of rain, the dirt runway went from bad to worse. Dan Preston called me on the radio from Ban Don and said, "Don't ask questions now. I'll tell you later. Just get Sergeant Collins and come out to Ban Don in our other plane. Have Collins bring a bunch of tools. And be careful to miss all of the damned wet places in the runway when you land. There's a whole bunch of them and they're soft. Your wheel can sink in the mud."

Dan was speaking from experience. There were several mud holes in the runway and Dan hit one of them with the left landing gear when he landed. He slowed enough that when the left gear sank into the hole, there wasn't any major damage. The airplane stopped very quickly and tipped forward onto its nose. The tail remained up in the air and the propeller remained stuck in the mud. Dan carefully climbed down with a disgusted red face.

By the time I got there with Sgt Collins in our other bird, Dan had enlisted the aid of a few Montagnards. They threw a rope around the vertical stabilizer, like lassoing a steer at the rodeo, and pulled the tail down out of the sky.

Dan spoke to the crew chief, "Well, Sarge, what do you think? Did I break our airplane?"

Collins replied, "I don't know, Captain. I can see there are a few buckled places on the engine cowling, but I think I can pound them out. My concern is for the prop and the engine. It looks like the prop screwed into the mud pretty hard. The resulting damage, if any, depends on how suddenly the engine was stopped. When we get all of the mud off, we can probably make a good visual inspection of the prop. What happened inside the engine will be harder to determine because we can't see in there. Maybe we'll be lucky."

Collins pounded out the dents in the cowling and we cleaned the mud from the prop and the front of the engine. Collins said, "Well, Sir, so far so good. I can't see any damage to the prop. Let's give it a thorough run up and see how it performs."

The engine checked out OK for a good run up, but I still had concern about possible damage we could not see. "Dan, do you think you want to fly it back now?"

"Yeah, let's give it a shot. You'll be on my wing if anything happens."

Nothing did happen. It all went smooth as silk. It was a happy ending to the unusual story about Preston's muddy airplane.

But the runway at Ban Don claimed another victim at the same time. The Army CV-2, Caribou, which hauled rice for the camp, couldn't land on the muddy runway until it dried a bit. The camp ran out of rice for the Montagnard strikers and they threatened to quit.

The population of about five or six hundred at Ban Don was typical for Special Forces Camps. About two or three percent were Green Beret Advisors. Another two or three percent were ethnic Vietnamese. The remainder, about ninety-four to ninety six percent, were strikers. If they decided to walk away, no one was going to stop them. To make things worse during the rice crisis, the Vietnamese Second Lieutenant in the camp continued a prolonged drunken rampage. He worsened the Montagnards' general resentment of the Vietnamese, a feeling that always simmered just below the surface.

Our FAC, Dick Overgaard, flew an Army major from the Green Beret team in Ban Me Thuot to the Ban Don camp. He assured the strikers that rice was on the way and did what he could to calm the local drunk officer. The crisis slowly quieted.

6.8 – Green Beret Capt Joe Foxworth, Ban Don Special Forces Camp Senior Advisor, provides taxi service from their muddy runway.

6.9 – An Army CV-2 Caribou misses a mud hole in the Ban Don runway.

6.10 – Joe Foxworth and an unidentified friend by a Ban Don machine gun bunker

6.11 – A Bird Dog FAC checks out the mortar pit at Ban Don Special Forces Camp.

At about the same time, things were happier at Lac Thien Special Forces Camp. On July 27, 1966, I had "dinner" with the Green Berets there and we talked about maps. On the return trip to Ban Me Thuot, I hauled two of their Vietnamese who needed to get there. They weren't very big and didn't weigh too much.

The next day I went back and gave them some maps and we talked some more. After takeoff, I circled back over the camp for some informal fun. Dan Preston and I rigged up a bracket to hold a smoke grenade. We could mount one bracket on each strut of the O-1. The bracket was located so the pilot could reach out the window and pull the pin on the grenade. Just before I came across the camp, I leaned out and pulled the pin on a grenade. The yellow smoke from the grenade trailed behind the plane as I flew over them.

They were quickly on the radio, "Hey, Baron Four Two! That's the coolest thing we've seen in a long time! And thanks again for the maps." It looked great and the gravel agitators on the ground really loved us. We, of course, were very modest. But they really knew for sure who we were.

I used the smoke grenade technology/gimmickry a couple of times on FAC missions, mainly to give the fighters something to talk about when they got back to their home base.

On a normal strike mission, the first contact between the FAC and the fighters was by radio. The FAC, at low altitude, usually looked up and easily located the arriving fighters. The fighters, however, frequently had trouble locating the FAC visually. This required the FAC to issue a few instructional calls to help the fighters see the FAC. That's where the smoke grenade was helpful.

On one particular mission I was prepared to let the fighters see something different to laugh about. We were already in radio contact with call signs exchanged and I could see them approaching over the target. "Yellow Bird Three One, this is Baron Four Two. I am at your eleven o'clock position low, trailing purple smoke -- now."

As I said the word "now," I pulled the pin on the smoke grenade, leaving a semi-spectacular trail of purple smoke.

Yellow Bird made a surprised response, "Hey, that's neat, Baron! How in the Hell did you do that?!"

On the more serious side, there was a semi-formal arrangement between our FAC squadron and the Green Berets attaching one FAC and one Special Forces Camp to work with each other. While flying out of Pleiku, I had that commitment with Ducco Special Forces Camp. At the request of Capt Josh Easley, the Camp Senior Advisor, I flew him around Ducco for some aerial reconnaissance in the vicinity of his camp. When we were in the air, I said to him, "Tell me just where you want to look, Josh, and I'll give you a good view of it."

I was taken aback by his response, "Dale, if you wouldn't mind, could I have it and look for myself?"

What?! Here's this Army ground pounding grunt telling me he wants to try to fly my airplane?! Well, what the heck. It could be fun watching him try. I shook the control stick and said, "Sure, Josh, you have it."

To my surprise, he flew the O-1 smoothly and capably for several minutes, telling me where he was going and then easily doing just what he said he would do. As we talked further, I learned he was a fully qualified Army pilot and had more experience and flying time in the O-1 than I had. Now he was the Senior Advisor of Ducco Special Forces Camp on the ground in Vietnam. He was a serious Army officer and had requested to be a Green Beret for "career broadening and advancement." Wow! I admired his ambition and dedication. I couldn't imagine asking to leave flying to run around in the weeds on the ground.

Later, in April 1966, things were hot around Ducco. Apparently Charlie came right back across the border from Cambodia as soon as the First Air Cavalry finished their big sweep through the area and chased them out. On April 12, 1966, things looked quiet for a while. Mervyn Unser had a 1st Lt paymaster in the backseat of his O-1 taxiing him to Ducco. However, as Unser neared Ducco, he received an urgent call for help. The paymaster passenger had the unexpected and unique experience of hanging onto 1,300,000 piasters, (about $13,000) in a box on his lap in the back seat of the O-1 when Unser abruptly abandoned his role as taxi driver and resumed being a FAC.

The distress call came from one of Ducco's own patrols. The patrol was just north of Chu Pong Mountain on the Cambodian border when they came under attack. Unser FAC-ed some A-1s and F-4s onto the source of the attack. Joe Everett later relieved Unser and put some more fighters onto the same area.

The patrol out of Ducco consisted of two Americans, two Vietnamese and twenty-seven Montagnards. Choppers later extracted eighteen uninjured and two wounded members of that patrol. Two others were dead and nine more were missing and thought to be dead. One of the two dead was Capt Josh Easley, the Ducco Senior Advisor. Easley was the Army O-1 pilot who had, to my surprise, capably flown my airplane when I took him for reconnaissance around his camp. By his choice he had left flying to become a Green Beret. So much for "career broadening and advancement."

I have great admiration for the Men of the Green Beret who served in the US Army Special Forces. They were brave, dedicated citizens working in very dangerous circumstances. They deserve our thanks.

Chapter 7
Our Frail Airplane

1965-66 – South Vietnam

The official Air Force designation of the airplane we flew was "O-1E," the letter "O" meaning "observation." That did tell part of the story. It was essential for the FAC to be able to observe what was going on in order to do his job. The use of the term "observation" was, however, also misleading, perhaps giving the impression the FAC's job was to sit in the fourteenth row and watch the proceedings. Nothing could have been more incorrect!

The FAC was not "an audience of one," holding a ticket for the show and subsequently reporting his views of how the performance went. The FAC was the director of the program, the conductor of the orchestra, the controller of the whole show. If he blew it, the entire production was a complete failure with very negative consequences.

To perform his task, the FAC had to <u>see</u> everything all of the time. First, he had to see the target and correctly identify what was to be struck. He then located the arriving fighter aircraft and gave them directions to visually find <u>him</u>. Then he marked the target with smoke rockets or smoke grenades and gave instructions to the fighters. During the strike, he had to maintain sight of both the target and the fighters. For more accurate placement of their ordnance on successive runs, the FAC usually issued refined instructions to the fighters.

The term observation alluded to what was probably the most valuable characteristic of the O-1, namely excellent visibility. With big windows everywhere, we could see very well in all directions.

Unless the weather was cold, we commonly flew with the side windows swung up, fastened open. The good visibility was enhanced by the aircraft's high maneuverability. Flying at only 75 knots, the pilot could slam the control stick to one side, stomp on the rudder and turn around on a dime. This was frequently necessary during an air strike to maintain sight of everything that was happening. It wasn't smooth flying, but it was effective.

The aircraft itself was essentially a Cessna 170 with a Cessna 180 engine. Cessna built a lot of them in the early 1950s and the US military bought them with minor modifications. In the Korean War, the US Army flew the plane and called it the L-19, the L standing for liaison. The term "liaison" described the Army's use of the aircraft for communication and general utility.

Early in the Vietnam War, the Air Force officially called it the O-1. It was unofficially known as the Bird Dog and the FACs who flew it in South Vietnam were called Bird Dog FACs. Later, the O-2, also a modified Cessna, made its appearance in South Vietnam as a FAC aircraft. It had one propeller pulling and one pushing. Later yet, the new OV-10, with two engines and some moderate strike capability of its own, arrived in South Vietnam for use by FACs. Over heavily defended North Vietnam, where an O-1 would not have lasted for five minutes, the F-100 sometimes served as a FAC airplane.

When I was in South Vietnam in 1965 and 1966, early in the war, the only aircraft used by FACs was the O-1. Nearly all of them were the E model, designated the O-1E. Late in 1966 we occasionally had an O-1F, with only slight differences from the O-1E.

The O-1 was a small slow airplane that weighed about as much as the Volkswagen Bug or the Toyota Corolla automobile. On a smooth straight road, either of those two automobiles might out run the O-1. It also had sturdy fixed main landing gear and a rear tail wheel, whose structure enabled it to land on rough surfaces.

The O-1E climbed at 80 miles per hour, cruised at 90 mph (75 knots) and landed at 70 mph with full flaps. The maximum allowable gross weight, which we always exceeded, was about 2,200 pounds. Equipped with four white phosphorus rockets and one pilot carrying his weapons and other gear, we usually operated at about 2,400 pounds. This was about nine percent over maximum allowable gross weight. Most of that extra weight was added by the rocket suspension racks under the wings and the rockets themselves. With an occasional observer in the back seat, the weight went up to about 2,600 pounds, about eighteen percent over maximum allowable gross weight.

7.1 – M-16 rifle, 38 pistol, flak vest, survival vest, map case, helmet bag and "picnic bag" containing an extra survival radio, canteen of water and energy bars

7.2 – Broken clouds over Pleiku.   *7.3 – Kon Tum, north of Pleiku*

The O-1 had no armament. I always wore one flak vest and normally sat on a second one. The back pack parachute was a standard item of issue, but was never worn. The standard practice for medium sized pilots like me was to prop the back pack parachute against the airplane seat to serve as a back rest. Most of the larger pilots left the parachute on the ground for more room in the cockpit and less weight for the plane.

The practice of not wearing the parachute for its designed purpose of bailing out of a disabled aircraft was not a matter of bravado or machismo. Bailing out was a bad deal. Given the conditions under which we operated, a preferable and safer procedure was to execute a good crash landing. A successful exit from the O-1 in flight, encumbered by a bulky survival vest, a heavy flak vest, a 38 caliber pistol strapped around the waist and wearing a parachute, was very unlikely. The O-1 wasn't designed for departure by parachute, and the extra equipment made a successful exit less likely.

That, however, wasn't the main factor. Our nominal operating altitude was 1,500 feet above the ground. If a FAC had trouble, he would probably first spend time addressing other possible remedies before considering bailing out, leaving less time available for the bail out procedure. Even if he promptly initiated the bail out attempt while at 1,500 feet, he was unlikely to make it in time. Furthermore, we spent much of our time at tree top level, not at 1,500 feet above the ground. I never heard of an attempted bailout by a FAC.

Every FAC I knew planned, if the engine quit, to put the plane down in the best available place using full flaps and flying as slowly as possible. If flight controls and flaps were still operable and a place without large rocks, trees or bad terrain was available, the chances of walking away from a crash landing were pretty good.

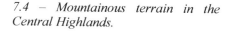

7.4 – Mountainous terrain in the Central Highlands.

7.5 – During an air strike, a Bird Dog FAC makes hurried notes on the window with a grease pencil.

The frail O-1 was routinely subjected to unreasonable expectations under harsh conditions. After all, it was designed to cruise with a passenger or two somewhere in the States when the weather was nice. In South Vietnam, overloaded, flown in combat, frequently in bad weather, it suffered repeated rigorous use and frequent outright abuse.

How well did the O-1 perform in some specific cases? In each of the following situations, did the performance of the aircraft itself merit a win, a loss or a draw? This analysis does not include the many O-1s and FACs flying them who were destroyed by enemy action. They are not part of this particular airplane performance review. It would be unfair to hold the O-1 itself responsible for being shot down when subjected to unreasonable conditions.

Here we go. WIN? LOSE? Or DRAW?

On January 27, 1966, I flew from Pleiku to Bong Son to deliver a heavy load of rockets, adapters, a gasoline pump and two parachutes. Our Operations Officer, Maj Archuleta, was at the flight line with me as I made the pre-flight inspection of the O-1. I said, "Wow! What is all of this junk? This airplane is no freighter and that stuff looks awfully heavy. Why are we hauling it anyway?"

Arch replied, "There's an operation starting tomorrow morning from Bong Son and they need all of this right now. You can see that the back seat is gone. It was removed so we could cram everything in."

I was seriously concerned about the overload. "This airplane has to be way beyond max allowable gross weight. How much does all of that weigh?"

Arch shrugged, "Who knows? Too much. And it's not only total weight that matters. With the load that far back in the airplane, the center of gravity is sure to be way out of whack. When you take off, be sure that the plane can first pick up the tail before you break ground. Be careful that you don't take off with the nose too high or the plane will stall out."

"This really doesn't sound like a Hell of a lot of fun for me, Arch. Do you think the bird can even get all of this stuff off the ground?"

"I don't know. It may not. We all know that it's way too heavy, but you have 6,000 feet of runway to find out. Give it a try. If it won't fly, you have enough room to abort the takeoff. If that happens, come back in and we'll unload some of the stuff."

It was close. The airplane may have set a record for high speed taxiing down the runway before finally staggering from the runway into the air. Climbing was still another question. It was uphill all of the way from Pleiku to Mang Yang Pass. It took full takeoff power all the way to make it over the top. That's called engine abuse. I got a closer look than I wanted at all of the crosses marking French graves on top of those hills. The struggling bird barely made it over the pass with precious little room to spare.

Once over the pass, it was down hill past An Khe and into Bong Son. The descent allowed me to ease off the unreasonable demand for power. The airplane's performance under unreasonable demands was easy to put in the WIN column.

A few months later, I over stressed it again. I hauled several overloads of abandoned groceries from the Boun Blech Special Forces Camp to the missionaries in Ban Me Thuot. The grocery loads were not quite as heavy as the stuff for Bong Son, but the runway was poor and short, and there were trees to clear right after take off. That put another mark in the WIN column for the O-1.

In the LOSS column, there was a serious matter regarding engine performance. Occasionally, without warning, the engine quit abruptly. This happened often enough to be called a characteristic failure. During my year in Vietnam, the specific cause of those failures was not positively determined.

Sudden engine failure was a very serious matter. Once my engine failed abruptly on final approach at Pleiku and I put the plane down in an abandoned mine field. When Otis Holmes crashed at the Tan Rai Special Forces Camp, sudden engine failure was found to be a possible cause for the accident.

In each of those two cases, and some others, a faulty fuel primer seal was thought to be the possible culprit. Although it was never determined with certainty why there were so many instances in which the engine quit, it was for darned sure that the engine did quit. An airplane engine is not supposed to quit in flight. The O-1 got a definite bad mark in the LOSS column on that issue.

Frequently weather caused trouble for the O-1 and the FACs who flew it. Heavy rain caused several mud holes in the runway at Ban Don Special Forces Camp. When Dan Preston hit one with the landing gear of his O-1, it wasn't the aircraft's fault it ended up on its nose with the propeller screwed into the mud. The fact the airplane survived that incident of severe abuse without any damage was a very large credit to the toughness of the bird itself. For enduring that incident undamaged, the O-1 gets applause and another mark in the WIN column.

Another incident of outright abuse involved a FAC from another squadron. The FAC flew over an artillery firebase at what turned out to be the wrong time and took a friendly artillery round up through the wing. The fortunate FAC landed safely to tell about it and the airplane was blameless for the incident. For surviving in one piece, the O-1 got another very big mark in the WIN column.

There were dramatic incidents which failed to produce a clear cut decision regarding the performance of the O-1. When I landed at Buon Ea Yang for hurried re-fueling, the Green Berets innocently gave me fuel contaminated with water. The incident reaffirmed what everyone knows. The internal combustion engine does not run on water but the O-1 was not at fault for the bad fueling error. That incident resulted in a "no call" or DRAW.

Similarly, the engine could not be expected to run very long without engine oil. Maj Dave Wiley had an engine fail because it suffered oil starvation. That engine failure was due to human error. The ensuing drama was in no way the fault of the O-1. Regarding the airplane's performance, the call in that situation was another mark in the DRAW column.

The little airplane we flew always came out second best when it ran into something large and hard. On July 2, 1966, a FAC in I Corps collided with an F-4C in the air. The F-4C landed successfully and the O-1 landed unceremoniously in a great number of small pieces with a dead FAC.

Five days later, a landing O-1 and a heavily loaded Army ammunition truck blithely rumbling across the runway suffered an unplanned meeting at the Oasis airstrip. Both the angry FAC and the suddenly alert truck driver scrambled away from the collision before the resulting fire ignited a large explosion which destroyed both the airplane and the ammo truck. Once again, the airplane's performance was not to blame.

Those two collisions with hard objects resulted in two destroyed airplanes, one destroyed Army ammo truck and one lost FAC. The rating for the performance of the O-1 itself was two more marks in the DRAW column.

A mid-air collision was nearly always disastrous for the O-1. On Aug 7, 1966, I had one while controlling an air strike. It was serious for me and my airplane, but even more serious for a very large black bird. I'm satisfied that if I could hear the big black bird's side of the story, he would report that he definitely came out the loser. Therefore, it seems implicit that the O-1 was the winner. We'll accept the bird's testimony as gospel truth and put another mark in the WIN column for the O-1.

In this informal examination of ten incidents, the performance rating of the O-1 produced five WINs, one LOSS and four DRAWs.

Could it be that the title of this chapter, "Our Frail Airplane," is an unfair reference to the O-1? Considering everything to which the aircraft was subjected and how it usually survived, would it be more appropriate to call the chapter "Our Tough Little Bird"?

Chapter 8

The Arrival of Large US Forces

Fall 1965 — Pleiku area

I arrived in Pleiku in October 1965, as part of "the big build up" of American forces in Vietnam. My FAC squadron was part of the "in country" system, numerically a very small part of the total American involvement in Vietnam. This book is focused on the activities of FACs in my area of operations. To repeat, we were <u>not</u> a part of any of the large American Army units which comprised most of the military people in Vietnam.

However, to fail to comment on those large units would be to neglect the principal numerical presence of American military forces in Vietnam.

Shortly before the big build up began, the military situation in the Central Highlands, in particular around Pleiku, was deteriorating rapidly and seriously. To appreciate the worsening military situation and the devastating impact it had on the civilian population, it is necessary to review events around Pleiku in the few years prior to the big build up.

A summary of those developments, from late 1960 until October, 1965, is presented here at the beginning of this chapter. This information is excerpted from the book <u>To Viet Nam with Love, the Story of Charlie and EG Long</u>, copyright 1995 by Christian Publications, Camp Hill, PA. The Longs were American missionaries in Pleiku. They worked under the auspices of The Christian and Missionary Alliance. This information is used with the permission of the author. Full credit and great appreciation are given to the author, Charlie Long.

(The following words are Long's. Thanks, Charlie.)

During the early 1960s the South Vietnamese government, with assistance from the United States, resettled thousands of coastal lowland Vietnamese into the Central Highlands. Le Thanh, west of Pleiku, was the westernmost resettlement village. I had assisted in the development of the Tin Lanh (Good News) Church in the town and had taught and preached there numerous times. Their leader, Pastor Tan, was a friend of mine.

In June 1965, Le Thanh was overrun by the Viet Cong. When the news got out, a relief convoy of provincial troops went to the rescue. Horns blared and citizen soldiers came running from all directions as the convoy formed in the streets of Pleiku.

The Toyota trucks carrying the assembled troops bumped and swayed down the main street of Pleiku and up the long grade to the junction of Route 19. This was a highway that ran like a belt around the middle of South Vietnam from the South China Sea on the East to Cambodia on the West. It was a possible line for cutting the country into two halves.

The rescue convoy was ambushed in the Le Thanh area and badly beaten by the VC. Two U.S. military advisors in the convoy were killed. The communists had clearly come to Le Thanh to stay.

Pastor Tan somehow managed to escape from the town of Le Tanh and made his way to Pleiku where he sought me out. "What should I do, Pastor Long? The Communists are killing all of the Christians that they can find. Should I go back to Le Thanh to be with my church or should I wait in Pleiku for a while? Will it ever be safe again for our brothers and sisters in Le Thanh?"

How do you advise a man who faces likely death whichever way he turns? "My friend, I can't tell you what you should do. Let's pray together now for God's guidance and then sleep on the matter overnight."

The following morning he was excited. I could tell that he had arrived at a decision. He said simply, "My place as the shepherd is with my sheep." We prayed together, shook hands and he departed for Le Thanh.

"God go with you, my brother. May He support you and your church."

Days later, I learned that Pastor Tan had been murdered by the communists. They had pitched his body by the side of the road. Some of his congregation found the body and buried it.

Soon the Le Thanh fighting resumed and threatened a nearby Special Forces Camp. South Vietnam threw some of its best units into the fray. This time the Viet Airborne Brigade and the Viet Marines came to the rescue. A young American captain, H. Norman Schwarzkopf (yes, that H. Norman Schwarzkopf) was the U.S. advisor to the Viet Airborne Brigade. This rescue party was also ambushed and suffered great losses.

More than 200 bodies of Vietnamese provincial soldiers were trucked back to Pleiku for their widows to identify and bury. Cries of "Dead already! Daddy's dead! Life is too miserable!" filled the air. Women collapsed in heaps on the ground. Some plunged themselves into the lake to escape their pain.

But there was something of greater significance in this series of battles. The last rescue party that came to the aid of western Pleiku province was an all-American unit, the 173rd Airborne. It was the first time I had seen an American combat unit in the fighting.

I knew that construction had been progressing on a new runway at Pleiku. One night I heard the whistling roar of incoming C-130 cargo planes. In a 30 minute period the whole 173rd Airborne landed on that unfinished runway. They quickly moved west on Route 19 to back up the hard-pressed Vietnamese units. The big American war was beginning.

There is no doubt in my mind that the arrival of American combat troops saved Pleiku. The war situation, so seemingly hopeless only days before their arrival, now took on new optimism.

(Thanks again to Charlie Long for his preceding words which I have used in introducing this chapter.)

Charlie Long states that the arrival of the 173rd Airborne saved Pleiku in the summer of 1965. Those few of us Americans on Pleiku Airbase in the fall of 1965 would have been glad to have a lot more units like the 173rd around the area. The security of the Pleiku compound itself was very questionable. The physical defenses were minimal and there was generally low confidence in the Vietnamese defenders. They appeared to be short on training, organization, firepower and dedication. The arrival of large American units appeared to make the Pleiku compound less vulnerable to the attacks regularly rumored to be coming.

In my nine months in Pleiku there was not an actual invasive assault on the compound. However, questions persisted about the many local civilian employees in black pajamas who regularly came through the gates. Might they have been a factor in the well targeted mortar attack that did hit the flight line and cause much damage to airplanes? Convenient access to the compound in the daytime could have been quite helpful in planning the nighttime attack.

8.1 – The Viet Cong launched a well directed and successful mortar attack on the A-1 parking ramp area on Pleiku Airbase. This A-1 took a direct mortar hit.

8.2 – A sizable fire followed the explosion of mortar rounds.

The "locals" might be paid employees in the daytime and Viet Cong mortar men at night. They might return the morning after the mortar attack and resume their paying jobs inside the Pleiku compound. The "round-eyed" Americans frequently couldn't tell a local good guy from a local bad guy. The "locals" could fade away into the local population and escape being noticed.

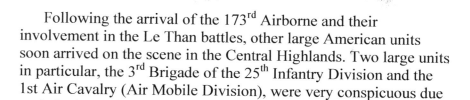

Following the arrival of the 173rd Airborne and their involvement in the Le Than battles, other large American units soon arrived on the scene in the Central Highlands. Two large units in particular, the 3rd Brigade of the 25th Infantry Division and the 1st Air Cavalry (Air Mobile Division), were very conspicuous due to their size and activity.

Our 21st Tactical Air Support Squadron (TASS) of FACs remained separate from these large new forces. However, as these large units arrived with their own FACs, we sometimes helped them "come up to speed" and occasionally augmented their numbers of FACs and/or airplanes on a temporary basis.

The "3rd of the 25th" arrived suddenly in Pleiku on December 24, 1965 in a massive effort called "Operation Blue Light." The event was documented by The Pacific Stars and Stripes newspaper in the following article which seems to be a combination of news reporting and cheerleading.

Operation Blue Light

"Operation Blue Light," the Air Force's airlift of 3,000 soldiers and 3,200 tons of cargo from Hawaii to Pleiku in the Central Highlands of South Viet Nam, ended early Sunday. The operation, conducted by the Military Airlift Command (MAC), began on Dec. 24. It moved elements of the Army's 3rd Brigade, 25th Infantry Division.

Lt. Col. H. Bowles, project officer for Operation Blue Light said, "This has been an exceptionally smooth operation. The Air Force did a magnificent job of transporting men and equipment to the Pleiku area. The operation went off with hardly a hitch."

Lt. Col. Russell J. Revel, of Hutchinson, Kan., the commander of the MAC airlift control force for Operation Blue Light, called the airlift an extremely well planned operation which combined the efforts of the Army and Air Force. Revel said, "This operation proved beyond a doubt that MAC can move a division-size unit and its equipment from a U.S. location into a combat area."

Some 270 men from MAC units were directly involved in the operation. About 80 men from other major commands also participated in the airlift. Air Force C-133 jet turbo prop and C-141 jet transports were the primary aircraft used in the operation. They were backed up by C-124 Globemasters and C-130 Hercules transports.

The airlift was indeed successfully completed. The 3rd of the 25th arrived in the Pleiku area and got settled. They didn't stay put for very long. They spent February 24-27, 1966, moving 2,000 men and equipment from Pleiku to Ban Me Thuot to launch an operation in that area. I learned on February 28th I would go the next morning from Pleiku to Ban Me Thuot to temporarily support their operation. I took Airman First Class Foxworth, flight mechanic, and O-1 #168 to support the operation which was already adequately supported without me. Our hurried dispatch to go help appeared to be completely unnecessary.

When organizations with great numbers of men and large quantities of equipment hurry into a mission, it's difficult to coordinate everything smoothly. On March 1st, their operation began near the Mewal plantation close to Ban Me Thuot. They had four attached FACs and two airplanes of their own available for the operation. Four of us FACs and four airplanes sent from Pleiku were not needed.

The 3rd of the 25th was a big outfit. Prior to their arrival, there had not been a large American unit in the Central Highlands. Their presence was big news. It attracted big time attention. At the "really big briefing" preceding the March 1st kick off of their operation near the Mewal plantation, General Westmoreland (Commander of Everything in Vietnam) was present.

When the big general showed up for the briefing and made a comment, people started jumping. Some jumped in the wrong direction. It would have been better if some had not jumped at all. But when the top military man in all of Vietnam said something perceived to be a directive, they did jump.

Maj Vertrees, the head FAC for the 25th, was briefing on the subject of aerial support for ground troops when Gen Westmoreland broke in, "Major, how many O-1s and FACs do you have for this operation?" Vertrees replied, "Sir, we have one plane and three FACs at present..." Before he could finish and say that he also had one more FAC and one more plane coming to make four FACs and two planes, which was their assigned strength, and that would be enough, Gen Westmoreland interrupted once more, "That's not enough, etc."

In the ensuing discussion with General Olmstead, someone muttered the word "six" and General Olmstead ordered our Pleiku squadron to provide four planes and four FACs effective immediately. People started jumping through their own shirt collars to comply with instructions. Furthermore, our 21st TASS airplanes and FACs weren't under General Olmstead's command anyway. That fact just added to the confusion.

It was so ridiculous it was almost funny. The four FACs and two planes that already belonged to the 3rd of the 25th were adequately working the operation. The four of us extra FACs and four extra planes from Pleiku made useless circles in the sky "flying intensive visual reconnaissance" for a few days in adjacent areas. That meant that we were just staying out of the way.

While we were there, it seemed that someone had realized there were too many FACs and O-1s for the operation and figured out how to get rid of one extra plane and one pilot. They scheduled one airplane for visual reconnaissance beginning with an extra early morning take-off in complete darkness from the unlighted dirt strip.

It wasn't a smart idea. It was, no doubt, conceived by someone other than the pilot who would be required to fly it. I drew the assignment and made it without hitting anything in the dark. They didn't get rid of me, so we still had four too many FACs and four too many O-1s for the operation.

Eventually the generals left Ban Me Thuot and returned to Saigon. Everything calmed down. When the top brass had been gone for a few days, the extra FACs and extra O-1s drifted back to their regularly assigned locations. The operation proceeded as though the generals had stayed in Saigon from the start.

If there had been names like Gen Amos T. Halftrack, Maj Greenbrass, Capt Sam Scabbard, Lt Sonny Fuzz and Sgt Snorkel involved, I would have thought that it had all come straight from the Sunday comics. My personal involvement in the operation was just a few days spent flying in circles, but those days counted toward the completion of a year, just the same as they would have back in Pleiku. At the time I didn't know that in Ban Me Thuot I was previewing the place where I would later spend the last three months of my tour in Vietnam.

That's how the 3rd Brigade of the 25th Infantry Division arrived in the Central Highlands and how we in-country FACs in Pleiku "helped" them on their initial South Vietnam foray in the Ban Me Thuot area.

The arrival of the 1st Air Cavalry (Air Mobile Division) was quite different.

On July 28, 1965 President Johnson announced on television, "We will stand in Vietnam… I have today ordered to Vietnam the Air Mobile Division." A huge logistical exercise quickly followed that announcement.

The newly designated 1st Air Cavalry Division feverishly prepared for deployment. The movement of over 400 aircraft, nearly 16,000 personnel, over 1,600 vehicles, and the necessary training for combat in just eight weeks was a monumental task.

In August four aircraft carriers, six troop carriers and seven cargo ships departed Mobile, Alabama to move the entire division to the other side of the world. The Army Warrant Officer helicopter pilots of the Air Cav were on the USNS *Croatan*. In September the armada arrived at Qui Nhon, a coastal town without any port facilities. Everything was successfully unloaded and the division proceeded inland to its new home.

An advance party of one thousand men had flown in earlier and begun the immense task of clearing the area for the huge base from which the division would operate. They were across Mang Yang

Pass, near the village of An Khe, about 40 miles east of Pleiku. Although the 1st Air Cav location was not geographically far from Pleiku, their operation with jillions of helicopters was completely different from ours, and we were seldom involved in what they did.

One area of involvement for our squadron with the 1st Air Cav was training and checking out their attached Air Force FACs. The 1st Cav had attempted the function of Forward Air Controlling from one of their attack helicopters. The attempt quickly proved to be totally unsuccessful. They desperately needed FACs flying O-1s. Some hurried cooperative adjustments between the Army and the Air Force were made to solve that large problem.

The Big Build Up in the fall of 1965 included other American units in other parts of South Vietnam. The 3rd of the 25th and the 1st Air Cav were the most notable units in the Central Highlands and it was good that they arrived when they did. Their presence may have saved Pleiku itself.

The big American forces commonly had more fire power than the Viet Cong and usually had more than the North Vietnamese Regulars. On the occasions when the bad guys would stand and fight, the Americans usually achieved a vastly superior kill ratio. The VC and the North Vietnamese knew that was the case and would avoid such engagements, which was smart on their part. The problem for the Americans was to locate and engage the VC and the North Vietnamese in combat. The bad guys were good at disappearing when things were not likely to go their way.

Since the large American Army units had their own FACs attached as part of their unit, we "in-country" FACs mostly stayed out of their operations. On occasion, we helped out and were appreciated for the resource that we could add to their effectiveness. We also learned how things went for Air Force pilots attached to large Army units. For the most part, it wasn't what an Air Force pilot would want.

On June 1, 1966, I talked with a FAC attached to the Army 1st Cav. He was an Air Force Captain like me, flying the same airplane and being a FAC. I wondered how it was to be with the Army for a year.

I asked, "How is life with the 1st Cav?"

"Just between us girls, it sucks big time. It's not worth a damn. I'm an Air Force officer and I never signed up for Army duty."

"Not so good, huh. How much flying time are you getting?"

"For the whole damned month of May I logged two hours and forty-five minutes in the air. Like I told you, it sucks."

"Man, I wouldn't like that either. We frequently have guys break a hundred hours of flying time in one month. What do you do when you're not flying?"

"I spend most of my time kicking around in the weeds with a bunch of Army grunts. Ya wanna trade jobs?"

I felt better after that visit. There was at least one job worse than being an Air Force FAC in Vietnam. That was being an Air Force FAC in Vietnam attached to an Army unit and running around on the ground with a bunch of grunts instead of flying.

Every Air Force FAC that I knew wanted no part of being attached to an Army unit as their FAC. Nevertheless, all of the Air Force FACs I knew were very glad the big Army outfits had arrived in the Central Highlands.

Chapter 9
Regarding Awards and Decorations

December 6, 1965 – Over the Ho Chi Minh trail

Military awards and decorations vary greatly in importance. They may indicate longevity, presence in a particular theater of service, a job well done, injury in action against the enemy or heroism/gallantry in action against the enemy.

A longevity award recognizes only length of service. An award for being present in a particular theater says only, "I was there," and makes no further comment.

In a book about war, the Purple Heart deserves particular comment. The award is made for "wounds or death in combat" and is perhaps the award most frequently presented in wartime. It may recognize a fatal injury, a very minor injury or anything in between. It is probably the military award most widely known and recognized by the people in our society. There is no requirement for gallantry, heroism or achievement for the award. The Purple Heart, however, is nearly guaranteed to strike a chord of sympathy among other people.

The higher military awards and decorations presented by the United States Military are given in recognition of gallantry or heroism in action against the enemy, for doing something. The medals and ribbons associated with combat action, awarded by the US Military, are as follows, in order of importance:

Medal of Honor - - awarded for gallantry and intrepidity at risk of life above and beyond the call of duty

Air Force Cross (Navy Cross/Army Distinguished Service Cross) - - awarded for exceptional heroism in combat

Silver Star - - awarded for gallantry in action

Distinguished Flying Cross - - awarded for heroism or extraordinary achievement in flight

Bronze Star - - awarded for heroic or meritorious achievement during military operations

Air Medal - - awarded for meritorious achievement in flight

In the FAC business there was a lot of action. Due to the nature of the job, FACs were always doing something. FACs were a highly decorated bunch of pilots.

Being a FAC was a very hazardous job and losses were high. During the year I was there, our loss rate of pilots was the highest in all of South Vietnam. (When loss rates in the North Vietnam air campaign were included, our loss rate was second to the F-105 fighter bombers. They flew into the most intense anti-aircraft defense in the history of aerial warfare.) Any FAC who did his job well and survived his one year tour of duty would most likely go home well decorated, deserving every award.

The paper work for an award, in the form of a submission (recommendation), must precede the granting of the award. The process can sometimes go afoul. Poor clerical staff work can impede proper action on awards. On one occasion I checked on the progress in Pleiku of a submission for the Bronze Star award for one of our Ban Me Thuot FACs. The sergeant who should have been handling the award said he knew nothing about it. When I delivered a second copy of the same submission to him, he found the original paper on his desk where it had lain unattended for more than a month.

Even when the paper work was in order, approval boards had a difficult job sorting out the most deserving submissions for awards. It was their task to decide whether a submission should be approved as submitted, downgraded to a lesser award or merely disapproved and returned.

In general, a mediocre accomplishment very skillfully described in superlatives on paper might appear to be more deserving than a much greater accomplishment poorly presented. It's tough for an evaluator to tell whether he is judging a particular action or judging the description written about that action.

In a very few cases, extreme heroism makes the approval process easy for the approval board. Bernie Fisher's rescue of Jump Meyers against unbelievable odds was completely amazing. Willie Wilbanks' personally taking on a vastly superior enemy force and giving up his own life while saving many other lives was heroic beyond question. Fisher and Wilbanks were the first two recipients of the Medal of Honor in all of the Vietnam War. The dramatic nature of those two events made the approval board's job easy.

Usually the facts were not cut and dried and the news media helped to make objective evaluations even more difficult. Capt Henry S. (Hank) Lang was one of our FACs who was deeply involved in the battle to hold the Plei Me Special Forces Camp. He was deservedly well decorated. The Pacific Stars and Stripes newspaper, hungry for glamorous stories, published a story about Hank as "Baron von Lang" (our call sign was Baron).

The generously overblown story reported Baron von Lang, "looking like a Prussian," flying with his five foot long red scarf emblazoned with the gold letters "Baron von Lang" trailing in the wind. It further reported Hank concocted home made bombs and dropped them from the O-1 onto a Viet Cong camp under an overhanging cliff, where the fighter bombers could not reach them.

United Press International picked up the article about "Baron von Lang" and published it as a feature nationwide. In the realm of news reporting, the story was greatly exaggerated, but it made attractive copy for readers wanting to see excitement and glamour in the paper. Such stories also complicated the official handling of awards and decorations.

There were others who would have relished that kind of press had they been able to attract that much attention. Maj Victor Vasquez, one of our FACs, on his third tour in Vietnam, managed to corner a large stash of purple smoke grenades and used them to mark targets whenever it was possible. With no modesty, he referred to himself as "The Purple Baron."

Some pilots hoped for, and even pursued, the acquisition of awards and decorations. The desire to "get my decorations" could be a seducing goal for a FAC who had been there for a while, but hadn't been decorated.

On December 6, 1965, I was innocently cast into the middle of such a pursuit launched by one of our FACs. During my "in country" check out I was flying front seat, conducting the mission. One of the "old heads" was in the back seat to see how the "new guy" did the job. It was a long day. At 5:00 AM Lt Mel Orwig woke me to go fly earlier than scheduled. We had a special target, staging first out of Kon Tum, 30 miles north of Pleiku, then continuing farther north and west to the target. It was a 'Tiger Hound' mission, one of those identified as more difficult and hazardous.

Many strikes in the area on the Ho Chi Minh Trail were planned, but nearly all of the fighters had been diverted elsewhere because of poor weather. We did get a flight of two Navy A-4s, from the aircraft carrier Bon Homme Richard, onto the target under the low clouds. They did a marvelous job. The lead A-4 managed to get down through a small hole in the clouds and acquire sight of me in the target area, a good piece of flying on his part.

The wingman got "shaken off" his leader's wing during the penetration down through the clouds and had to make a quick pull up to clear the top of the clouds. In formation flying, it is the wingman's task to maintain his aircraft position relative solely to the leader's aircraft. If it becomes impossible for him to maintain his position, much like staying on an extremely short leash, he is suddenly cut loose, shaken off, with no visual reference of his own to anything else. If that happens in the clouds, he must immediately switch to the use of his flight instruments. If he is in the vicinity of mountainous terrain, he must also initiate a pull up.

I proceeded with the attack with only the leader of the two ship flight. I marked the target and gave the lead A-4 instructions for his bombing run. He scored good hits on his first two passes. Meanwhile, the wingman was circling above the clouds trying to find his flight leader and me.

As I was clearing the lead A-4 onto the target for his third and final run, his wingman successfully came down through a little hole in the clouds. The smoke created by the leader's bombs showed the number two man where we were. The wing man had barely enough fuel left for one bombing pass. I cleared him onto the target to jettison every thing he had on one pass. He dumped it all right on the money in one excellent bombing run.

Maneuvering around the mountains under the low ceiling took a lot of skill and the two A-4 pilots did it quite well. With the strike complete, the two fighters pulled up through the clouds and returned to their carrier. They did an excellent job of flying in what turned out to be a very successful strike.

For most of the other fighters on that day, things were different. Because of bad weather, most of them were diverted onto relatively unimportant secondary targets or wasted their ordnance, dropping it into the ocean, to avoid the extra hazard of landing with live bombs.

For our strike, we reported nearly 30 buildings (loose definition of "building") destroyed and three large secondary explosions with the fireballs reaching an estimated 300 ft into the air. The target was reasoned to be a fuel storage area supporting infiltration from the north into South Vietnam.

I later learned Orwig and I had been submitted for the Distinguished Flying Cross (DFC) for action on that mission. That prompted some interesting questions in my mind.

The first question was whether our actions were deserving of the DFC. My own appraisal of all of the events of the day led me to say no. True, the mission was outstandingly successful, but I couldn't see we did enough to be awarded the DFC.

Yes, it was a particularly long hard day. We started very early and performed very well under difficult conditions. We succeeded while most of the attempts by others failed due to weather. We returned to our base in the dark with one fuel tank empty and the other one nearly dry. Yes, we did extremely well under unusually difficult conditions, but as I saw it, if anyone deserved special recognition it was the two A-4 pilots. They demonstrated perhaps even more achievement than the FACs did.

The second question in my mind was who made the submission on our behalf? There were only four people who saw what happened. I had no thought of seeking any special award, so that left three. Two of the remaining three were the two A-4 pilots. It was theoretically possible they could have somehow researched the identity of the FAC(s), told what a wonderful job he/they did and submitted from the Navy, the recommendation the Air Force FAC(s) be specially recognized. That seemed extremely unlikely.

That left only one person who could have told how wonderful we were. That was my back-seater, Lt Mel Orwig. It seemed implicitly obvious he gave a glowing report of the mission to one of his buddies in the squadron and his buddy made the submission. I didn't even know for some time the recommendation was made.

And there was a third question to address. The award submission was for Orwig and Amend, two FAC pilots in one airplane. I flew the airplane, located the target in an unknown area by correctly reading the topographical maps, made the successful rendezvous with the fighters in bad weather, marked the target accurately, and controlled the highly successful strike.

Orwig held down the back seat for one reason. As the old experienced head, his job was to observe the new guy and report on how the new guy did the job. So, if there was an award of the DFC, as requested, should it have been for two pilots or for one, and for which one?

Had I considered the possibility of some award, and if it had been left to me, there would have been no submission for any award. I didn't think our achievements had been sufficiently meritorious to earn the award of the DFC. Furthermore, I had been raised to believe modesty was a good thing and "self praise stinks." I understood it was not a good thing "to toot your own horn."

In the real world, however, there was a conflicting adage: "If ya don't blow yer own horn, it ain't gonna get blowed." It appeared to me that Orwig understood that selfish adage, and vigorously blew his own horn, trying to get his DFC.

The whole matter turned out to be academic. The approval board downgraded the DFC submission anyway and made it the award of a one-time Air Medal.

Big deal! FACs were awarded one Air Medal for each 25 missions flown because all of our flights were over enemy territory. We flew lots of missions and appropriately received lots of Air Medals. Now Orwig and I had one more. This one, however, was different since it was awarded for one very successful mission.

The recommendation for the award of the DFC for that particular mission faded into insignificance. On that occasion, in my opinion, the awards board got it right.

Chapter 10

The Boss Decides I Can Write

November 1965 – Pleiku

After the intense activity during the fight to save Plei Me Special Forces Camp subsided, the 21st TASS was able to assimilate Jenkins, Youngman, Holmes and me into the squadron.

We learned the Squadron Commander and the Operations Officer were great guys, but three of the lower ranking FACs gave us the kind of welcome frequently accorded an FNG. (An FNG was a "fuckin' new guy." It was a term of disdain and contempt, showing aloofness on the part of one who had been there a little longer and presumably knew it all).

The "old heads" somehow learned the FNGs were university graduate engineers. These old heads were good at "stick and throttle" for flying airplanes, but had little or no college education. Furthermore, they had just successfully proven themselves as FACs in a serious conflict. Their superior and resentful attitude was understandable.

Being the newest FNG wasn't necessarily fun. Fortunately for me, a surprising incident on Nov 2, 1965, nine days after my arrival in Pleiku, dusted some of the newness from my FNG status. It occurred at the end of a routine FAC mission which was part of my "in-country" checkout. One of the old heads, Lt Orwig, was in the back seat to observe the new guy.

When I returned to Pleiku, the tower cleared me for a practice touch and go landing per my request. I remained in closed left traffic after the touch and go. Everything was normal. Then on final approach at approximately 300 ft with 1600-1700 rpm, the engine quit completely. I switched fuel tanks and recycled the throttle, mixture and carburetor heat. The fuel selector was on the fullest tank, the mixture was full rich and the auxiliary fuel pump was on, all having been in their same respective positions since approximately one minute prior to the first landing. There was plenty of fuel in either tank when the engine quit. There was no reason for the engine to quit.

I landed the aircraft straight ahead with full flaps in full stalled condition and rolled approximately one hundred feet through very heavy grass about 200 yards short of the runway. There was no damage to the aircraft.

10.1 – The engine quit suddenly. I put it down 200 yards short of the runway in an abandoned mine field.

We learned later that I landed in a former mine field. The field had been cleared of mines only recently in conjunction with the building of the new runway and there was no danger from mines. That was interesting news to me, but it wouldn't have mattered if the mine field had been live and I had known it. With full flaps and a completely dead engine, the bird was coming down! Fast. No choices.

There was no fault on my part. In fact, there were favorable comments regarding my landing the aircraft without damage. Of course, it was fortunate there was a half-decent place to put it down. I did something unique none of the big ego, "old heads" had done. I rather enjoyed it all.

Unrelated to the dead engine landing, four hours earlier I was appointed Accident Investigating Officer for an accident involving one of our FACs and his airplane near Bao Loc. I wondered if that task, in addition to my regular flying duties, was because no one else wanted to push the paper job, or if perhaps LtCol Oliver thought I would do it well.

The project appeared to be an insignificant bother to merely fill the necessary squares following the loss of the Bao Loc airplane. At the time, I hadn't the least clue this developing sequence of paper jobs, which I really didn't want, might eventually contribute to my longevity.

The accident I was appointed to investigate happened the previous day near our operating location of Bao Loc. The aircraft burned completely after it crashed in bad VC country and was not recovered. There was no physical evidence to be examined. The investigation was a paper project all the way.

The following day I hopped an Army CV-2 Caribou, an Army transport about three fourths the size of an Air Force C-123 with a similar mission. The two Warrant Officer pilots were very accommodating. They changed their first stop destination from Tan Son Nhut to Bien Hoa to take me there. On the trip down they fed me a can of C rations for chow. At Bien Hoa they let me fly the traffic pattern and land this airplane I had never even seen at close range. How accommodating can you get? It was fun!

10.2 – US Army CV-2 Caribou and FAC hitchhiker

10.3 – Final approach to landing, viewed through the wind screen of the Caribou.

At Bien Hoa I talked with the Flying Safety people, got some accident investigation manuals to study, and found an empty bed belonging to some guy who was gone for the night. Before I left Bien Hoa there was enough time to get another pair of wrong size jungle boots from supply. I hoped to trade them for a right size pair somewhere. I bought laundry soap and an ironing board cover and found the Bien Hoa dispensary still had no gamma globulin for hepatitis prevention.

The next day, November 4, 1965, I caught the C-47 courier ten-minute flight from Bien Hoa to Tan Son Nhut and found a flight from there to Nha Trang where all the maintenance and aircraft records for the clobbered bird were kept. At Nha Trang I found Capt Gary Iverson of the Flying Safety Office. He helped me on procedures for the investigation and found me a bed for the night.

The following night in Iverson's room I sat on the edge of the bed with an upside down drawer on my lap for a table and started to write the report.

"Gary, I'm reading something interesting in these other O-1 accident reports you gave me. Do you guys here know anything about a fuel primer seal problem?"

"We don't know anything definite. So far it just looks like a possibility there could be a problem with it."

"I'd like to know more. My engine quit on final approach at Pleiku three days ago and I plunked it down in the tall grass on an abandoned mine field short of the runway. These reports you have here sound a lot like what I had. Could a faulty fuel primer seal be a factor in the Bao Loc accident, my own engine failure and other engine failures? Boy, if that's true, lots of pilots flying this bird would like to know."

"I don't have a definite answer, but we think that could be true."

The next day I rode at least fifteen miles around Nha Trang on a clunky old bicycle with the seat too low. It beat walking, though, and I finished filling all of the necessary squares on paper work there. A Nha Trang FAC gave me a lift to Bao Loc to conduct personal interviews regarding the crash.

I met with Maj Marvin Oglesby, the pilot, and Sgt Mike Easley, the Crew Chief, who was in the back seat as an observer. They were of no help. Oglesby said the engine quit suddenly without warning. Easley said he was in the back seat and couldn't see much, besides, he wasn't a pilot anyway. They both got out unhurt and the airplane burned completely after the crash. I already knew all of that, but the interviews filled another square for the investigation.

The information gathering phase was complete. All that remained was to write up the report. On the day I got back to Pleiku, I learned I was to be the "Assistant Operations Officer" for the squadron. That translated to a nothing job where I would get the dead horse paper work Arch didn't want to do. Whoopee!

The biggest part of the new paper work as Assistant Operations Officer was administering the FAC training program for quite a large number of arriving pilots who had no previous experience in the O-1. Our squadron would check them out in the O-1 and train them to be FACs. There were also routine Office Instructions to write for the new squadron and miscellaneous records to be kept. All of this was in addition to writing up the Bao Loc accident report and continuing my regular flying duties. I had more than my share of work, but it all helped the year go by more rapidly.

I completed the Bao Loc accident report, along with the other paper work, and still did my share of the flying. LtCol Oliver thought my report was well done and decided I could write. At the time, the accident investigation report appeared to be an unimportant paper pushing project. I had no idea it would be important to me later.

Another much larger accident investigation, with unpleasant political implications, was just around the corner. No one knew this next investigation was coming, and I certainly didn't know it would have my name on it. Neither did I know it would involve a friend, a fellow FAC who was presumed to have screwed up big time, killing himself and seriously injuring his flight mechanic.

There was no doubt about some of the obvious facts surrounding the investigation. The FAC was dead, the crew chief was seriously injured and the airplane was trash. However, certain folks in Saigon presumed the pilot had exercised very poor judgment. Was it fair to rush to that conclusion or were there more factors needing evaluation? Those questions accompanied the accident investigation. It was all dumped into my lap.

Chapter 11

Shining His Ass on the Grass???

March 1966 – Tan Rai Special Forces Camp

I had just started writing my daily letter home on March 21, 1966, when LtCol Oliver, our Squadron Commander, walked into my room. I wasn't expecting him. "Hey, Boss. What's up?"

He sat down on the edge of my bed and motioned for me to sit back down. "Have you heard about Capt Holmes?"

"No, Sir, I haven't. I heard that an O-1 crashed near Bao Loc this morning. Was that Holmes?"

"Yes, it was. It was actually about seven miles north of Bao Loc at a new Special Forces Camp under construction. It's called Tan Rai.

"I'm really sorry to hear that. Otis was a friend of mine. What happened?"

"They were making a mail drop at Tan Rai. His crew chief, Sgt Easley, was in the back seat and they crashed on the perimeter wire of the camp. Holmes was killed and Easley was seriously injured. I'm appointing you Accident Investigating Officer and I need to tell you more about the situation. Although we won't jump to any conclusions, the initial report is they were <u>not</u> shot down.

"The Seventh Air Force Headquarters Flying Safety Office has been making noises about reports of FACs doing some irresponsible flying. They're trying to stop FACs from "buzzing" or "shining their ass on the grass." (No pilot ever wanted to have those words officially attached to his name). It's inescapable the FAC business is inherently dangerous, but the Flying Safety guys are trying to keep FACs from taking chances that aren't necessary. That's OK. That's Flying Safety's job.

"I'm telling you this because you need to know the people from Saigon are going to be looking over your shoulder while you conduct this investigation. You did a good job on the Oglesby accident investigation four months ago and I know you'll do a good job on this one. That first one was small. This one is going to be big, with political implications attached."

All of that was bad news. Really bad news. I was saddened at the loss of a friend, and selfishly wanted someone else doing the investigation. The situation had already attracted some high level attention and some conclusions had been reached before the investigation even began.

Capt Otis Holmes was more than "one of our FACs." He was my good friend. Holmes and I together were two of the seven pilots in Combat Crew Training in Florida. We discovered on the long trip across the ocean, leaving behind the country we loved, he and I could talk openly and comfortably about serious matters. Much of the conversation focused on our wives and families in Mena, Arkansas and Cheyenne, Wyoming.

We felt the same void in our lives growing larger as the airplane took us farther away from those families. Our basic theological beliefs were similar. Although neither of us was a Bible thumping evangelist, we were both Christians who tried to live what we professed.

During the long flight to another continent, Otis and I together reached a wise decision. Two Army Captains whipped out the cards and invited us to play bridge. We accepted their offer. The wise decision on our part was our response about the stakes, "No, let's not play for money. Let's just play for fun." They cleaned our clock so badly it was tough to call it fun.

A month before Holmes' crash, Otis and I enjoyed a good visit in Nha Trang when we were both there to leave airplanes for

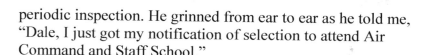

periodic inspection. He grinned from ear to ear as he told me, "Dale, I just got my notification of selection to attend Air Command and Staff School."

"Congrats, Otis! Will you have time to finish your tour here?"

"No, the assignment people tell me my Vietnam tour will be shortened to nine and a half months to enable me to meet the professional school schedule. I'll still get credit for a completed one year tour. Isn't that great?!"

"That's super. And selection for the school is nearly a guarantee you'll make Major on the next go around. I'm really happy for you."

Everything looked good for Otis Holmes. Now I drew the assignment to write an official report about how he died. I also had some personal grieving to accomplish over the loss of my friend. That part wouldn't go into the official report.

The accident investigation promised to be a large task for several reasons. The crash itself was unusual and had generated a lot of interest. The logistics would be difficult, too. There were six different locations to visit to conduct the required research. Hopping available flights from place to place or getting my own O-1 to fly would be challenging.

First came a trip to Bao Loc, Holmes' operating location. Capt John Everitt, the Summary Court Officer, went with me. Everitt wasn't part of the actual investigation. It was his job to assemble all of Holmes' personal effects and send them to his next of kin in Mena, Arkansas. The Summary Court Officer represented the United States Air Force in rendering comfort, consolation and assistance to Capt Otis Holmes' widow.

11.1 – Picturesque Bao Loc, only seven miles from super ugly new Tan Rai Special Forces Camp

11.2 – Maintaining a machine gun in the muddy Hell hole called Tan Rai

11.3 – Tan Rai, a miserable place

11. 4 – Tan Rai laundromat

11.5 – Tan Rai automatic dishwasher

11.6 – Tan Rai kitchen

The crash site was a real mess. Tan Rai Special Forces Camp was little more than a large number of holes dug in the mud, surrounded by a generous amount of perimeter barbed wire. It was a muddy Hell hole of a place. Construction was under way, but living conditions were terrible. The FACs did all they could to alleviate the misery of the Green Berets and their native Montagnard strikers (soldiers). Otis Holmes frequently dropped cigarettes and mail to them as his contribution toward morale.

According to interviews at Tan Rai, Holmes had the practice of dropping the mail and then giving the troops on the ground a bit more for their money. He would make the necessary low pass over their compound to drop the mail bundle out the window and then disappear out of sight down into a ravine beyond the edge of the camp. Dropping the mail out of the window of the O-1 was quite a bit like dropping a smoke grenade to mark a target during an air strike.

Exactly what happened after his disappearance into the ravine on that fateful day was impossible to determine from "after the fact" interviews. My only certain conclusions were that Holmes dropped the mail, disappeared into the ravine, popped back up into view and then crashed on a subsequent pass. The charred remains of the airplane tangled in the perimeter barbed wire looked so bad I wondered how Sgt Easley in the rear cockpit survived.

I stood there and stared at the mess. "What a Hell of a way for a friend to go. Otis had everything going right for him. I saw him just a month ago in Nha Trang. It doesn't seem fair. The Big Wigs in Saigon have already concluded he did it to himself and I haven't even begun the damned investigation. I wish someone else had this shitty job."

For quite a while I remained transfixed, captivated by the ugly pile of junk and the many resulting implications. We were short one more FAC. That was obvious. But what about Otis?

Otis wasn't going home to attend Air Force Command and Staff School as scheduled. Some unidentified guy on the list of alternates to attend the school would be happy when the phone rang and he was told there was an opening for him. Otis wasn't going to the school. He was going home in a box. And there would be another opening on the majors list in the next promotion cycle. Otis' military career was over. He was forever a Captain.

Survival, it is said, is the first law of nature. The events before me forced me unwillingly to think of my own survival. What if Otis and I switched places? My first thoughts were of my family.

What memories would my children have of me? At nine years of age, Steve would remember quite a bit about his father. I hoped his memories of me would all be good. Jim was two years younger and would remember less. Would it be good? Marshall turned four a few days after I left home. It was unlikely he could recall my departure. Elaine was sixteen months old the last time I saw her. She would later learn to point to a certain picture and say, "Daddy." She would know nothing about me.

Where would they live? As my survivor, Nancy would receive part of a Captain's pay. It wouldn't be enough to pay rent and buy groceries. Would she move in with her sixty-seven year old widowed mother? Gram Garfield had a modest house that was large enough to accommodate everyone, but possessed little else materially. Would Nancy have to work at a full time job for them to get by? Would the resulting huge load of child supervision be suddenly and unfairly forced upon Gram Garfield?

What about their longer term future? Nancy was a trim good-looking thirty-three year old. She was a wonderful woman with an effervescent personality and a cheerful smile for others. She would be attractive to some reputable man wanting a fine quality serious woman for life. She was fiercely devoted to her children and would probably bring along four kids for their first "get acquainted" date. Would that end a promising opportunity?

I hoped a good man would fill my place in their lives if circumstances sent me home in a box. I hoped he would be a good husband and a good father. My musing was full of meaningless conjecture. If it all happened, I could be certain of only one thing about the new man in their lives. His name wouldn't be Dale Amend.

The entire fictitious imaginings of "what ifs" nearly overwhelmed me. I prayed that Nancy and the kids in Cheyenne would never face the harsh news recently delivered to Otis' wife in Mena, Arkansas. Otis had no more worries on this earth, but what about his family?

From Tan Rai I went to the 85th Field Hospital in Qui Nhon to interview Holmes' crew chief, Sgt Easley, who was in the back seat. Coincidentally, Easley was also in the back seat during the Oglesby accident I investigated. His injuries this time were critical and he was soon to be evacuated to the States. He was not able to provide any useful information about the crash.

After interviewing witnesses, the next step was to find out what was learned from the examination of what was left of the airplane. At Bien Hoa airbase I met with Capt Mike Quinn. He told me, "We tear engines down to analyze all of their components. The purpose is to determine their condition immediately prior to the crash. Was everything operating normally, or was there a problem that could have contributed to the crash? We also send engine oil samples to Clark Airbase in the Philippines for analysis. We can't do that here."

I asked him, "Will you be able to tell me if Holmes' engine failed? Did it stop suddenly? Was it operating normally at the time of the crash?"

"Sometimes it's possible to make that determination. In this case, I don't think we will be able to give you a specific answer. I wish we could."

The regular maintenance, corrective maintenance and periodic inspections on the aircraft had been performed in Nha Trang. I scanned the records of all of that work for information which might give insight into possible problems.

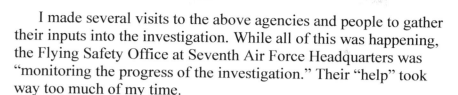

I made several visits to the above agencies and people to gather their inputs into the investigation. While all of this was happening, the Flying Safety Office at Seventh Air Force Headquarters was "monitoring the progress of the investigation." Their "help" took way too much of my time.

They had heard rumors and already concluded Holmes had flown carelessly or recklessly and the accident was his fault. The Saigon boys made up their minds before I began the investigation. They were fishing for a determination of "Pilot Error" as the primary cause of the accident.

There was no escaping the reality that FACs in Vietnam were indeed a high profile group. It was hard to miss some of their exploits which were put into print by news writers seeking glamorous stories. A lot of it was true but some was considerably overblown. To a safety officer sitting in a comfortable chair in Saigon, it was easy to judge this incident as an example of excessive swaggering bravado gone bad. Those darned FACs needed to be reigned in.

The FACs didn't see things that way. They had great disdain for the "Saigon Warriors" sitting at desks in secure offices. Occasionally a Saigon Warrior would hop a morning flight to Pleiku to buy a crossbow made by a Montagnard tribesman and then get out of Pleiku with his souvenir before dark. I tried deliberately to ignore the inherent differences between the Saigon boys and the FACs and get on with my assigned task.

Once at Bao Loc on a hot day I hoped for a shower but the water was off. Fortunately, rain was falling. I borrowed a bar of soap and a towel and went outside. I shucked off all of my duds and had a good shower outside under a roof drain. Neither the village passersby nor I were concerned with any thoughts of modesty. They did their business and I did mine. It was a refreshing bath.

In great contrast, one flight that I hopped to another place was on a T-39 (civilian equivalent, Saber Liner). Cruising in air conditioned comfort at 35,000 ft was pretty fat! Flying that executive transport looked like a plush job compared to my job as a FAC sweating at low altitude.

But I was still a FAC. On one investigating trip I had my own airplane for transportation and was cruising back home to Pleiku at a comfortable 9,000 ft. I heard another FAC down on the deck controlling a strike in support of the good guys at an ambush site. At low altitude he was having trouble getting his radio calls out. I circled the ambush site at 9,000 ft and relayed radio calls for him. It's nice to be helpful.

A trip to Saigon on March 26, 1966, provided an inside look at some living arrangements there. I stayed at a place shared by five officers, including one of the Flying Safety guys who worked with me that afternoon. Their place, the top floor of an apartment building, was fabulous by Pleiku standards. They had lots of room, a maid who did the laundry and cleaning, and enjoyed a fine supper cooked and served at a nice table in pretty good style, all for about $100 per month.

They were living well, making money from their extra allowances and had no hazards like those of us who were out there fighting the war. It was absolutely no wonder those like me resented those like them. They were good men doing their jobs, but they sure put a face on the term "Saigon Warriors." Those guys in particular, however, treated me well and I appreciated it.

The traveling and evidence gathering were finally done. It was time to write. My longhand writing was typed up by a mediocre clerk typist at a mechanical typewriter. It took quite a while, but it finally got done. The report was long and included several attachments. Most people, however, would be interested in only the bottom line.

11.7 – "Saigon Warriors" relax by the pool

11.8 – The Saigon Officers Open Mess and Bar on the fifth (top) floor of the Rex Hotel --- Nicer than another can of cold C rations in the dirt?

The findings concluded it was impossible to positively define the "Primary Cause" of the accident due to the lack of specific evidence. The "Possible Cause" was sudden engine failure at low altitude leaving inadequate time for recovery. A "Possible Contributing Cause" to the engine failure was a faulty fuel primer seal. Several faulty fuel primer seals had been recently documented for the O-1.

The report went to Seventh Air Force Flying Safety Office in Saigon. They didn't like it. No surprise there. They wanted something that at least implied the pilot had been responsible. They didn't know that to be true and neither did I. My signature wasn't going onto something I grabbed out of the air.

I told it like it was. Period.

The Saigon boys wanted to make an issue of the general question of FACs flying recklessly. Was Captain Holmes showboating and "shining his ass on the grass"? The answer to that question could likely depend on who was giving the answer, a FAC on the job out in the weeds or a staff officer in Saigon.

Not long before Holmes' accident I was flying a visual reconnaissance mission when I heard, "Baron Aircraft, this is Black Cat Six Two."

"Black Cat Six Two, this is Baron One Zero. What can I do for you?"

"Hey, Baron One Zero, we're at your two o'clock position in a clear area. Glad to see you. It's been a boring day for a hike in the weeds. Rock your wings if you see us."

As was the usual case, they had seen me before I saw them. I looked more closely and found the Special Forces patrol moving through rather open terrain. I rocked my wings for them, "I have you now, Black Cat. Anything happening today?"

"Naw, it's pretty dull."

I made a couple of slow circles over the patrol. We continued the empty chatter and then the leader of the patrol said, "Hey, Baron One Zero, how about coming down and giving us an altitude check?" It was an obvious invitation, really more of a request, for me to fly over them very low and blow off their "Bum Fuck Hats."

When the Special Forces were on patrol, they abandoned their Green Berets in favor of olive drab hats with soft wide brims turned up on one side. They were more practical and were still distinctive in appearance. We FACs called their patrol hats Bum Fuck Hats "because those guys really have a bum fuckin' deal. They walk around in the weeds carrying a gun looking for trouble. If they find trouble, then they wonder if they will get back to camp alive."

I discussed the hat and job terminology with one of the Special Forces guys. He said, "Hell, no! That's not true. You guys are the ones who have the bad deal. I can hide behind a rock or a tree. Blowing you out of the sky is as easy as shooting a duck." We agreed that he could keep his tree and I'd keep flying my little airplane. Neither of us really had a choice.

I went down and "blew off their hats," flying low enough to make them duck and then gave them a reading from my altimeter. I wouldn't have hit any of them, but if even a small airplane comes directly at you on the deck at ninety miles per hour, you'll probably hit the dirt. That raises a question. Was *I* shining my ass on the grass? I preferred to look at it as strengthening the good working relationship we enjoyed with the Special Forces guys. That's what FACs did routinely.

When my report arrived at the Flying Safety Office of Seventh Air Force Headquarters, they quickly bounced it back to Pleiku on the next courier flight. Their official comment included the words "suggesting further review." I discussed the issue with LtCol Oliver. He said, "Your job is to gather all of the available information and write the report the way you see it, doing everything by the book." I said, "Yes, sir. I have already done that and they sent it back."

He already knew all of those details. He said, "Then, take it back to them the way it is."

I made one last trip to Saigon for the investigation. I hand carried the report back to the Flying Safety Office at Seventh Air Force Headquarters and returned it to them without changing one word. They didn't like it, but they had their honest report, based on a thorough investigation.

Chapter 12

There But For The Grace Of God...

April 1966 – Pleiku

While I simultaneously worked on the paper war of the accident investigation and did my share of the flying in the shooting war, a new development arose.

At lunch on April 3, 1966, LtCol Buskirk, the II Corps Air Liaison Officer, informed me, "I am transferring you and three other FACs to an assignment called Operation Cricket. You will leave Pleiku with an airplane and all of your belongings for extended TDY (temporary duty). The duty station is in Thailand. Operation Cricket is a special assignment similar to Operation Tiger Hound." (Everyone knew a lot of bad things about Tiger Hound.)

Our Squadron Commander, LtCol Oliver, confronted Buskirk regarding his plan for assignments to support Operation Cricket. "Buster, we can't send Amend on Operation Cricket. He's the Accident Investigation Officer for the Holmes crash at Tan Rai. Right now he's half way through that project. We don't have anyone to replace him.

"Furthermore, the investigation is a big job and Seventh Air Force Flying Safety Office is already looking over our shoulder. Removing Amend from this investigation would waste time, travel and research already expended on that job. Some parts of the investigation might not be possible to duplicate and would be lost. If we pull him out right now, we'll all look really stupid."

A few hours after LtCol Buskirk told me I was going on Operation Cricket, LtCol Oliver told me I wasn't. "You aren't going on Operation Cricket. You're not going anywhere right now.

Keep working on the investigation. Forget what you heard from LtCol Buskirk at lunch."

Buskirk conceded belatedly that Oliver was correct and came up with another plan for more efficient manpower utilization. Capt Chris Davis, one of our FACs in Ban Me Thuot, would replace me on Operation Cricket. As soon as I finished the investigation, I would go to Ban Me Thuot and replace Davis. It was a reasonable and simple solution. That switch, however, ultimately determined which one of us went home right side up and which one went home in a box under the flag of our country.

Adequate manpower for the 21st TASS was a serious problem. We were already thirty-five FACs below authorized strength for our squadron. The shortage was shared among the squadron's thirteen operating locations scattered around II Corps. After Operation Cricket took away four more pilots, we would be thirty-nine FACs short of what we should have. We were operating between one third and one half of our authorized pilot strength. Our FACs were very busy.

I was nearly done with the big paper work job on April 21, 1966, when we received bad news. One of our FACs on Operation Cricket was shot down by 37 or 57 mm flak and 50 caliber machine gun fire. The FAC was Capt Chris Davis who had just replaced me several days earlier on Operation Cricket. Another FAC, Vance Ryan, flying top cover in another O-1, watched the whole thing. A third FAC trying to see about Davis was hit by 50 caliber machine gun fire but survived. An A-1 pilot, Keith Thompson, was shot down and killed in a futile rescue operation.

What is there to say? Two weeks earlier, the Tan Rai accident investigation forced switching two FACs. Davis replaced Amend on Operation Cricket. Amend replaced Davis in Ban Me Thuot. Why was Chris Davis shot down and killed and I wasn't? There, but for the grace of God was I.

I wondered if Davis, like me, had left a wife and four kids at home.

Chapter 13

Letters To and From Home

1965-66 – Pleiku, Ban Me Thuot and Cheyenne

During my year in Vietnam, it was US Air Force policy to have the Air Force member back in the states on or before the 365th day of his tour of duty. My "year" fit that policy definition almost exactly. I made it home on the 357th day. On 96.1% of those three hundred fifty seven days I wrote to the most important woman and children in the world. It was the most direct and supportive thing I could do for them. The final count was three hundred forty three letters home.

13.1 – Another letter home, logged in as #38 upon arrival in Cheyenne

During that year, Nancy wrote nearly three hundred letters to me. Receiving one of her letters was the most welcome and cherished thing that could highlight any of my days. While I mourned the day when there was no letter from her, I recognized if it had been my task to constantly care for four energetic kids, my letters might have been even less frequent.

There were also letters to and from other family members and friends. I was uplifted by the many I received, but it was beyond my ability to acknowledge all of them. I noted many names to Nancy and asked her to tell those people thank you for writing. The number of cards and letters from family and friends at Christmas time was humbling and heart warming.

Mail service between Pleiku or Ban Me Thuot and the US was generally quite good. From the start, Nancy and I carefully used a numbering system to track every one of our letters. This allowed us to know if a letter was lost and also enabled us to use a dialog form of "conversation." I could refer to "your letter #XXX dated XXX" and then respond specifically. It took time, but it was effective. Anyway, we had a year to "discuss" things.

Not all mail delivery was that effective, but it wasn't necessarily the fault of the mail service system. When I went on R&R to Bangkok, Thailand, one of my buddies had a friend stationed in Bangkok. Lt Jeff Dillon was the US mail service officer for all of Southeast Asia. He showed us a building the size of a large residential double garage completely full of material that looked like something dumped by a convoy of Post Office trucks.

I said, "Wow, Jeff, that's a real haystack of letters! Is all of that really personal mail intended for military people?"

"Yes, it is. But we can't deliver it."

"Why not? Isn't that your job?"

"It sure is, but all of that mail is undeliverable. It was sent from the United States to military men somewhere in Southeast Asia, but has incorrect or incomplete addresses. The senders may have used the wrong addresses or the addressees may have moved. We can't find them."

"Boy, Jeff, that's a sad situation. I must be looking at thousands of letters that failed to reach their intended addressees."

Jeff responded, "It's more like tens of thousands of letters. That huge pile of stuff in front of you is the worst part of my job and I can't fix the problem. I feel sorry for every one of those guys somewhere who didn't receive his mail. And it's equally sad for someone back home who sent the mail and wondered why there was no answer to something important."

Mail also failed to get through on an individual basis. My friend and roommate in Ban Be Thuot, Dan Preston, watched wistfully as I sent and received mail to and from home. Although Dan didn't talk much about it, I sensed that things weren't very smooth between him and his wife. Their communication seemed limited. Maybe there was a bit of alienation between Dan and his wife. Perhaps that was one reason Dan was completely absorbed in the perfect accomplishment of his job.

Our letters between Vietnam and Cheyenne also served another purpose which was un-anticipated, but later became very important. The letters I received were important. I treasured them. But somehow none of them made it back home with me. Fortunately, Nancy carefully kept all my letters intact. Decades later, they comprised a complete body of written reference material available for the writing of this book. Those letters also included supplementary enclosures from newspapers and periodical magazines.

My personal daybook was always current and accurate, but was limited to what I could cram into the sixteen square inches of space allotted to one day in the book. For the same day, however, my letter home might consist of several pages containing much more information about the same subject. The two references complemented each other well.

Letters in both directions were good, but wouldn't it be wonderful to talk directly for even just a few minutes? The possibility did exist. The system was called MARS, Military Affiliate Radio System. It was a somewhat complex arrangement consisting of several various components and requiring some good luck. First, the military guy in Pleiku had to wait in line quite a while until it became his turn to try. Second, the radio link between Pleiku and McChord Air Force Base on the west coast just south of Seattle, had to be successfully established. Third, the radio signal at McChord had to be connected to the Strategic Air Command (SAC) Automated Voice Network (Autovon) telephone system. Fourth, the Autovon telephone system had to be available for non-official use. Fifth, there had to also be a SAC base located near the desired destination telephone (Warren Air Force Base was suitable for a Cheyenne call). Finally, when the SAC base called the civilian number, Mama had to be home and answer the darned phone.

The radio link, the key to success, was also the least dependable element. The clarity of the conversation varied from pretty fair to worthless depending on atmospheric conditions between Vietnam and Seattle. Even if the radio link was functioning clearly, most people were not familiar with the use of a radio connection. It was essential for the two parties to alternate talking and listening. Otherwise, they blocked each other and no one heard anything. This was common when a family member back home answered the telephone and, having no instruction, didn't know what to do on the radio.

Most attempts for a two way conversation ended as disappointing strikeouts, but the occasional success kept people trying. Two days after Christmas 1965 the radio link was established and I waited my turn to try a call home. Everything was working and I held my breath excitedly as the telephone rang at our home in Cheyenne. It rang and rang. The air fizzled out of my balloon. Ten thousand miles away there was no answer.

I still had hope as the telephone rang at Nancy's mother's home in Fort Collins, Colorado, fifty miles down the road. Maybe she had taken the kids there for a visit. No answer. In a few minutes I went from eager anticipation to flat disappointment.

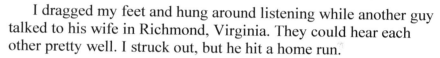

I dragged my feet and hung around listening while another guy talked to his wife in Richmond, Virginia. They could hear each other pretty well. I struck out, but he hit a home run.

Usually the disappointment outweighed the chance for success and kept me from wanting to try. Only one time, on February 19, 1966, things worked and I talked briefly to Nancy and all of the kids. They all sounded wonderful. Just wonderful. When the call was finished, I didn't know whether to bawl and settle the dust on the floor or kiss the staff sergeant who was operating the radio. I was elated from talking with them.

Letters sometimes produced unexpected results. Local newspapers seemed eager to put a face on the Vietnam war by making it personal. They published actual names which might be recognized locally. My sister pushed the action which resulted in an article in the Timnath, Colorado newspaper where she lived.

Timnath Cub Scouts are going to make a door to door canvass of Timnath and the surrounding area on Saturday, May 7 and again on May 14. They will be collecting items to help the 21st Tactical Air Support Squadron gather supplies for a hospital being built in Pleiku for the Montagnard people in Vietnam. The Air Force calls this a "Civic Action Project" and Capt Dale N. Amend is the Project Officer...

Newspaper articles weren't actual letters, but sometimes they accomplished quite a bit of communication. A most unusual article appeared in the Indianapolis Star on September 6, 1966.

FACs Look like Miracle Workers

Well, From the Ground, They Do

Copley News Service

Ban Me Thuot, South Viet Nam. Air Force Capt Dan Preston, 33 years old, strode into his room at the US Military Assistance Command Viet Nam compound here after a hard day of flying.

He opened a can of beer, poured a jigger of whiskey into a glass and threw himself into a chair.

"That business about being miracle men is ridiculous," Preston snorted.

"Of course it's ridiculous, Dan," said Air Force Capt Dale N. Amend, 34, who had opened a can of lemon-lime soda pop and taken another chair in the room the two men share. "But you can see how it seems like a miracle to some of those people on the ground.

"They get into a firefight and they call for an air strike. A couple of minutes later the planes come in and they are right on target. It seems pretty miraculous to them—so fast and so accurate."

Preston and Amend were talking about their jobs as FACs, which means Forward Air Controllers, for the Air Force in Darlac Province, South Viet Nam.

Preston, who comes from Joplin, Mo., is tall, slender and handsome. He has wavy brown hair and blue eyes. He has a wife and three children in Joplin.

Amend, of Rocky Ford, Colo., is short and wiry with sandy hair and gray eyes. His wife and four children are waiting for him in Cheyenne, Wyo.

"There's nothing miraculous about the job of a FAC," Preston said. "It's just hard work. I come in every day, and I'm not satisfied. I don't feel I've done enough."

"You're a perfectionist, Dan," Amend put it. "You never will be satisfied. A lot of us won't be, but we do the best we can."

Preston tossed off the whiskey and took a sip of beer.

As FACs for their sector in II Corps, Preston and Amend are responsible for directing air strikes in Darlac Province. Under the Air Force tactical air control system in Viet Nam, there are FACs in each province who direct all air strikes by Air Force or Navy fighter-bombers in their area.

The FAC gets the target by radio from troops on the ground, locates it and marks it with white phosphorus smoke rockets for the striking planes. The FAC flies a tiny, unarmed O-1 Bird Dog spotter plane.

Preston said he flies up to 150 hours a month. A short day might be one or two hours in the air. A long one might run to eight hours or more. "Every FAC does the job differently," Preston said. "Me, I believe in knowing the people I'm working with on the ground. I want to be briefed on the operation before it starts. I want to know where they're going, what they may run into. I want to know what air support we have and where it will be.

"I want to know the voices on the radio. That way we can save time. We don't have to go through all that jazz about call signs and proper radio procedures that waste a lot of time. We can just talk to each other."

Page 136

Preston has been in the Air Force for 13 years. He has been a FAC in Darlac Province since December.

Amend, an 11-year veteran of the Air Force, has been a FAC in Viet Nam for nine months. He has been in Darlac Province only two weeks.

An Army advisor to the 23rd Division poked his head into the door. "Hello, flyboys," he said.

"Hey, who was controlling the artillery today?" Preston asked.

13.2 – A 105 millimeter Howitzer was at Boun Ea Yang Special Forces Camp.

"Why?" countered the advisor.

"Because that dumb gook told me that the artillery was shut off before I went in to call the air strike," Preston said. "Then the artillery fired two more rounds while I was in there, that's why! I don't go for that stuff!"

"Aw, some ARVN (South Viet Namese soldier) had a round in the gun, so he yanked the lanyard," said the advisor.

"Well, give that guy the word just the same," Preston said. "I don't mind the Viet Cong shooting at me, but I don't want to be shot down by friendly ARVN artillery. That's stupid."

The article in the "Indianapolis Star" was completely authentic and accurate. The unusual part was how it got into my hands. A Copley News Service reporter, operating out of San Diego, was in Ban Me Thout looking for news. He interviewed a Capt from

Wyoming and a Capt from Missouri for the content of his report. A friend of mine from Cheyenne was in Indianapolis on a business trip. He clipped the article from the newspaper and gave it to another friend in Cheyenne who gave it to Nancy. Nancy sent it to me back in Ban Me Thuot.

Closer to home, the <u>Wyoming State Tribune</u>, the largest newspaper in Cheyenne, chose to appeal to Christmas sentiment when it published the following article. The article also used a local name which a few people might recognize. It appeared on Christmas Eve, December 24, 1965, in a rather large front page spread, along with a picture of the author of this book.

Letter from Viet Nam

Stand and be Counted

By Carolyn Denton

A little more than a year ago, Capt Dale Amend, USAF, sang the romantic lead in a Cheyenne Symphony production. Today he's in Viet Nam.

His family, Nancy, and four children, Steve, 9, Jim, 7, Marshall, 4, and Elaine, 18 months, who reside in Cheyenne, will attempt to enjoy Christmas at the home of relatives in Fort Collins without Captain Amend.

As the holidays approached, Amend wrote:

"Tonight, we are at the Air Force Officers quarters where talk is centered on Capt Paul McClellan, who was killed in the crash of his A-1 Skyraider today during an air strike against the Viet Cong.

"His sacrifice will have been more worthwhile if, through my faltering words, you gain a greater understanding of our country's need for loyal, patriotic citizens. We need citizens who are proud of their country and are willing to stand and be counted in the fight against world communism.

"Foolish acts like burning draft cards and volunteering supplies and blood to aid the enemy border on treason to our country.

"Be proud of the United States of America and stand faithfully behind its cause of preserving freedom for all people.

"Last Sunday was a day of contrast, incongruities and inconsistencies from start to finish. Catholic mass and the Protestant chapel service were held consecutively in the "theater," a very loose term used to describe a room between the bar and some living quarters on one side and a mortar bunker outside.

"There were Army and Air Force personnel at each service.

"It was communion Sunday at the chapel service and the Chaplain's short message was interrupted occasionally by the noise of a low flying helicopter or airplane.

"Men dressed in flying suits, fatigue work uniforms and civilian clothing knelt at the communion rail or received the bread and wine at their seats.

"Some of these men were the ones who would fly the strike aircraft that were to hit target areas west of Pleiku.

"It would be my job to find the target, mark it with white phosphorous smoke rockets and control the strike aircraft onto and off the target.

"This would be a small part of the free world's fight against the domination of world communism, that others may enjoy the freedom of worship, among other freedoms.

("The lights just went the way of the water—temporarily, I hope. I'll continue by the light of my big candle.)

"After the Chapel services many men returned directly to their duties. This isn't an area of the 40 hour work week. It's a seven day a week job and we never know what is coming next from the Viet Cong or where they will strike next."

Amend was stationed at Warren Air Force Base three years prior to leaving for Viet Nam. He was graduated from Colorado State University in 1954 and from the University of Colorado in 1962. He is a veteran of over 11 years' service.

Newspaper articles were wonderful. It was uplifting, and yet humbling, to think that someone cared enough to print news articles that showed interest and support for what we were doing a long way from home.

Letters and packages from home arrived in various sizes and in varying condition. Cookies were always welcome, even if they got there looking like they had been run over by a truck. An hour before I left on R&R in April 1966 I received a package from Mrs. Trumbull, our church organist in Cheyenne. Inside were home made cinnamon rolls. Wow! They looked and smelled delicious. I ran one finger through the frosting for a quick taste and re-wrapped them securely. They would keep well in my steel locker until I got home from R&R five days later.

Back in Pleiku, I opened them to enjoy Mrs. Trumbull's culinary expertise. I discovered my very own penicillin farm. The cinnamon rolls had evolved into an impressive bumper crop of mold. They still smelled good but looked really bad. I thought it best not to eat them. In my next letter I asked Nancy, "Please give Mrs. Trumbull my sincere thanks for the gorgeous cinnamon rolls. Tell her they arrived in beautiful condition and I appreciate her thoughtfulness and kindness. That's true. Don't tell her the details about why I threw them away without taking one bite."

The size and shape of a package can be quite deceptive. I received a package that from the outside resembled an eighteen inch section of the handle on a garden shovel. As I handled the package, the texture of the contents felt rough. There seemed to be a hard central core surrounded by several rough skinny pieces up and down the sides. I wondered what Nancy had sent.

It was mid-December and, knowing that woman as I did, I should have guessed what it was. Inside the package was a crude little pre-fabricated Christmas tree. The central stick was the main trunk. The various length pieces of wire were twisted around shreds of green plastic "foliage." The wire "limbs" fit into holes pre-drilled up and down the trunk. When assembled, the conical shaped little monstrosity stood erect on its own base. There were even miniature decorations to adorn the scraggly dwarf bush. I was suddenly the proud owner of what may have been the only Christmas tree in Pleiku.

My Yuletide prize from home stood on my shipping crate "dresser" where a passerby couldn't miss it. It prompted interesting reactions.

One guy, when he recovered from laughing said, "Ya know, Dale, I think that's probably the ugliest damned Christmas tree I have ever seen." He was still chuckling as he walked away.

13.3 – Physically ugly ---symbolically beautiful

In a few minutes he was back. He stood in the doorway motionless and without comment for quite a while looking at the tree. After several moments of reflective meditation, he said pensively, "But it <u>is</u> a Christmas tree. I like it."

He left slowly and quietly. I didn't disturb his thoughts.

Chapter 14
Silver Star or Court Martial?

November 1965 – Near Plei Djerang Special Forces Camp.

Anderson and Turner cheated death. They <u>really</u> cheated death.

Sunday, November 21, 1965 began as a routine day. It didn't end up that way. I took an airplane to Nha Trang and left it for periodic inspection. Since there were two airplanes ready to bring back to Pleiku after periodic inspection, Major Jack Turner went along in my rear cockpit and flew back on my wing in the second airplane. It was a simple matter of ferrying airplanes back and forth. To make things more interesting on the way home, we did some formation flying. That was fun.

14.1 –Bird Dog FACs in the O-1 flying formation just for the heck of it

14.2 – Jack Turner flew home on my wing, to ferry the airplane from Nha Trang to Pleiku.

My permanent personal call sign as a FAC flying out of Pleiku was Baron One Zero. When Turner flew back from Nha Trang on my wing, he was known as Baron One Zero Alpha, since he had no call sign identity of his own.

When we landed back at Pleiku I said, "I have the pickup here, Jack. Do you want a ride up to the compound?" He said, "No, thanks, Dale. I'm going to stay down here at the flight line for a while." I knew Turner and Master Sergeant Anderson, our lead maintenance man, had become friends and it seemed quite normal that Jack was going to spend some time at the flight line with Andy.

Master Sergeant Donald "Andy" Anderson was in Vietnam on 180 day TDY (Temporary Duty). He was an excellent mechanic and a hard worker, dedicated to keeping our airplanes flying. He worked with limited tools and equipment, but possessed unlimited skill and resourcefulness. Once when I performed the engine run up before take off for a strike mission, the engine had a magneto drop which mandated aborting the take off. If I failed to rendezvous on time with the fighters over the target, they could not deliver their ordnance. They would loiter for a few minutes, as

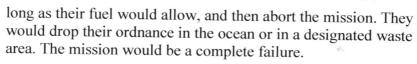

long as their fuel would allow, and then abort the mission. They would drop their ordnance in the ocean or in a designated waste area. The mission would be a complete failure.

I taxied back into our maintenance area. Andy was waiting for me. He had watched to be sure I made my take off. He walked quickly to the cockpit and shouted over the engine noise, "Don't shut it down, Captain! What's wrong?" I said, "I got a bad magneto drop, Andy." Andy said, "Keep it running and stay strapped in." He stood by the engine in the air blast from the whirling propeller only a few feet from his elbow. One misstep in the wrong direction, and he could be dead.

He lifted the cowling, took a grease pencil from his pocket and made grease pencil marks on the hot engine manifold. In a few seconds he identified the bad spark plug by the residual grease mark on the only cold portion of the manifold. He took a new spark plug and the wrench, which he also had in his pocket, and deftly replaced the defective plug. I taxied back out, made a good run up, took off and made my target time with the fighters. Andy's skill and experience had saved the mission.

Andy was very good. I wasn't the only one who knew that. He was recognized as "Enlisted Man of the Quarter" for all of South Vietnam in Airman Magazine, an official Air Force publication. But he made a serious mistake when he and Turner hatched what turned out to be a very bad idea.

Major Jack Turner was in Vietnam on 120 day TDY. He was an experienced pilot assigned to a non-flying job. He was one of four officers who worked at II DASC selecting and approving targets.

Pilots assigned to fly desks were commonly a very restless bunch. A lot of flying needed to be done and Turner wanted to fly. He was very restless. He wasn't a FAC, but he could ferry an O-1 from one place to another.

Monday morning Turner, Anderson and an airplane were missing. It became evident they launched an ill fated adventure which did not appear to be something spontaneous and unplanned.

Late Sunday afternoon, about twenty minutes after I left Major Turner at the flight line, he and Anderson taxied out for their "mission." They had, in fact, no mission to fly and no authorization to take the airplane. In the number one position, just short of the runway, Maj Turner called the tower, "Pleiku Tower, Baron One Zero, for take off." The tower responded, "Baron One Zero, you're cleared for take off."

In that short radio exchange, Jack Turner had just essentially told the tower, "This is FAC Capt Dale Amend, assigned to the 21st Tactical Air Support Squadron." A FAC's call sign was always a unique expression. It designated one particular FAC and no one else. Turner had just stolen my identity. He and Anderson launched their unauthorized, illegal, stupid adventure and things only got worse.

They took off on their own private war and flew to a place 30 miles west of Pleiku, just across the large river from the Plei Djerang Special Forces Camp. Turner flew at tree top level and Anderson fired his M-16 assault rifle out the rear window at some grass huts.

Official records after the incident state they were shot down. I tend to doubt the accuracy of that statement, although it could be true. Allegedly some Special Forces troops at Plei Djerang reported there were holes in the airplane caused by bullets passing from the bottom, up through the top.

Whether or not they were hit by ground fire is questionable in my mind. Whether the engine quit before or after the airplane hit the trees will never be known. It was certain they crashed into the trees on the west side of the river. The Plei Djerang Special Forces Camp was east of the river. Both men survived the crash. Anderson, in the back seat, was only slightly injured. Turner received cuts above and below his right eye, which probably wouldn't have occurred had he been wearing a helmet. He was close to losing that eye. Anderson helped Turner out of the cockpit, got him down to the ground and patched up his bleeding cuts. They hid and rested until nearly dark.

Just before dark, they made their first attempt to cross the large, fast moving river to get to Plei Djerang. They pushed off on a big log and tried to paddle across the river. It didn't work. Some time later, in the dark, they beached on the same side from which they had launched far upstream. They spent the rest of the night cold, wet and scared under another log on the river's edge where they beached. It took them four hours the next morning to walk back upstream to the initial launch point. They found another log which looked suitable for crossing and launched again. The results of the second attempt were the same as the first. They were still on the west bank across from the camp, but this time they were not as far downstream.

While Turner and Anderson continued their efforts to cross the river, all available airplanes and pilots in Pleiku were in the air searching for them. No one knew where they were, but I knew of one possibility. Before I took off on one of those search missions, I told my back seat observer, "I'm going to fly over the area across the river from Plei Djerang. I know that another FAC took Andy to that area a couple of days ago so he could shoot his M-16 out the window. They may have gone back to the same place. Watch closely on the west bank of the river."

My guess turned out to be correct. I flew over them at 0745 the morning after they crashed. Andy later said to me, "Man, you flew right over us!" But they had no signaling devices. They had discarded a radio beacon because they thought it wasn't working. I probably could have received their signal if they had used it. Although we looked in the right place, neither my observer nor I saw them.

After their second failed attempt to cross the river, Turner and Anderson returned to the initial launch point. The injured Turner was fatigued and needed to rest. Anderson was an excellent swimmer and thought he could make it across the river. This attempt, the third try, was also unsuccessful. He shed his 45 pistol and his heavy flight boots in midstream and barely made it back to the river bank, exhausted, half drowned and still on the wrong side of the river. He made his way back to the injured Turner and said, "Jack, I'm going to rest a while and try it again. I still think I can make it."

He rested for an hour, took off all his clothing except his T shirt and pants cut off to the crotch, and got ready to try again. Turner, a fatigued, injured, poor swimmer could do nothing but wait and hope. It seemed possible during all this time Charlie could have had them, but may have been waiting for something more valuable to shoot at, like a rescue chopper. On this attempt, his fourth try, Anderson successfully struggled onto the east bank of the river.

He ran barefooted the two and a half miles to the Special Forces camp. A rescue party took a boat back to the river and exchanged small arms fire with Charlie on the other side of the river while rescuing Turner. A chopper from Army Camp Holloway, near Pleiku, retrieved both men from Plei Djerang. Anderson was soon back in Pleiku for a shower, food and bed. Turner was taken for more first aid and then to Saigon for a check on his eye and surgery on his cuts.

Andy was back at work a bit "shook up" the next day. Turner was back at work about a week later with no permanent eye damage. Thanks to some good surgery, he had only two scars on the right cheek bone and eyebrow and a couple of fading black eyes. He had only a few days left on his 120 day TDY and was soon back at his home base in Alabama.

In retrospect, the whole story was something that should never have happened. Two good men teamed up to satisfy their respective passions and together made some extremely bad decisions. Anderson had a passion for shooting the M-16 and

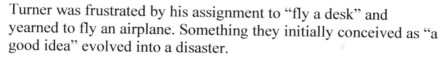

Turner was frustrated by his assignment to "fly a desk" and yearned to fly an airplane. Something they initially conceived as "a good idea" evolved into a disaster.

Official records of the incident show they were "shot down" on a "visual reconnaissance mission." Since the aircraft was a "combat loss," no investigation was required. Each man received The Purple Heart for his injuries. Anderson received the Silver Star, the third highest military decoration, for saving Turner's life. There was no doubt he did save Turner's life… while saving his own skin.

For taking the airplane on an unauthorized flight and for everything that followed, Maj Turner received an official reprimand in the form of an Article 15, a disciplinary letter placed in his personnel file. An Article 15 meant this letter would later be officially removed from his records and become non-existent if there weren't any further unfavorable personnel entries on his records. MSgt Anderson was not disciplined for his part in their escapade.

Was this a proper and just conclusion to this bizarre event? Was Anderson, the one with the passion for shooting the M-16 from the back cockpit, any less deserving of official reprimand than Turner, the frustrated pilot who wanted to fly? Should they both have been court martialed for equal collaboration in taking and crashing an airplane while endangering their own lives and the lives of others? The reader may decide.

Chapter 15

Missionaries--The Real Warriors Through the Years

1882-1995 – Southeast Asia

In order to present the subject matter of this chapter more completely and more meaningfully, information beyond my personal experience is included. Much of the introductory information is from the book <u>To Viet Nam with Love</u>, the Story of Charlie and EG Long, copyright 1995 by Christian Publications, Camp Hill, PA. This information is used with the permission of the author, Charles E. Long.

The fly leaf of my copy of that book is inscribed "Charlie and EG Long, April 18, 1995. Isaiah 8:13. Dale, thanks for your part in Vietnam!" It is in Charlie Long's handwriting.

How typically gracious and modest of Charlie! That <u>he</u>, the veteran of seventeen years of risking his life to bring Christianity to an ethnic minority element of the Vietnanese people, would thank <u>me</u>! I had done little but enjoy the privilege of claiming him, his family and his friends as my friends for the nine months I spent in Pleiku. When I was transferred from Pleiku to Ban Me Thuot for my last three months in Vietnam, his associates in Ban Me Thuot were automatically my instant friends. Thank you, Charlie, for everything!

15.1 – Two of the most wonderful, dedicated, courageous people I have ever been privileged to call friends.

After my one year tour, when I returned to the United States, Charlie and his wife, EG (Elma Grace), were still in Vietnam. Charlie worked frantically to finish the translation of the New Testament and the Psalms into the Jarai native language and EG worked on a hymnal in Jarai. After their service in Vietnam, they returned to Raleigh North Carolina where Charlie served as Senior Pastor of the North Ridge Alliance Church. Nancy and I maintained contact with them through annual Christmas letters.

When Charlie and EG began their work in Vietnam, he adopted Isaiah 8:13 as his personal message from God regarding the work to be done. The King James Version of this verse reads, "Sanctify the Lord of hosts Himself; and let Him be your fear, and let Him be your dread." Charlie took this to be God's command. Charlie was to have no fear save the concern he might fail to adequately accomplish what God wanted him to do. Charlie was absolutely fearless!

When things were at their most dangerous for the Longs in Vietnam, Charlie discussed with EG the possible need for her to leave the work and return to the United States. He said, "We shouldn't leave our children orphaned with the loss of both parents." EG responded, "I will go anywhere in the world with you, and nowhere without you."

You call military people brave and committed?!

My own introduction to the missionaries came through the Chaplain in Pleiku. I met Chaplain (Captain) Brian Wesley soon after my arrival in Pleiku and we quickly became friends. But before introducing my personal experience into this chapter, it's necessary to examine general missionary activity mixed into the history of Southeast Asia over a broad time line of many years. This chronological review fixes regional, local and personal events in their relative places. It is presented from the missionary perspective. Political and military events are intertwined with missionary activities.

1882: Albert Simpson, the founder of the C&MA (Christian and Missionary Alliance) "looked compassionately" at the Indo-China peninsula.

1911 through World War I: C& MA was the only Protestant Mission establishing churches in what later became Vietnam.

After WW I: The British returned Indo China to the French. Ho Chi Minh assumed de facto control of much of Northern & Central Vietnam.

February 1929: "Dalat School" was established in Dalat, South Vietnam, for the children of missionaries serving in all of Southeast Asia. Because of increasing danger from the Communists, the school was moved to Bangkok in 1964 and to Malaysia in 1965. It retained the name Dalat School.

1953: North Vietnam vanquished the last French forces in the battle of Dien Bien Phu.

August 16, 1958: Charlie and EG Long arrived in Vietnam. They were part of a wave of new missionaries who intended to serve about 1.2 million Montagnards. The largest of these tribes of "mountain people" was the Jarai tribe.

January 1959: The North Vietnam Central Executive Committee (Communist) adopted Resolution #15. This announced their change of posture toward South Vietnam from "political struggle" to "armed struggle."

November 1960: President Eisenhower pledged the U.S. to help maintain South Vietnam as a separate state, free from North Vietnam domination. Some 800 US "military advisors" were already in South Vietnam to assist in the training of an army of 243,000 men.

November 1960: President Kennedy was elected.

December 20, 1960: North Vietnam announced the formation of the National Liberation Front. Military incursions into South Vietnam followed.

1960: The C&MA operated a large hospital in Ban Me Thuot, primarily for the treatment of leprosy patients.

February 1961: The Communists tortured and murdered Ga Hao, the leading national Christian pastor in the Jarai tribe of 200,000.

1962: President Kennedy ordered Green Berets to South Vietnam to begin training village men as counter-insurgence defense groups against the Viet Cong.

March 1962: Charlie Long began serving as auxiliary chaplain at the Pleiku detachment of the Military Advisory Group. He frequently preached in three languages, Vietnamese, Jarai and English, before lunch. He conducted the memorial service for US Army Warrant Officer Holloway, a helicopter pilot, for whom Camp Holloway, next to Pleiku Airbase, was named.

1962: Charlie Long survived serious hepatitis.

May 26, 1962: Communists isolated the leprosarium hospital ten miles outside of Ban Me Thuot. C&MA personnel were fortunately unharmed.

1962: EG Long survived her third miscarriage and endured the D&C operation performed by a Vietnamese doctor without the benefit of anesthesia.

October 1962: The U.S. Air Force deployed a second Air Division to Vietnam.

Early 1963: The South Vietnam Army suffered its first major defeat.

Later 1963: A US Senate panel reported 12,000 US troops in Vietnam on a "dangerous assignment."

July 1963: After four years in Vietnam, the Longs began a one year furlough in the US.

August 21, 1963: President Ngo Dinh Diem ordered military attacks on Buddhist pagodas harboring communists.

November 1, 1963: The South Vietnam government was toppled by a military coup.

November 2, 1963: President Diem and his brother were assassinated.

November 22, 1963: President Kennedy was assassinated. Lyndon B. Johnson succeeded him as president.

February 7, 1964: President Johnson ordered the withdrawal of all American dependents from Vietnam.

July 1964: Charlie and EG Long and their three children returned to Vietnam to begin their second four year term.

August 7, 1964: Congress passed the Tonkin Gulf Resolution beginning the undeclared war on North Vietnam.

Fall 1965: American combat forces began to arrive in Vietnam. "The Big Build Up" was underway. The 173rd Airborne landed on the unfinished "new Pleiku" airstrip near the Pleiku base under construction.

1967: This was a busy year for the Longs with the construction and funding of the Pleiku Leprosy Center. It was an emotionally draining period. For three and a half years the gunfire and the explosions never stopped.

January 29, 1968: The Communist "Tet Offensive" began.

February 2, 1968: All C&MA missionaries in Ban Me Thuot except Marie Ziemer and Carolyn Griswold were killed or captured. Carolyn died in surgery. Essentially all C&MA facilities in Ban Me Thuot were destroyed. All C&MA facilities in Pleiku were extensively damaged.

February 1968: The new Leprosy Treatment Center in Pleiku opened. The funds for construction were mostly donations from American military servicemen.

February 1968: Charlie Long recovered his translation of the book of Matthew into Jarai from underneath the rubble of his bombed-to-pieces office in Pleiku.

July 1968: The Longs started their second one year furlough in the US.

Summer 1969: American troops began the withdrawal from Vietnam.

1969: The Longs returned to Vietnam for their third four year term. Mixed with other work, Charlie worked frantically on translating the scriptures into Jarai and EG worked on the production of a hymnal in Jarai.

1969-1972: There was a period of large growth of Christian churches in the Central Highlands around Pleiku and Ban Me Thuot.

1973: The Longs extended their third four year term into five years to allow the completion of the scriptures and the hymnal.

1973: All American combat units were gone.

June 1974: The Jarai hymnal came off the press. The first printing of 5,000 copies sold out in one month.

July 1974: Two weeks before their July furlough, all 810 pages of Charlie's translation of the New Testament and the Psalms into Jarai were finished and ready for printing by the United Bible Societies in Hong Kong.

February 16, 1975: The Jarai translation of the New Testament and the Psalms reached the Jarai people. They were dedicated and presented to the Jarai people at the Tin Lanh church in Pleiku on February 16, 1975.

March 9, 1975: The Communist assault on Ban Me Thuot began. This led to the Vietnamese government abandonment of Ban Me Thuot, Pleiku and all of the Central Highlands.

April 30, 1975: South Vietnam capitulated into Communism.

October 1975-1985: There was a ten year news blackout regarding all Montagnard people in the Central Highlands.

1985: News finally came out of the Central Highlands. Five Montagnard tribes had survived intense interrogation, imprisonment, beatings and fearful mistreatment at the hands of the Communists. They united to form one "Mountain Nation." The great revival of 1971 continued. Montagnard tribespeople became Christians by the thousands. In 1972 there were about 53,000 Christian and Missionary Alliance baptized church members in Vietnam. In 1992, that number reached more than 248,000. Jarai tribe believers made up 62,000 of that total number.

1995: <u>To Viet Nam with Love</u>, the Story of Charlie and EG Long, copyright 1995 by Christian Publications, Camp Hill, PA became available to the public.

The missionaries I knew in Pleiku were Charlie and EG Long, Dave and Jeannie Frazier, and Gale and Irene Fleming. They had come to bring Christianity to a third world people who were barefooted, half dressed and lived in grass huts with dirt floors. The Montagnard people were held in disrespect and shunned by the ethnic Vietnamese.

The Montagnards hunted with the home made cross-bow and did limited farming with pointed sticks for tools. They believed the liver and intestines, not the heart, were the deep seat of human emotion. How would you feel if a dear one said to you, "I love you with all my liver and intestines"?

The cultural gap in thought and belief between "them and us" was a great impediment to communication. The missionaries had first to learn the Jarai language and then try to understand their culture. Only after learning to understand the Jarai people, could the missionaries begin to teach them about Christianity. It was an enormous undertaking.

The Longs, the Fraziers and the Flemings had been working at the task for six years when I arrived in Pleiku. Observing first-hand some of their dedicated work was a unique privilege for me.

Chaplain Brian Wesley had already become acquainted with the missionaries. Wesley introduced me to these kind friendly people through their Sunday afternoon hymn sing. They welcomed military members and civilian employees to their compound for cookies, tea, singing and visiting. It was a most welcome change from the military environment.

In my FAC business of flying, Sunday was just like all of the other days of the week. The common expression was, "The only thing different about Sunday is that's the day that my watch turns red and I take my malaria pill." Diarrhea on Monday commonly followed the malaria pill on Sunday.

The flying schedule was always busy and took precedence over everything else. The "town" was also usually "off limits," but sometimes the Chaplain's special exemption allowed us to pile into his jeep and go to the missionary compound anyway. I liked the music, the people and sitting on real grass. I went to the Sunday hymn sing every time I could.

One of the missionary wives pumped vigorously on the foot bellows of a field organ and did a good job on the limited keys. The Chaplain brought several copies of the Armed Forces Hymnal, but most of the people ignored them and just followed along. Those who could actually sing were readily noticed, especially if they could read music and carry a part other than the melody.

On one of my first visits to the missionary compound, Charlie Long, the lead missionary in Pleiku, conscripted four of us visitors and declared us to be a male quartette. Surprisingly, we made what actually sounded like real music. Charlie then told us that he wanted us to sing later that evening for the worship service at the Tin Lanh (Good News) Church in Pleiku. It turned out to be an unforgettable experience.

To start with, the "city" of Pleiku was never safe, and especially not safe for "round eyes" (Americans) out after dark. Night time was the best opportunity for the folks in black pajamas who smiled and sold things for American dollars along the dirt streets during the day, to wait around the corner and shoot the same customer at night. There were good reasons for the town to commonly be off limits.

The Tin Lanh Church was a small building with a pitched roof and exterior walls covered with old white plaster of some sort. It was unfurnished except for wobbly wooden benches which seated a little over one hundred people. There were doorways and window openings but no doors or window coverings.

A widely varying conglomeration of people gathered there for worship. Most of them were Montagnards, more of the Jarai tribe and fewer of the Raday tribe. The men wore a wrapped breech cloth and a discarded piece of army fatigues or some other shirt. The women wore the traditional piece of brightly colored native woven material about three feet wide wrapped around the body. It covered the body from the ankles to the waist, leaving the rest uncovered. None of them wore shoes.

A few ethnic Vietnamese, mostly of Chinese descent, and some American missionaries rounded out the crowd. In the midst of this incongruous gathering of souls were four very out of place white guys Charlie Long recruited to sing four part harmony from the Armed Forces Hymnal. To say we stood out in the crowd was a great understatement.

The service resembled an extended family gathering in the park. The small talk continued, uninterrupted by planned proceedings. Various dogs walked freely in and out, up and down the central aisle. Babies cried and were fed at Mom's bare-breasted lunch facility which was always openly on display and readily available. The casual atmosphere prevailed until the main event. Charlie Long was the main event.

When Charlie stood to address the assembly, everything changed. His lanky six foot four frame towered above the typically short Montagnards and Vietnamese. The real difference, however, was these people obviously knew and respected him. Everything fell silent and all distraction ceased. Charlie spoke to them in their language, Jarai, and they listened intently to his every word. I didn't understand one single word, but it was clear the Jarai people took in everything Charlie said.

At the end of the service, the entire group sang, "When the Roll Is Called up Yonder I'll Be There." The musical score was slaughtered in English, Vietnamese, Jarai and Raday simultaneously. Any music critic worth a nickel would have said the horrible cacophony of competing bellowing and shouting had absolutely no resemblance whatsoever to music.

However, remembering the Biblical admonition to "Make a joyful noise unto the Lord," I could imagine seeing God smiling, applauding and saying, "Well done! Very nice joyful noise."

Our attendance at the Tin Lanh Church service had gone very well, but things did not always go well. Less than three weeks later, our "quartette" had an invitation to dinner with hosts Dave and Jeannie Frazier, at the C&MA compound. This was a rare treat and I looked forward to it with considerable anticipation. The night before our invitation, there was a rumble among some ARVN (VN Army) troops in town, a common occurrence. They managed to end up with one of their own killed in the fight and the town was off limits again. We unavoidably stood up our hosts and later explained and apologized.

While my personal experiences with the missionaries were good and pleasant, I knew that their very survival was regularly in jeopardy. The Communists hated Christian influence and persecuted the Montagnard Christians mercilessly. The Communists particularly resented Jarai Christians who became effective leaders. Two years into their first four year tour, the Longs learned how serious that was.

Ga Hao was the leading pastor in the Jarai tribe. In February 1961 the Communists tied his hands behind his back, threw the other end of the rope over a tree limb and pulled on the rope until his body was suspended in the air. They took a Jarai sword and started chopping.

Feet.

Ankles.

Calves.

Thighs.

Piece by piece.

When they finished, Ga Hao was dead, and the Communists had sent a message regarding what they thought about Christians. No one knew who might be next. There would be many.

While the C&MA missionaries were well aware their lives were in constant danger, they were not deterred from persisting in their purposes. Neither were they selfish when it came to helping others.

Doctor Martin Newburgh and his wife, a registered nurse, arrived in Pleiku in February 1966. They were the on scene representatives of the Mennonite Central Committee of the United States, with plans to build a Leprosy Treatment Center in Pleiku. The C&MA had no ties with the Mennonites, but the Longs hosted the Newburghs and helped them get started in Pleiku.

They introduced the Newburghs to "an Air Force pilot" (guess who) that might be able to fly Dr. Newburgh to Dak To, sixty miles north of Pleiku, to visit a refugee camp. In the camp were some 13,000 Montagnards, many of whom had leprosy. I hadn't seen that task coming, but it landed in my lap anyway.

On February 20, 1966, I took LtCol Oliver, our Squadron Commander, and LtCol Conway, our Air Liaison Officer, to the C&MA compound for refreshments and to meet Dr. Newburgh. We then went and looked at a stake in the ground at the corner of the property in Pleiku where the Mennonites planned to build the new Leprosy Treatment Center. My bosses liked the idea and appointed me Project Officer for our squadron's Humanitarian Project to lend support to the Newburghs and their project.

The very next day I took an O-1 and flew Dr. Newburgh to Dak To, the site of the refugee camp. Dak To was also our staging base for Tiger Hound missions on the Ho Chi Minh Trail. Dak To was bad country. I didn't like flying out of there and liked even less being on the ground there. From the airstrip we took a jeep and drove over four miles through the jungle to the village where Dr. Newburgh took pictures for his project.

When we returned to the Dak To airstrip, the good guys (I think) were running through the village with rifles chasing the bad guys (I think). I cranked up my little airplane and we left without delay. After shooting some aerial pictures of that area and another village, we returned to Pleiku. The new Leprosy Treatment Center project was underway.

The initial construction was funded by $15,000 from the Mennonites and two other national Protestant agencies in the US. It was the first Protestant Mission hospital in Vietnam. Much subsequent funding came from donations from American military members. Since I was our squadron's Project Officer, I was gratified that so many military members in Pleiku, and their families back home, supported our Humanitarian Project.

The support for the project from American military members continued and grew. Six months later when I was in Ban Me Thuot, Dan Preston delivered a message from Art Cannon, the new Project Officer, who replaced me after I was transferred and left Pleiku. "Tell Dale about twenty boxes from his Cheyenne return address arrived and I delivered them to Dr. and Mrs. Newburgh. They were very happy to have the goods."

In my next letter home I asked Nancy to relay my thanks to our home church members who had been generous. The one who deserved the real thanks was my wife, Nancy, who led the effort and made it all happen.

There was another side to my relationship with the Pleiku missionaries. The family atmosphere in the Long household was much like home. Charlie & EG's little Susie and I hit it off immediately. She liked me and I liked her. We quickly formed our own mutual admiration society.

When I arrived at the missionary compound, I would kneel on the grass on one knee and Susie would run to me with open arms for me to pick her up and hold her. One evening at the Longs' dinner table, Susie wailed loudly, stopping her father, Charlie, as he was starting to offer the prayer, "I wanna sit by Uncle!" EG graciously and quietly moved Susie's high chair next to my chair. Susie and I were both very pleased with the improved seating arrangement. God and everyone else just had to wait until Susie was happy for Charlie to resume his prayer.

Later when it was time for Susie to go to bed, she selected "Uncle" to carry her and put her in her crib. She warmed my heart and broke it into pieces with home sickness all at the same time. How I wished I could hold my own sweet loving little Elaine, at home in Cheyenne! Susie and Elaine were two beautiful little blond girls, the same age, the same size and 10,000 miles apart on opposite sides of the world. I was missing a year of Elaine's sweet little girl charm that could never be recovered. It hurt.

When I was transferred to Ban Me Thuot for my last three months in Vietnam, I soon found the missionaries there were the same dedicated servants as those in Pleiku. I had a ready introduction from the Pleiku missionaries and was glad to meet their Ban Me Thuot associates.

The Ban Me Thuot missionaries played tennis. Good tennis! I was pleased to play a better variety of the game with them and some of the Army MACV people there. It felt good to fit into their game so comfortably. They played it rather passionately. Sharing vigorous physical exercise creates good friendships quickly and I enjoyed new friends.

They also conducted regular worship services in the military facilities and included me in their music. The entire situation seemed quite civilized. On July 30, 1965 I got down from flying and found that I had a call from "the missionaries." I hurried to the court for a good competitive game of tennis with Bob Ziemer and Ken Swayne. We had an impromptu supper at their compound and I practiced a simple music number with Bob McNeil to sing in church the next day. The C&MA mission compound was a small oasis of civilization in the desert of the war. Make no mistake; the war was large and real and all around. The missionaries were in constant danger.

There were six C&MA missionary families and several single women nurses in Ban Me Thuot, a total of nearly thirty people. The focus of C&MA activity was the leprosarium, which had been in operation for many years.

On September 14, 1966, I enjoyed my last visit and supper at the Ban Me Thuot compound of the C&MA. Our host and hostess were Bob and Marie Ziemer along with three other missionary couples and four single nurses. At Marie's invitation, my immediate boss, LtCol George Olson, was also there. Another FAC, Dick Overgaard, was invited to come but got stuck out at the Boun Blech Special Forces Camp and didn't make it.

The food for our meal, in this land of rice and more rice, was a real surprise. It was Pizza! And Ice Cream! Could you believe it? How in the world did they manage that, clear across the world from home? And then they explained. This was part of the several airplane loads of food I hauled from the Boun Blech Special Forces Camp and delivered to the missionaries.

Ten days later I left Vietnam and went home. The "home cooking" pizza party at the Ziemers was my last memory of those marvelous people, "the missionaries" in Ban Me Thuot.

Sixteen months later, on January 29, 1968, the Communist Tet Offensive began. The Communists destroyed the C&MA missionary compound and leprosarium. All the missionaries and nurses were systematically slaughtered. For the C&MA it was the largest single loss of missionaries since the 1900 Boxer Rebellion in China. They missed only one of the entire group of missionaries in Ban Me Thuot. Our kindly pizza and ice cream hostess, Marie Ziemer, was the sole survivor.

Marie's husband, Bob Ziemer, was my good tennis partner and friend. Now, after nearly two decades of devoted missionary service together, Bob was dead and Marie was seriously injured. She had no home in either Vietnam or the United States. All of her colleagues in Ban Me Thuot were dead. Her first priority now was to go back to the United States to bury her husband.

The missionaries were indeed the Real Warriors. Who could doubt it?

Chapter 16

A Place to Eat and Sleep

1965-66 – The Pleiku compound

For my first two days in Pleiku, I dragged a suitcase and a duffle bag around and looked for a mattress on the floor somewhere for the night. That worked if there wasn't already a body on the mattress. For the remainder of the week, two other guys pushed enough stuff around to make a sleeping corner for me in their small room.

At the end of the week, the next wing of the building was marginally ready. I had a room and a bed. That was good news. The base facilities folks gave me some green mahogany and some nails which I mangled into crude shelves to go with a salvaged baggage crate. I had furniture.

Then I scored a major victory. I captured my own steel wall locker and recruited a sergeant named Marvin to help me move it to my room. As we maneuvered around corners and up a couple of steps, something inside the locker slammed from side to side. Marvin said, "It sounds like there's a brick banging around in there." When we had the locker upright in its place, I opened the doors to check on the brick.

"Well, look at that, Marv. My brick is a four pound fruitcake."

"Yeah, and a pretty damned ugly one at that. I'd say the guy who abandoned it made a good decision."

I kicked the fruitcake to one side on the floor and ignored it for several weeks. Not even the rats, regular visitors in the room, were interested in trying it. Then curiosity prompted me to look at it more closely. My standards regarding culinary creations had slipped considerably and the fruitcake's appearance began to improve. I peeled it open, and although it was as sticky as fly paper, it tasted better than I expected. With minimal help from roommates, we ate the whole darned thing.

Our "room" was a cubicle partitioned by drywall nailed to upright studs. A larger area had been divided into six smaller spaces called rooms. There were no ceilings and no doors. The walls stopped a foot above the floor. The building itself appeared to be a temporary structure of World War II vintage. It had, in fact, been built only six or seven years earlier by local contract. It was shoddy and ugly and just looked old.

16.1 – Pleiku Airbase Officers Quarters, Home Sweet Home for nine months

But it was home and I was glad to have it, especially with a bed of my own (most of the time). Although we had mosquito netting, I didn't use it during the dry monsoon. When the wet monsoon arrived, the mosquitoes encouraged me to use the netting. The more humid atmosphere during the wet monsoon also prompted some action to keep things dry.

One of the sergeants in Civil Engineering got me a 60 watt light bulb, a reflector, a socket, a large tin can, some plugs, some conductor wire and some tying wire. The marvelous creation hung in the bottom of my locker so a little bit of heat could rise. The heater was effective enough to almost prevent mildew on clothing.

The officers who occupied the "new" wing of the building were all lieutenants except me. As the senior officer, a captain, I had first choice and invited Frank Munson to share a room. In such a small space, it would be nice if we got along well. I was white, a captain, a pilot, a Protestant, married with kids. Frank was black, a lieutenant, non-flying, a Roman Catholic, single. We were different. We got along great.

Frank was a quiet and unassuming personnel services officer in the base support group. It was only through an article and photo in the Air Force Times newspaper I learned he was an accomplished athlete. He was a silver medalist in the pentathlon in the Tokyo Olympics in 1964, a year before coming to Vietnam. His five rugged events were obstacle course horsemanship, fencing, pistol shooting, free style swimming and cross-country running. He hadn't even told me about the silver medal. Frank trained by running on base and hoped to compete in the Mexico Olympics.

He played his guitar, quietly, of course, demonstrating about the same lack of skill I had on my baritone ukulele. Frank was scheduled for "in-country" R&R at Nha Trang on the coast. "I'm going to take my guitar, my running clothes and my swimming suit. That's all I'm going to need."

"Frank, you're going to have a relaxing time running on the sandy beach and swimming in the ocean. It will be a great change of pace from Pleiku. When I go to Nha Trang to exchange airplanes from periodic inspection, I'm always anxious to get out of there. Your R&R schedule sounds a lot better than my maintenance schedule."

16.2 – Roommate, Lt Frank Munson. Strong, quiet, Olympic Silver Medalist

I hoped Frank and I would be the only two in our room, but soon we had two more. There were four of us crowded into the room. Occasionally we had wall to wall bodies as others came and went. The third and fourth regulars in our room were Warrant Officer Josh Ellis and Lt Theotokopolous Papadiamantis Dyonisios.

Ellis was a quiet, easy going older guy who worked in the personnel office. With Josh, I made my only walking trip of the year into the "town" of Pleiku to buy souvenirs for my kids. We also bought woven grass mats to serve as carpet of sorts. The mats merely rearranged the dirt on the floor. Ellis and I later waged a spirited on-going contest in the rat trapping business. Rats provided some of the best entertainment available. Josh was an excellent roommate.

Lt Dyonisios worked as a radar controller. He was different enough to keep life interesting. "Don't try to say Theotokopolous Papadiamantis Dyonisios. Don't even try to say Theotokopolous. Just call me Theo, or better yet, just call me Greek. That's a lot easier."

Greek was lively and energetic and seemed to enjoy life more than most people thought was allowed in Vietnam. After another trip to the Vietnamese government operated whorehouse, he came back all aglow and wanted to tell me about his night. "I had a really nice girl! She was a real sweetheart. I couldn't say her name, but I'm going to try to find her again next time."

16.3 – Downtown Pleiku with roommate, Warrant Officer Josh Ellis

"Stay away from me, Greek. I don't want any of your whorehouse bugs jumping onto me. These people have diseases with names harder to pronounce than Theotokopolous Papadiamantis Dyonisios, and they resist the medicines that the doc has to fight them."

Greek wore T shirts with large bright Batman and Superman emblems emblazoned on the chest and liked to sing along when I played my baritone ukulele. He admired pictures I got from home and was fascinated I had a wife and four kids.

"What grades are your boys in at school?"

"Steve is our oldest and he's in the fourth grade. Jim is in the first grade. They attend an elementary school two blocks from our home in Cheyenne."

"I want to do something special for them. I'm going to write a letter to them in English and Greek. I'll write one line in English and then write the same thing on the next line in Greek. I'll alternate lines like that all the way through the letter. They can take it to school for their teachers and the kids to see."

Greek did send the letter in both English and Greek to my boys. Figure 16.4 shows what the letter looked like. He wrote (presented here in English only):

16 April 1966

Dear Steve, Jim and Marshall,

I am writing you this letter from Pleiku, Vietnam where I am with your father. We are roommates and good friends. I thought with your father that you would like to receive a letter written in Greek.

My home is in Mobile, Alabama where I have my parents and one brother, John and one sister (Amalia). My sister goes to the university in Washington, D.C. and she is a good student. My brother works with my father as partners.

Vietnam is an interesting country. It has many things that America doesn't have. It has elephants, tigers and big snakes. Some day when peace is made you will come and see it all.

With love,

Theotokopolous Papadiamantis Dyonisios

Inside those comic book T-shirts was a young man who was intelligent and articulate. While he prompted a lot of my unspoken disapproval, I couldn't help but like him. He gave me something to think about other than flying and directing air strikes. When I left Pleiku to spend my last three months in Ban Me Thuot, I think he was sorry to see me leave. "My family has a large famous Greek restaurant in Mobile, Alabama. I would like to have you and your family come for a visit and dine there as my guests."

He wrote out specific instructions for me. I'm sure he was sincere.

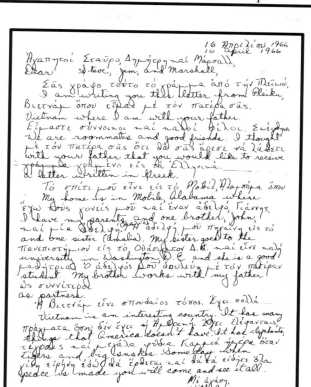

16.4 – Greek's letter to my boys, written in both English and Greek

Climate-wise, Pleiku wasn't a bad place to live. Most of the population of Vietnam lived on the hot, humid coastal plains or in the equally uncomfortable Mekong River Delta. The Central Highlands were 2,400 feet above sea level and enjoyed a cooler dryer climate. Even a "nice house" in Pleiku, if there had been one, and there wasn't, wouldn't have been equipped with heating or cooling. In cool weather, one blanket was plenty on my bed. In warm weather, I used nothing for covering.

Sometimes we enjoyed the luxury of water and electricity in the quarters. The main problem for the electrical power system was the lack of fuel to run the generators. Fuel was commonly stolen and sold on the black market. The generators then ran out of fuel. My back-up lighting system, a big candle mounted in a Coke can full of dirt, was quite adequate. It provided enough light for the Scrabble game or letter writing to continue uninterrupted. The rats weren't impeded by darkness. They saw better in the dark than I did. They frequently ran past my feet while I wrote letters by candlelight.

The water system in the compound was less reliable than the electrical system. Adequate supply wasn't the problem. Lake Bien Ho, a large spring-fed lake, provided plenty of good water. The problem was delivery and distribution of the water. The system was built by the French to supply four or five hundred people. With the "Big Build Up" the demand for water suddenly mushroomed to several times the capability of the system. Breakdowns were common and long lasting.

Furthermore, the locals stole fuel from the water pumping station as easily as they stole it from the electricity generating station. The result was the same. The pumps quit running. The water user in the compound couldn't tell if the latest problem was mechanical equipment failure or fuel starvation for the pumps. In either case, there was no water.

After a long day of flying I looked forward eagerly to showering my hot, dirty sweaty body. However, if it didn't happen, the only consequence was personal discomfort. In terms of the entire compound of many people, it was a greater problem. On one occasion, the water was on for only two hours of eighty consecutive hours. That posed a serious challenge for washing dishes at the chow hall and flushing toilets.

I developed a sequence of priorities for getting a shower. First I went to the adjacent latrine and tried the shower. If there was no water, I went down the little hill to the latrine in the next building. If that didn't work, I came back to the first latrine. Frequently I could drain enough water from the lowest pipe to fill my steel helmet.

If there was no water in the lowest pipe, I took my steel helmet to the fire barrel outside under the roof drain. I brushed away the bugs and cigarette butts and dipped my helmet full of water. With a wash cloth and the helmet full of water on the shower floor, I got a pretty good bath. The maid laughed at my procedure as she walked by, but neither of us cared.

My last resort regarding water was the sturdy plastic Clorox jug Nancy sent at my request. I seldom used it for more than wetting the rag and wiping down the body. I reserved that last gallon for drinking.

Food was seldom a problem. The Army MACV Mess Association ran a tight ship and did it well. They acquired all the food, paid the employees and served the meals. Each member of the Mess Association was charged a pro rata share of the total costs. Of course it wasn't mom's home cooking and there were limits on what they could do, but it was very satisfactory.

FACs frequently had a problem beyond the Mess Association's provision. We flew missions that caused us to miss meals they served on their schedule, which differed from our flying schedule. I kept a stash of C rations in my locker for those occasions.

On November 18, 1965, I taxied in, parked the plane and caught our senior flight line maintenance guy. "Hey, Andy, was that C-123 this afternoon hauling any C rations?"

"Yes, Sir, it was. They had several pallets of "C"s going on up to Kontum for an operation the 101st Airborne is about to start. We helped those guys rearrange some of their cargo."

"Great! I'm glad you helped them. I hope you stole some grub for me. My locker back at the compound is nearly empty."

"Aw, c'mon now, Captain. We don't ever steal anything. But, ya know, several boxes fell off a pallet and happened to land in my pickup. You know we take care of our FACs."

Andy was superb working on our airplanes and also knew how to take care of his FACs. I brought back four packs of C rations for my locker. The "entrées" were

Ham, fried

Ham and lima beans

Chopped ham and eggs

Beans with franks

That was OK. I like ham. There were also other items like crackers, bread, cookies, jelly, peanut butter etc. C rations were very satisfactory - - occasionally. They filled in well when we missed what the Mess Association had to offer.

The quarters where we lived were intended for military men like me, but we were not the only inhabitants of the building. At night the rats were everywhere and in the daytime the maids took over. We did our best to kill the rats and co-exist peacefully with the maids. We didn't have much influence over the activities of either. I had the same degree of success in communicating with the maids as in talking with the rats.

The maids were local Vietnamese women employed under a general agreement intended to direct what they did and how they were paid.

The monetary exchange rate was $1.00 = 118 piasters. A local haircut cost 25p. The five foot by seven foot woven grass mats Ellis and I bought in town for the floor cost 150p, about $1.30 each.

For 200p per man per month the maid swept the floor (rearranged the dirt), polished the boots and made the bed. For another 100p she did all laundry not requiring ironing. Flying suits and jungle fatigues cost another 20p per set. In the interest of simplicity and generosity, the guys gave the maid 500p per month and skipped the details.

In hopes of recovering my own clothes after the laundry process, I put my name on my clothes with a black marker. The maid had already marked some of my things "RON" which I didn't understand. Later I figured out her system. She marked laundry for individual men with the last three letters on their uniform nametag. She mistook my call sign, "Baron 10" on my uniform, to be my name and extracted the letters "RON" from "Baron." She used those letters "RON" for her laundry mark on my clothing.

Now, what in the heck would she do if she had men named Olson, Johnson, Wilson, Swanson, and Munson? Who knows? Would she mark all of their laundry with the last three letters of their names? If she did, all of their laundry would come back marked "SON." Who would sort that mess? Her system didn't work.

The maids' treatment of laundry was absolutely brutal. They used minimal soap and water, laid the garment flat on a concrete surface and beat it severely with a brick.

16.5 – The maids take a break from pounding the laundry on the concrete.

Predictably, the life of clothing decreased rapidly. My flying suits developed holes, hastening my use of jungle fatigues instead of flying suits.

Communication with our maid was barely more than zero. We pointed, smiled, gestured and shrugged our shoulders. The only gesture mutually understood was nodding or shaking the head for yes or no. Even that had no meaning if you couldn't identify the question or the subject being discussed. Yes or no about what?

Early in the game I tried to tell the maid I needed my socks back from the laundry. I made several gestures trying unsuccessfully to explain. Finally her puzzled expression changed into a broad smile and she disappeared. She soon returned with all the black boot socks she could carry, at least enough for a dozen men for several days. She dropped them in the middle of the floor, took a small step backwards and gave me a triumphant grin.

All black military boot socks look pretty darned similar. I sorted through the pile and did my best to retrieve only my own socks. I wondered if the last guy recovered his own socks. Did he get any socks at all?

All the maids were short, lean and lithe, allowing them to effortlessly employ the relaxed "Asian squat." The feet were flat on the floor, the knees were fully flexed, the buttocks rested on the heels and the torso leaned forward with the armpits on the kneecaps. The hands were free to gesture, to drink tea at break time, to push rice from a bowl into the mouth with chopsticks or perform their tasks as maids.

In the squatting position, they pounded the laundry and ironed on a blanket on a grass mat on the floor. For them it was a natural posture. A fuller bodied American or European cramped in the Asian squat position for five minutes would need two good friends and a stretcher to get to the chiropractor. Recovering the use of his legs and back would probably require much therapy.

In a vain attempt to save certain items of my laundry from the maid beating the Hell out of it with a brick, I learned my only words in Vietnamese. The words were "dung giat," pronounced "doong yak." They meant "don't wash." I held up my laundry bag, pointed to its contents and said, "dung giat." She nodded and smiled, but it didn't help. When I was gone she gave everything another vicious pounding. The maid always won. I gave up.

On one special occasion, my poor laundry did get a short respite from torture. For the national TET holiday observance, everything in Vietnam came to a halt. The war was put on hold and both sides quit shooting at each other. My laundry was left ignored in a big pan of dirty water under my bed for four days. It didn't matter. As usual, it came back pounded and still as grungy as when it left.

Our maid was always congenial and smiling. After Christmas, she tried to communicate with me something about the small decorated Christmas tree Nancy sent me. Through the exchange of several gestures, I realized she admired the small, round, colored ornaments hanging on the tree. I couldn't tell if she had any concept of the true meaning of Christmas. Neither did I know if she understood the tree was a symbol associated with the custom of giving gifts.

It hadn't been long since one of the guys looking at my little Christmas tree struggled through his laughter to tell me how ugly it was. Now here was our maid quite strongly attracted to it. It seemed she was asking if she might have the ornaments. I gave her the tree and all of the decorations hanging on it. That gesture produced the most smiles she ever gave.

For the most part, by comparison with lots of guys in Vietnam living in muddy holes in the ground, our "place to eat and sleep" wasn't at all bad. I had a little bit of space that was mostly my own. I sat on a chair to eat most of my meals from a plate on a table. Most of the time, I was able to find a way to wash up and I had a bed to sleep in. I didn't complain.

Chapter 17
The Worst Ever Air Force Officer

1965-66 –Pleiku and Ban Me Thuot

He was commonly known as Buster the Bastard, or BTB for short. "Buster the Bastard" was about the kindest, most complimentary name anyone who knew him could assign to the worst ever Air Force Officer. He was also called all of the nasty, hateful, disrespectful names available in the entire Air Force vernacular, and those names were appropriate for Buster.

17.1 – Buster The Bastard, (BTB), second from the right

His parents christened him Bosworth T. Buskirk and somewhere along the way he became Buster. I often thought he must have caused his mother great pain and anguish prior to his birth. Otherwise, why would she have hung such a clumsy moniker on an innocent baby? Or did the father help with the name selection?

Then again, perhaps the father was un-identified. In that case, Webster's dictionary would also define BTB as a genuine bastard. That possibility provided enjoyable speculation to those of us who had the misfortune to know him well. It also reinforced the validity of the "Buster the Bastard" label.

When LtCol Buskirk arrived in Pleiku, he promptly made a fool of himself by visiting one of the Special Forces Camps with his personal machete dangling from his belt. He sought out some of the experienced Green Berets and initiated a conversation regarding the best techniques for chopping through the foliage of the jungle. The Green Berets smiled and said,"Aw, Colonel, we don't do that. We just walk around it."

If BTB had been merely an ordinary fool, he might have been harmless. He was, however, the Air Liaison Officer for the II Corps area, with supervisory authority over all Forward Air Controllers. He was a disaster for all of us FACs.

My first personal experience with BTB came during a search mission for one of our FACs who was down. Maj Mark Caswell left Qui Nhon in an O-1 headed for Cheo Reo but never arrived. He was never heard from again. In Caswell's back seat was an F-4 pilot from Cam Ranh, on exchange to learn something about how FACs controlled F-4s and other fighters on air strikes.

On the morning after they failed to arrive, I was one of four FACs who flew out of Cheo Reo along the arrival route which we thought Caswell would have flown. Two more of our FACs searched along the Qui Nhon departure end of their flight. There were six FACs looking for Caswell. Each airplane also had an observer in the back seat. Twelve sets of eyes scanned the area for Caswell. No one saw anything.

It was on one of the search missions for Caswell my luck ran out. BTB had been in Pleiku for nearly a month and I had avoided trouble with him. On March 5, 1966, he was my back seat observer. I quickly confirmed everything bad I had heard about him. He was a <u>real loser</u>! He was extremely conceited and took personal credit for anything good the Air Force did. He had been everywhere, done everything, knew it all, and told everyone how to do everything. The worst part was he was <u>our</u> boss of flying operations. In that capacity, he made himself obnoxious to all FACs. He had clashed with everyone with whom he had flown, and I didn't spoil his record.

We flew all morning, looking continuously and listening for a signal from an emergency radio. There was nothing. None of the others saw or heard anything. The only good part of the morning was I didn't have a run-in with BTB in my back seat. As noontime approached, I thought to myself, "Well, that wasn't so bad. If running his mouth in overdrive keeps him happy, I can stand it for a while."

We landed at Cheo Reo to refuel and get a quick bite of lunch. Cheo Reo's hard surface runway was much longer than most of the poor dirt runways from which we frequently operated. I made a good landing, touching down well past the approach end of the runway in order to shorten the required long taxi distance to the intersection where we turned off. I slowed normally and turned off comfortably without delay onto the taxiway. It was a perfectly executed expeditious landing and taxi run.

To my complete surprise, BTB blew his stack, "What in the Hell are you doing, Amend? Can't you fly this airplane? How long have you been here, and still can't fly? You landed so long you barely made the turn off! Any longer and you would have tipped the plane over trying to turn off going too fast. Do you realize that <u>I</u> am responsible for everything that <u>you</u> do in this airplane? If you can't fly any better, it will be my job to write the letter to your wife expressing my sympathy you killed yourself because you couldn't fly!"

I was dumbfounded and grossly insulted by this idiot in a superior position of authority who had just crashed into my life. I was a very good pilot. All FACs who survived were good pilots. We flew a lot and were highly proficient. And then out of the blue, here came this imbecile! I managed to hold my tongue and say, "Yes, Sir."

The afternoon flight brought more of the same results in searching for Caswell and the F-4 pilot. Ironically, the F-4 pilot's tour of duty in Vietnam ended in an airplane that flew about one fifth as fast as the F-4 he regularly flew. Time dragged as we listened for an emergency radio signal and looked for the missing O-1.

I never stopped steaming while BTB was in my back cockpit.

At the end of the long afternoon I landed on the same runway at Cheo Reo, but in different fashion. I approached at slow speed with full flaps and touched down perfectly on the very first part of the runway. I braked the airplane smoothly and promptly to a full stop, a good normal short field landing. Sitting still on the runway, I raised the flaps, added a minimum amount of power, and taxied putt-putt-putt-putt ever so slowly the long distance to the intersection to turn off the runway.

The explosion from the back seat met all my expectations. "Now what in the Hell do you think you are doing, Amend? Do you think that was funny? Why did you do that?"

"Sir, I know you want to be satisfied all of the pilots under your supervision are proficient and can fly the O-1. This morning there seemed to be considerable doubt in your mind I can handle this airplane. I knew you would want to observe I can indeed put this airplane down on the end of the runway and stop it safely."

I had just joined the club of those pilots BTB hated. There was no particular distinction in belonging to that club. It wasn't an exclusive group. BTB hated everyone, especially those who were under his authority. He was out to hurt all of them. He was a bad guy.

After a second and third day, the search for Caswell was abandoned. As we left Cheo Reo, Dan Preston, who would later be my roommate and immediate boss in Ban Me Thuot, was in the back seat. We commiserated over our experiences with Buskirk. Although BTB had been in Pleiku less than one month, he had already caused Preston in Ban Me Thuot a world of grief. I told Preston about flying with BTB out of Cheo Reo and Preston told me everything he had already endured under BTB's authority as the new II Corp Air Liaison Officer.

Preston said, "Damn it all! It just isn't fair! Why do we have to have him on our side all of the time? They should have him on their side some of the time to even things out. Ya know, Dale, one of us has to make the big sacrifice and shoot that worthless son of a bitch."

Immediately after making that comment, Preston realized his radio control switch in the rear cockpit was in the wrong position. Instead of talking on the intercom, he broadcast his words over the radio to anyone listening on that radio frequency. BTB was in the air at the same time. We never learned if he heard Preston's remarks.

Back in Pleiku, after the unsuccessful Cheo Reo search missions, BTB continued spreading chaos and discontent among the people who worked for him. I felt particularly sorry for Maj Joe Everett, our Pleiku Sector FAC. Everett worked directly under BTB. Buskirk was so amazingly incompetent, conceited, brash acting to cover his own inferiority complex, full of hot air, insulting, irrational, overbearing, threatening, etc. ad infinitum that it was impossible to work for him.

He commanded no one's respect and everyone disliked him immensely. The tragic part was how miserable he made things for those required to associate with him. He was absolutely the worst I had ever seen for disturbing all of those who had contact with him and for destroying morale of those who worked under him. Joe Everett was ready to ask for a transfer to escape working directly for him.

Conflict and strife among members of the same team is always destructive. With BTB imposed as a member of our team, conflict existed wherever he was present. I am a believer in the practice of living at peace with all men insofar as it is possible. Where Buster the Bastard was concerned, that was a noble but insurmountable task. I really did try. It seemed I was slowly winning him to the point of association without friction. One of the best ways to get rid of an enemy is to turn him into a friend. However, with him I doubted it was possible.

BTB didn't have any friends. As I pursued peaceful coexistence, I became concerned that my efforts toward a reasonable working relationship might have been more successful than I had hoped. On June 13, 1966, Buskirk finally caught up with me to play tennis. He horned in quite awkwardly into a doubles game already in progress.

He was obviously an unwelcome "fifth wheel" creating an embarrassing situation. My playing partner, Chaplain Brian Wesley, "graciously bowed out" so Buskirk could have his place. Wesley obligated me to accept BTB as my new partner. I was trapped with no way out. I endured it.

At my first opportunity afterwards, I jumped all over the Chaplain. "Brian, you were chicken! You know all about Buster the Bastard. You looked gracious relinquishing your place on the court, but you took the easy way out. You dumped him on me."

A few days later it looked like things were getting worse for me. It appeared I was going to be stuck as BTB's assistant for the rest of my time in Pleiku. Fortunately, I was moved to Ban Me Thuot where my roommate and immediate boss was Capt Dan Preston. We both worked for Maj Karl (Doc) Dawkins. Doc was a great guy, a real gentleman and a fine officer. We were also ninety miles away from BTB in Pleiku. Yea!

We were still responsible to Buster the Bastard, but now the leash by which he jerked us around had ninety miles of slack. For communication Pleiku and Ban Me Thuot were connected by a US Army land line field phone which at best worked poorly and much of the time did not work at all. The large heavy instrument Dan Preston was obliged to answer when BTB called was located in our room. Dan would answer, talk for a while and then give me the signal to be very quiet.

He then proceeded with "the BTB disconnect." He moved the instrument's mouthpiece farther and farther from his mouth while saying, "Sir, the signal is getting weak. What was that, Colonel? I can't hear you, sir. The line's bad, Colonel. No, sir, I can't understand what you said. What was that, sir?"

When he had extended his arm as far as he could and lowered his voice enough, he quietly shut off the field phone. When BTB called back, there was no reason to answer. Dan had already told him the phone wasn't working. We always wondered if Buskirk ever figured it out.

Dan Preston was exceptionally hardworking and capable. Since Buster the Bastard preferred to harass the best people who worked for him, Dan Preston was a favorite target. On one occasion, Buskirk attacked Preston and in the process upset the commander of the Vietnamese 23rd Division in Ban Me Thuot. General Nguyen strongly supported Preston and smacked BTB down a couple of notches.

More good people of influence learned that BTB really was a worthless bastard. I still hoped for the success of the exchange program with Uncle Ho Chi Minh, so BTB would go fight on their side for a while.

Even when he wasn't harassing his own people, chaos followed BTB's path. He was the only one known to fire his weapon in his room and put a hole in his own ceiling. The black cloud of coincidence also followed him. It was his jeep a disconsolate airman stole. The airman left Pleiku alone, presumably headed for

Saigon. He was seen being taken away under guns by the VC. Neither the airman nor BTB's jeep was ever seen again.

Buster's incompetence was not limited to mismanagement of people under his supervision. As the Air Liaison Officer, he was, at least on paper, qualified as a FAC. His actual qualifications were highly questionable. His reputation as a FAC pilot was bad.

On May 29, 1966, the word leaked out about the incident which substantiated just how bad he was. Things like this were hard to keep quiet. About a month earlier BTB directed fighters onto a friendly Montagnard village killing about sixty people. It was his personal mistake. It was the worst mistake by any FAC in all of South Vietnam during my one year tour of duty. No follow on action was ever taken after the tragic event. Everyone just hoped it would quietly go away.

BTB didn't kill any Americans, but he damaged the careers of many fine officers under his authority. The Officer Effectiveness Report (OER) is essentially the "report card" that largely determines the future of an officer's assignments and promotion in rank. Buskirk routinely gave low ratings to officers who worked for him. He also lowered the ratings made by other rating officials on their subordinates. BTB hurt a lot of good people. It was a tremendous injustice.

Following my move from Pleiku to Ban My Thuot, I served under Preston barely long enough for him to write an OER on me before my tour of duty in Vietnam was finished. It was a very good OER and would strengthen my personnel file. BTB, however, always ready to hurt one of his own people, challenged the validity of the OER.

He asserted the length of time I served under Preston's supervision was three days too short and said the OER was illegal. FACs moved around a lot, and the actual dates of my service in Pleiku and Ban Me Thuot were poorly defined. My personnel file for the entire period in Vietnam was adequate without that OER, but it would have been better with the inclusion of the OER by

Preston. Once more BTB chose to damage the records of one of his own people.

BTB aggressively pursued the issue of the dates of service on that OER. He tracked down the OER in the squadron office, which was in Nha Trang, having been moved from Pleiku. He was successful in having it destroyed, but was frustrated when told there was still a copy of it in Ban Me Thout. He worried the copy in Ban Me Thuot might be resubmitted through personnel channels without his notice and become effective in my official records. He ordered LtCol George Olson and me to report to him in his Pleiku office to address the situation.

There is a very sound Air Force maxim which says, "Never get into a pissing contest with a superior officer. You will lose." It was also just good common sense, especially if the superior officer happened to be your boss. Unfortunately, that was where I was headed. Going into the confrontation, I had two aces BTB didn't know about tucked up my sleeve.

For my first ace, Colonel Warren DeWeese, Commander of the 633rd Combat Support Group in Pleiku, accompanied LtCol Olson and me as a witness when I reported to BTB. DeWeese was not in our chain of command, but he was the ranking officer in the area and a highly respected officer.

Col DeWeese, LtCol Olson and I walked into LtCol Buskirk's office. I reported formally at attention in front of Buskirk's desk and rendered a smart salute. Before BTB could finish his lame return of my salute or say anything, Col DeWeese spoke, "Good afternoon, Buster. I'm here at Capt Amend's request. I know a lot about Amend. He's a fine officer and I'm pleased to honor his request to be present. I'm sure you won't mind my sitting in." He casually pulled up a chair and made himself comfortable.

Col DeWeese knew me from my previous activities in Pleiku. He was very supportive. Perhaps more importantly, he knew a lot about Buster the Bastard and what a bad officer he was.

Won't mind? Buskirk was visibly upset at DeWeese's presence but couldn't really ask him to leave. He redirected his attention from DeWeese to me and the pissing contest began.

"Capt Amend, where is the copy of that illegal OER?"

I took the copy of the OER from my folder, showed it to him from a safe distance where he could see it but could not reach it, tore it into a large number of small pieces and laid it on his desk. "There it is, Sir."

Buskirk wasn't done. "Capt Amend, your conduct in this matter is inexcusable. You have attempted to falsify official records to promote an illegal OER to benefit yourself." He ranted on for a while and then, "Because of your inappropriate devious conduct I am seriously considering taking legal disciplinary action against you through official Air Force channels."

"Sir, I will respond to that. The OER in question was a legal Air Force document which you ordered destroyed. The last copy lies on your desk. Capt Preston, who prepared and signed the OER, LtCol Olson, who endorsed and signed it, and I all state that it is a proper, legal OER. Only you say it is not.

"Without that missing OER in my records, the personnel file of my year in Vietnam is still a good strong report. With that OER in my file, as it should rightly be, my personnel file would be better and stronger. You have chosen to damage my career. You have shown yet again how you treat good officers under your supervision. Nothing devious or illegal was done by Capt Preston or LtCol Olson. Furthermore, I have done nothing wrong."

Then it was time for the second ace which I had up my sleeve. "And now you make threats about how you plan to further sabotage my career by taking action against me with your false statements. I must tell you, Sir, if you do that, I will retaliate. More people than you realize already know about the friendly Montagnard village that was wiped out by an air strike directed by an un-named FAC out of Pleiku. If you choose to pursue action against me using your <u>false</u> statements, I will go forward through official Air Force channels with <u>true</u> statements detailing the sixty skeletons you have hidden in your closet. I will pursue legal action against you."

BTB turned five shades of red and shouted, "What are you talking about?! I demand you tell me exactly what incident you are talking about!"

"Sir, I respectfully decline to make further comment. If you choose to pursue action and sully my good name, I guarantee you a very large number of people will know all of the details of that incident."

When I refused to tell him what I knew about the skeletons in his closet, he became more infuriated. We both knew I alluded to the sixty dead Montagnards in the friendly village attacked by fighters he controlled as a FAC. It was <u>his</u> personal mistake and the most egregious error made in Vietnam by any FAC in the 1965-66 time period. The pissing contest had suddenly become a draw.

Col DeWeese made what proved to be the final comment of the nasty confrontation, "Buster, I'm sure you know Capt Amend is correct. *I* know about that incident and more people than you want to believe also know about it. You should be glad it hasn't already been made public. If that information becomes common knowledge, it will be the biggest kettle of shit to hit the news papers in the US in a long time. And if that happens, <u>you</u> will be the <u>star</u> of the show. You will be <u>in</u> that kettle. Don't you suppose it's time for all of us to go home today?"

I hadn't actually won the pissing contest, but as the Captain up against the LtCol who was my boss, neither had I lost. Somehow it made me feel like I won.

Chapter 18

The Monsoon--Wet and Dry

Seasonal – Every year. Southeast Asia

Most folks, if asked to define a monsoon, would probably say something like, "That's weather that causes lots of rain. It's good for growing rice." That statement, although quite incomplete, is mostly correct.

The word "monsoon" is derived from an Arabic word meaning "seasonal." The dictionary defines monsoon as "A wind system that influences large climatic regions and seasonally reverses direction, esp. the Asiatic monsoon that produces dry and wet seasons in India and southern Asia." That definition hit Vietnam right on the money.

In general, the weather in the Central Highlands could be summarized as the wet monsoon and the dry monsoon. The wet monsoon in Pleiku was approximately May through October and brought an average of nearly one hundred inches of rain. The dry monsoon was approximately November through April, during which the seasonal wind blew from the opposite direction and there was little rain.

The rain and clouds of the wet monsoon seriously limited the operational capability of the O-1. The airplane officially had no all-weather capability. We were limited to visual flight rules (VFR) operation. This meant we could fly only when we could directly see the ground, cloud buildups, other airplanes, mountains, etc. The airplane did have basic flight instruments for limited flying in clouds. Its only navigation aid was a radio compass which could "home in" on an AM radio station.

There was an unreliable commercial AM radio station in Pleiku which operated intermittently. There was no published procedure by which a pilot could make an instrument let-down through weather using the Pleiku radio, even if the station did happen to be operating. There were also mountains around Pleiku to add to the hazard. Any pilot planning to make his own self-designed let-down in clouds had to know exactly what he was doing. If he didn't, the result would be one more airplane flown into a mountain.

I developed my own instrument let-down procedure which I used a few times. Of course it was illegal. So what! The alternative could be running out of fuel trying to find another place to land. Besides, the other place might also be socked in. If I had to do something illegal to get down, I'd rather do it where things were familiar.

We broke a lot of rules, usually in situations where it was the reasonable thing to do. FACs had a commonly used bottom line regarding such circumstances, "What are they going to do to me? Send me to Vietnam and make me a FAC?"

Wet monsoon weather commonly kept us grounded or limited the flying we could do. We spent many hours waiting to see if we could take off, sometimes with success, and many times cancelling the flight. On one occasion after much waiting, I took off and flew half of the length of the Pleiku runway before running into a solid wall of clouds. I wheeled about abruptly and logged a flight of five minutes. No flying on that day!

Weather was critical to the outcome of many conflicts. Air power frequently decided the final outcome and if the airplanes could not fly, the advantage of air power was lost. The Viet Cong and the North Vietnamese knew this and struck when bad weather prevailed.

Airplanes weren't the only equipment affected by wet weather. Frequently the ground vehicles were completely disabled by the mud. Jeeps, tanks, armored personnel carriers and artillery pieces were rendered helpless. They had no footing. No matter how fine the equipment, it sat useless in a mire of deep impassable mud.

The 3rd Brigade of the 25th Infantry Division was stationed near Pleiku. In September 1966 <u>The Pacific Stars and Stripes</u> newspaper featured a picture story showing the immobility of their equipment. The area's red dirt and clay was a quagmire of thick muck. No equipment moved. Troops trying to walk struggled in the mire up to their knees. Everything stopped.

The weather also produced interesting natural phenomena. On an otherwise dull reconnaissance flight out of Pleiku, I saw something not visible from the ground. On the sunny edge of a rain shower, I looked down for several minutes on a complete circle rainbow. It was very clear and bright, double for much of the circle. It was the only complete circle rainbow I've ever seen. From the ground, it is possible to see only a half circle rainbow at the most, since the earth blocks the bottom half of the rainbow from the viewer's perspective.

On another occasion during the wet weather of May, I watched another show. Water from a heavy local rain five hours earlier ran from smooth hills and rice paddies southeast of Pleiku and gathered in a low area. It then drained suddenly into a stream just above the point where it dropped rapidly into a valley. The stream and its large volume of clay-reddened water flowed over a waterfall.

At the same time on the same stream, the water level at a smaller waterfall about a mile downstream was low. The water there was relatively clean, a light tan-brown color. As the leading edge of the flood crest progressed down the stream bed, the color of the water changed markedly and the water level swelled higher.

The outstanding part was the arrival of the flood crest at the second waterfall. The volume of water crossing the fall suddenly multiplied by perhaps ten times and the stream was transformed from a silvery threaded misty waterfall into a dirty red roaring torrent. It was dramatic. It will all happen again sometime when

Mother Nature once more does her stuff. I wonder if someone else will watch and appreciate the show.

In complete contrast to the wet monsoon, the dry monsoon was pleasant. The temperature was warm in the day and cool at night, but the dust was extremely bad everywhere. It covered everything. A foot stomped on the road or a sidewalk raised a cloud of dust. Even a tennis ball on the court did the same thing. Those living in tents in the dry powder dust were miserable at best. I didn't envy them.

The condition of living quarters, however, was a trivial matter compared to the operational problems the dust caused for mechanical equipment. Any machine that had an internal combustion engine and breathed air was severely affected. Air filters commonly had to be cleaned daily or engines would be choked down and quit for lack of combustion air.

The air blast from airplane propellers created huge choking clouds of dust. Personnel trying to get into or out of a helicopter idling on the ground were blinded to the point of incapacitation by the cloud of dust completely enveloping the chopper.

All weapons, simple or sophisticated, were affected by dirt. Keeping them clean, oiled and operating smoothly was an unending difficult job. If you got tired enough of dust to wish for rain, you could just wait a while and see if you really did prefer operating in the mud.

Chapter 19

The Demise of an Alcoholic Commander

February 26, 1966 — Pleiku

Alcohol ruins countless lives and kills untold numbers of people, both good and bad.

Col Johnson, the Commander of the Combat Support Group at Pleiku, was one of them.

The combat support group was the "house-keeping" organization which existed for the purpose of building and maintaining the facilities which housed the people and equipment used in fighting the war. They constructed the buildings, tried to keep the water and electrical systems operating, fed the people and did everything needed to support the combat organizations. There were many dedicated people who worked diligently with woefully inadequate supplies, tools and equipment. Their jobs were made more difficult by weather and the combat environment. Their alcoholic commander made things even worse.

Col Johnson was not the leader/manager they needed. To the contrary, he was a great detriment to their cause. He spent much of his time wasting the efforts of people who worked for him as they tried to satisfy his crazed ego. He was their boss and they tried to keep him happy. He demanded such things as his personal vehicle to drive, although there was no place to go. He could have walked the short distance to the club to continue his excessive drinking.

He demanded his personal reserved parking space in front of the small bar known as the officers club, although space was critically limited. When another vehicle was parked in "his space," his enraged bellowing could be heard for a great distance. He cursed the one who parked there and cursed his own people for allowing it to happen. Everyone stayed far away while he shouted his demands for the immediate removal of the offending vehicle.

However, he had an amazingly different side. I observed his polished demeanor when he hosted Rev. Charlie Long and his wife, EG, and two more C & MA missionaries on base for lunch. He was a perfectly smooth, polite gentleman, graciously hosting important visitors.

The officers working under Col Johnson were in an extremely difficult position. He was their direct boss and wrote their Officer Effectiveness Reports, OERs, which had great bearing on their career progression or lack thereof. This was especially true in the case of the Flight Surgeon, Capt Walt Rivers and the Chaplain, Capt Brian Wesley.

The Chaplain was Col Johnson's favorite target for insults and demeaning public comments. He put Wesley down severely at every opportunity. He made a ridiculous ceremony out of his own specially contrived presentation to the Chaplain. The gift was a 16 x 20 inch color photo nicely framed and covered with glass. It featured three good looking women standing on a beach and smiling for the camera in full frontal nudity. The obvious purpose was to embarrass the Chaplain and insult his sense of decency and propriety.

Brian took it all in stride and displayed the picture prominently in the hallway on the wall immediately outside the door to his room. He discreetly clothed the ladies in two piece swimming suits carefully cut out of black electrical tape and stuck in the appropriate places on the glass. It was a clever treatment of Col Johnson's insult. Round Two was won by Chaplain Wesley.

Unfortunately, his ingenious style show didn't survive. The first guy to walk past the Chaplain's door in the morning might pause a while to admire the ladies in the photo. After choosing his favorite lady for the day, he would lift her two piece swimming suit from the glass with a finger nail and relocate it. One piece might be on her right knee and the other piece on her left elbow. Satisfied his favorite lady now looked better, he would leave subsequent improvements of the photo to the next guy who came along.

Col Johnson was in Pleiku in the midst of "The Big Buildup" in Vietnam. More people were arriving all the time. Many men were housed in an area called Tent City near the runway. Tent City was about a mile from the main housing compound and had meager facilities. Chaplain Wesley responsibly did his best to meet a particular need for the men who lived there. He tried to persuade Col Johnson to provide a modest floored tent building near the airstrip for worship services. Col Johnson was not the least bit supportive, but the Chaplain faithfully persisted. Johnson rudely brushed him aside saying, "Chaplain, you can hold your God damned services under a fuckin' tree."

Besides his dislike for the Chaplain, Johnson showed many other reasons to be judged incompetent to perform his job. After much soul searching and discussing the overall situation, the Chaplain and the Flight Surgeon went together as a team to 7th Air Force Headquarters in Saigon and presented their case that Col Johnson was unfit for command. Their recommendation that he be removed was a very serious charge brought against the commander by two of his subordinates. It could have been career suicide for both of them. Their case, however, was strong and well presented. A team of doctors came to Pleiku and took Col Johnson back to Saigon for evaluation.

In Saigon, under the spotlight of being examined, Johnson shifted gears and put on the smooth, polished, gentlemanly air he used in hosting the missionaries for lunch. He talked himself out of the hole. In a few days he was back in Pleiku, back in command and back to being the same old drunken, raging, bellowing, crazy bull. On February 26, 1966, the over-due heart attack hit him. He was evacuated to Saigon and died a few days later. Col Johnson's heart attack put an end to his alcoholism, his bad manners and various other character flaws.

Chapter 20

18,000 Rounds Per Minute From That Old Airplane?

December 1965 and continuing – Pleiku

The venerable DC-3/C-47 is frequently referred to as "the most successful airplane ever built. " It first flew on Dec 17, 1935, which was, by coincidence, the 32nd anniversary of the Wright Brothers' first flight at Kitty Hawk on Dec 17, 1903. Neither "first flight" drew much attention from the public. No official press photographer was present to record either event. However, in retrospect, both events were enormous in the realm of aviation history. Over several decades that followed, Douglas Aircraft produced more than 800 civilian versions and more than 10,000 military versions of the DC-3/C-47.

The DC-3 put many commercial air carriers in business around the world. Civil air fleets were created where none had previously existed. The airplane was so successful that for decades it was said the only replacement for a DC-3 was another DC-3. Of the many names by which it was known world wide, the most popular was "Gooney Bird."

The most widely used military version of the DC-3 is the C-47, C standing for "cargo." That designation implies a wide range of uses. In World War II the C-47 delivered cargo to isolated locations, transported troops, served as a medical evacuation plane, dropped paratroopers behind enemy lines, towed gliders for the D-Day invasion and performed many other functions.

The Commander-in-Chief of Allied Forces, General Dwight Eisenhower, later President Eisenhower, had extreme praise for the C-47. He is quoted as saying, "Four things won the Second World

War: the bazooka, the Jeep, the atom bomb and the C-47 Gooney Bird." Famed aerospace historian, Douglas Ingalls, referred to the C-47 as "The Plane That Changed the World."

After World War II, the Soviets blockaded and isolated the city of Berlin. Over one hundred C-47s participated in the "round-the-clock" Berlin Airlift that eventually broke the blockade.

The conflict in Vietnam saw the introduction of a new mission for the old Gooney Bird. The concept of a side-firing gun on an airplane had been previously explored but never developed. On the C-47, the side-firing concept was married with the technology of the "Gatling Gun" and its multiple rotating barrels. The result was a gun that fired at an extremely rapid rate, ninety degrees to the left of the aircraft heading.

Richard Jordan Gatling (1818-1903), was an American inventor. He spent most of his life improving agricultural methods, but is best known as the inventor of the Gatling Gun. His gun was the first practical, quick-firing machine gun developed in the United States. It was patented in 1862 and was used to a limited extent during the Civil War.

The principle advantage of the Gatling hand-cranked multiple barrel gun was its rapid rate of fire (600 rounds per minute). As one barrel fired, all of the other barrels cooled until their respective turns to fire. By the 1960s the principle was the same, but huge advances had been made in technology. The "mini-gun" on the C-47 in Vietnam used the NATO standard 7.62 millimeter round (equivalent to 30 caliber) and fired 100 rounds per second. That's 6,000 rounds per minute.

Each fourth or fifth round was a tracer, so the bullets created a visible red stream from the airplane to the ground. The fiery breath and the loud roar of the guns led to calling this latest version of the old Gooney Bird "Puff the Magic Dragon." The name was a take-off on the folk song popularized at that time by Peter, Paul and Mary.

The name "Puff" was informal. When the "new" airplane arrived in Vietnam, it was officially assigned the designation FC-47, meaning Fighter/Cargo-47. That terminology produced an immense howl and great ridicule from fighter pilots.

"What!? You're going to call that thing a 'fighter'? I fly fighters and that thing isn't any fighter! And it looks spooky."

The result was interesting. The airplane was officially re-named the AC-47, meaning Attack/Cargo-47, but the moniker "Spooky" stuck and became the operational radio call sign for the AC-47.

20.1 – The "Spooky" bird. Note the open back door.

When the Spooky birds arrived in Pleiku in December 1965 the planes and their mini-guns were ready for action, but the crews were not. The pilot, in the left seat, knew how to maintain a steady banked left turn while firing a burst from the guns onto the target. He visually followed the stream of tracers to the target, like aiming a stream of water from a garden hose under high pressure. He made corrections by changing the aircraft heading and angle of bank. The crew also included a co-pilot in the right seat, a navigator and perhaps a crew chief/flight engineer.

Unfortunately, in the beginning none of the crew knew where they were or how to find the target. A "quick draw" solution to this problem was directed by higher headquarters. Our squadron was tasked to provide a FAC as an additional crew member on each Spooky Bird. The FAC was intended to control the strike from the AC-47. That created another problem. FACs were already over committed and this worsened the situation. Furthermore, the FACs' workload wasn't the only limitation.

On December 29, 1965, shortly after the Spookys arrived, I flew on an AC-47 on a FAC mission north of Pleiku. Controlling an air strike from a Gooney Bird was impossible. There were two seats in the cockpit occupied by the pilot and the co-pilot. I leaned forward between them and tried to see out the windshield or a side window. It was mandatory for a FAC to have visibility and maneuverability. I had neither. I couldn't see the target, much less other airplanes in the area.

Two days later I flew on Spooky 21 on an armed reconnaissance mission. My job was to control some fighters if a strike became necessary, and/or to control the firing of the mini-guns from the AC-47. My second flight as a FAC on the Gooney Bird confirmed what was already obvious on the first flight. My presence was worthless. I couldn't maneuver. I couldn't see anything. I had no smoke rockets to mark the target which I couldn't see anyway.

Two immediate changes were absolutely mandatory for the entire Spooky Bird program. First, FACs simply could not control air strikes from a C-47. Second, for effective manpower utilization, the Spooky crews needed to be self-sufficient. There were not nearly enough FACs available to do their own jobs plus flying on the Spooky birds as crew members.

The reasonable answer to the problem was simple and straightforward, i.e., teach the Spooky crews what they needed to know to fire their own guns on their assigned targets <u>without</u> a FAC. We FACs were assigned the job of teaching them. All Air Force pilots were already proficient in general radio communication procedures, so that part was easy. However, developing proficiency with the maps we used was a new undertaking.

FACs were extremely dependent on the 1:50,000 scale topographical maps which we used every day. The success or failure of the mission, and the life or death of the people on the ground, was dependent on the accurate use of the map by both the FAC and the people on the ground. The Spooky crews needed to acquire enough proficiency with these maps to be self-sufficient.

Most Spooky pilots had been flying other airplanes before coming to Vietnam. They and their navigators had flown mostly in the United States and other areas using only radio navigation aids and radar support from the ground. If they had even touched a map of the surface of the earth in the last several years, it was probably a 1:1,000,000 scale aeronautical chart where about four and one half inches of paper covered sixty nautical miles of the earth's surface.

The 1:50,000 scale maps depicted twenty times the detail shown on the 1:1,000,000 scale maps. About seven and one half inches of paper on the 1:50,000 maps covered about ten klicks (ten kilometers) (six nautical miles) on the surface of the earth. Even our low and slow O-1 at 75 knots went across ten klicks on the map in about four minutes. Initially it was a shock for a pilot or navigator to realize he had just flown off his map and didn't know how to recover his orientation.

In addition to adjusting to the great change in scale, it was also necessary for the AC-47 crews to learn to "read" the topographical presentation of contour lines. Contour lines on topographical maps connect points of equal elevation. Contour lines packed closely together represent an area of steep sloping terrain and contour lines widely spaced indicate relatively level terrain. Some experience is needed to interpret the lines on the map and "see" the steep slopes or flat plains which exist on the ground.

My emphasis on the subject of 1:50,000 scale maps may sound overstated. It is not. It was quickly obvious to FACs the only deficiency the Spooky crews had was lack of familiarity with maps they had never before seen. While the higher headquarters folks were adjusting to that fact, I flew two more times with the Spooky boys. On a mission with Spooky 23, after working on the maps, there was little left to do. They spent the rest of the time on "armed reconnaissance" i.e. looking for something worth shooting.

I wished I had brought my camera to take some interesting shots in the back of the plane. One of the rear cargo double doors had been removed leaving a hole roughly four feet wide by six feet high in the side of the plane. The crew chief sat on a little loose box by the open door looking at the ground through a pair of seven power field glasses. A few straps tied across the open door were intended to lessen the probability of someone being tossed out if the plane bumped around too much.

I thought that all of that stuff out the back door looked interesting, so I walked forward and talked to the pilot.

"Dave, I think I'll stand back there at the cargo door and watch while you pop off some practice rounds. How soon are you going to be ready to fire?"

"We're ready now. I'll give you a couple of minutes to go back and get ready by the door. I guess I don't need to tell you to get a good grip on the top of the door frame. The air is pretty smooth now, but we could hit a bump. I'd hate to become the infamous Spooky pilot that pitched a FAC out the back door."

20.2 – The Spooky Bird's open rear door. Watch out for the first step!

I stood by the open door, just a few inches inside the plane. With my arms almost fully extended upward, I rested my hands on the top rail of the door frame. That was comfortable, and what a view! It was impressive to watch as the three guns on "Puff, the Magic Dragon" fired. Each gun fired 6,000 rounds per minute. That's 18,000 rounds per minute total. Wow! That was a lot of lead. But I already knew that was going to happen.

There was, however, another factor I had not considered. The guns created an enormous roar and I was standing a few feet away from them and had no ear plugs. I couldn't put my hands over my ears because I was quite sincere about holding onto the top rail of the door frame. That first step down was a big one. Tipping my head far to one side I could press one ear against my shoulder while the other ear hurt. I couldn't put both ears against both shoulders at the same time. Next time I would darned sure remember the earplugs if I was going to stand by the guns while they fired.

Much of the Spooky Birds' purpose in Vietnam was nighttime support of Special Forces Camps and outposts. Until they were cleared to fly without a FAC on their airplane, we continued our overload. My last such day with Spooky was another long one. On January 22, 1966, I flew visual reconnaissance all day in the O-1. I also made a mail exchange for the guys at Plei Me Special Forces Camp and flew Capt Josh Easley, the Senior Advisor at Ducco, around his Special Forces Camp to look at a future patrol route.

That should have been enough for one day, but that was where the overload started. I then flew the long haul on the night local AC-47, Spooky 62, as the "readily available FAC" if needed. We took off a few minutes after midnight for a local airborne alert mission. My air mattress and blanket worked beautifully and I slept most of the time until we landed at 6:30 AM. All was quiet around Pleiku and we did no more than kick out ten flares during the period.

We FACs were glad when the Spooky crews were officially declared to be self sufficient, not needing a FAC either as a crew member on their airplane or nearby in an O-1. It relieved the overload on us. We hadn't been of value anyway, except for some instruction on maps that were new to the Spooky boys.

There was a story the Viet Cong and the North Vietnamese were instructed to avoid shooting at Puff because that might anger him and he would unleash his fury on them. I thought that was hogwash. It was similar to the supposed reasoning they shouldn't shoot at the FAC lest the FAC put an air strike on them.

It was my belief the bad guys knew a more effective way to avoid the wrath of either Puff or the FAC. The more effective method was to blow them out of the sky. That method worked better than hiding from them. Statistics supported my contention. The AC-47s had been in Vietnam slightly less than six months when, on June 4, 1966, another Spooky Bird went down in Southeast Laos west of Pleiku. It was number six lost of the original twenty brought from the states. The AC-47 put out 18,000 rounds per minute, but it also took some hits coming back in the other direction. Sometimes it took too many hits and didn't survive.

Chapter 21

Entertainers from Home

1965-66 – Pleiku

The United Services Organization (USO) is a federation of six voluntary agencies. It was founded in 1941 to serve many needs for members of the armed forces in the U.S. and overseas. The most widely known service performed by the USO is bringing entertainment from back home to troops serving overseas.

Bob Hope was "Mr. USO" for several decades. His shows entertained many tens of thousands of men and women of all branches of the services during World War II, the Korean War and the Vietnam War. Bob Hope was famous, respected and much loved by people wherever he took his shows. In addition to Hope's personal talent, his big production shows had great logistical support and featured additional well-known performers of the highest caliber. He made the USO look good around the world.

And then there was Pleiku.

Let's face it. Pleiku wasn't exactly the prime venue of the show business world. The entertainment that came to Pleiku was nothing like the Bob Hope productions. The quality of the shows varied from good, to fair, to poor, to "should have been flushed." That was no surprise. Why should civilians with any real performing talent volunteer to come to Pleiku? Most of the military people in Pleiku were <u>not</u> volunteers and didn't like Pleiku as an assignment.

But the entertainers did come. We owed them our thanks for their presence.

One group I dubbed "The Downtowners" chose a central theme of going "Downtown." That theme missed the mark in Pleiku. New York's Times Square and San Francisco's Fisherman's Wharf were good places to go for a night out "downtown." If a "round eye" went to Pleiku for a night out "downtown," he might not be around the following day.

None of the song's lyrics related in any way to "good ol' Pleiku." But that was not the point whatsoever. The performers weren't singing about Pleiku, they were singing about home, and "Home" was a good subject.

The Ann Margaret show in a hangar at Army Camp Holloway featured a big name performer. The two guitarists and the drummer made lots of noise, and the Army grunts who made up most of the audience loved Ann Margaret. Again, thanks go to her. She did come.

The Kathy Nolan show, also the courtesy of the USO, played to about four or five hundred in a crowded courtyard patio. It was a pretty good show and an enjoyable change of pace. Miss Nolan and two more girls did the featured singing and dancing, backed up by two male musicians. Kathy Nolan did a clever and entertaining job of parrying the continuous comments from the all male audience.

Nolan: "And now the three of us girls have something very special for all of you guys."

Audience GI: "There's not enough to go around!"

She wasn't taken aback or offended. She handled it all smoothly and capably. The show was well appreciated.

Not all "entertainment" came "from home" to entertain the troops. The "3rd of the 25th" had a bunch of guys in boots and fatigues who <u>were</u> the troops and they were already <u>in</u> Pleiku. The Infantry Division Band sounded better than anyone expected. I liked them.

21.1 – These are <u>not</u> singers, or dancers, or beautiful women, or strippers, or sports heroes or stand up comics. They have no USO support. The 3rd Regiment 25th Infantry Division band played pretty good music in the Pleiku compound.

Entertainment wasn't limited to singing, dancing and stand-up comedy. And not all entertainment was sponsored by the USO. An independent program at the club on April 16, 1966, featured two strippers, Candy Barr and Princess Negula, both from Australia. Their audience was about 200 men of the quite horny variety and the place was really jumping. The rain dampened the audience, but the show itself moved from the volleyball court to the covered walkway and continued full blast.

Early in the show, LtCol Rick Oliver briefly left the rainy audience to get a coat. He went into his room and to his complete surprise ran smack dab into a good looking woman standing there in only a g string. He retreated in shock and embarrassment muttering something that included the word "raincoat." She smiled and casually asked, "Do you know a Captain Williamson?" Oliver stammered, "I don't know anybody. Just let me out of here."

He quickly rejoined the wet audience, still with no coat. Unbeknownst to him, the strippers had commandeered his quarters as a dressing room. Tough. War is Hell.

Both ladies went down to only very small g strings. A prize winning set of bare boobs bouncing happily in the pleasant night air didn't exhibit great talent, but the audience of normal healthy males hadn't seen anything like it for a long time. It held their rapt attention. One of the ladies brought one of the guys up from the audience to dance with her. As they danced, she appeared to be proceeding to also remove her g string.

Colonel DeWeese, the Support Group Commander, had previously stationed himself strategically in the front row. He quietly and discreetly stepped forward and let her know she had reached the allowable limit.

It might be surprising that clearly the best entertainment brought to Pleiku while I was there had no good looking women, no comedians, no singers and no dance routines. It was a USO "thank you" expedition, featuring four very well known US citizens. They came to Pleiku to express their appreciation to the military men representing the country which they also loved.

These men were prominent in their field and were widely recognized for their great accomplishments. A high percentage of Americans regularly saw their faces on TV and said, "Oh, that's so & so," calling them by name. Yet, these citizens were not in Pleiku to entertain us by doing what they did back home.

They walked around shaking all the hands they could reach and said, "Thank you. We appreciate what you are doing for our country." They sat down next to us and talked like we were old friends. Then they showed films of what they did for a living back home.

These four citizens were Frank Gifford, Willie Davis, Sam Huff and John Unitas of the National Football League. Every one

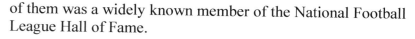

of them was a widely known member of the National Football League Hall of Fame.

These four very decent people were on the pinnacle of success in a field which was highly celebrated in our society. They chose to come down and assume the rank of "average citizen" to tell other average military citizens in Pleiku thank you for what we were doing for our country.

The point was not that football itself is so extremely important. These famous individuals set aside their personal fame and glory. They came to us on the common man level to sincerely tell us thank you. To me it was extremely gratifying. I deeply appreciated their expression of thanks.

Chapter 22
The Bullshit Bomber

January 1966 – Near Cheo Reo Special Forces Camp

Psychological warfare was waged with words, not bullets and bombs. The words were delivered by an airplane known informally as "The Bullshit Bomber" because of what it spread in generous quantities over large areas. The purpose of the Psychological Warfare program was to influence VC and North Vietnamese troops to defect and join with the South Vietnamese.

The two weapons used by the Psy War airplane were large powerful loudspeakers and paper leaflets. The audio messages were recorded in Vietnamese and the leaflets were printed in Vietnamese. Chosen areas were targeted for the dropping of leaflets and blaring of loudspeakers.

The airplane that did the job was unusual in the US Air Force inventory. It was the Helio "Super Courier," a unique, high wing, single engine tail dragger. It had full-span leading-edge slats, four seats and was powered by a Lycoming 295 horse power engine turning a three-bladed propeller. It had remarkable short field takeoff & landing capabilities and was procured by the USAF for special operations missions.

The Air Force official designation for the aircraft was U-10. Its operational call sign was appropriately "Litterbug."

The broadcast recordings told surrendering soldiers where they should go and what they should do in order to be granted asylum and be repatriated into the friendly forces. It was nearly impossible to know if the intended enemy troops ever got the message. The whole program seemed to be of questionable effectiveness.

The Psy War bird could also broadcast over a live microphone located in the cockpit. The conclusion of a mission in the Pleiku area was frequently signaled by a live triple forte blast from the pilot, Shorty Cochrane. This message, though, was in English, not Vietnamese, and the target was the Pleiku compound. The whole area reverberated with, "Hey, Flip, bring me a beer." Flip Edwards, the other Psy War pilot, sprang from the starting blocks and the race was on.

Flip grabbed a cold one, cranked up the jeep and sprinted for the flight line about a mile away. He roared through the mud or dust, depending on the season, and met the landing Psy War bird at the parking ramp. When Shorty climbed down from the U-10, Flip handed him the beer. No one knew if the VC got the message that day, but everyone knew that Shorty got his beer.

We FACS never had it that good. No one ever greeted a hot and sweaty FAC with a cool one.

The second Psy War weapon was the leaflet, or rather thousands of leaflets, dropped in selected areas. The leaflets were three by six inches, printed on reasonably good quality paper. They carried the same general message as the one broadcast over the loudspeakers. Leaflets were commonly known as "Montagnard toilet paper," a not very subtle reference to the person who might pick one up and what he might do with it.

Depending on the workload of both outfits, FACs sometimes loaned a helping hand and airplane to the Psy War boys. On one occasion I picked up a sergeant from the Lac Thien Special Forces Camp and took him to drop leaflets on two nearby locations. Lac Thien pounded these areas with artillery the day before and the leaflets were a follow- up mission. The hope was the VC would rather fight on the government side than be pounded by artillery.

In later years, Litterbug crews pitched boxes of leaflets from their U-10 at higher altitude for less vulnerability to ground fire. These boxes were twelve to eighteen inches per side and equipped with time delay fuses which blew them open at a lower pre-set altitude. In the 1965-66 time period, however, things were more primitive. When FACs "helped out for the day" it was a matter of a leaflet man in the back seat of a low flying O-1 with a much larger box on his lap.

22.1 – A "safe conduct" pass, guaranteeing a Viet Cong repatriation without harm

22.2 – Preserve the family. Avoid the Viet Cong

SAFE-CONDUCT PASS TO BE HONORED BY ALL VIETNAMESE GOVERNMENT AGENCIES AND ALLIED FORCES

Đây là một tấm Giấy Thông Hành có giá trị với tất cả cơ quan Quân Chính Việt - Nam Cộng- Hòa và lực lượng Đồng- Minh.

N⁰ 88229 E

22.3 – A 3-inch by 6-inch piece of paper turns enemies into instant buddies. Really?

I flew several Psy War leaflet drop missions, the most memorable on January 18, 1966. We took a large corrugated cardboard box full of about forty pounds of leaflets. The three or four cubic foot box held about twenty thousand. Our target area was about fifty miles southeast of Pleiku, near Cheo Reo. I flew back and forth over the designated trail while my backseat "leaflet flinger" reached into the box on his lap and threw a handful at a time out the open window.

My leaflet man was Tommy McCloskey, a well liked FAC who had what was surely the most marvelous mustache in Pleiku. It was jet black and immaculately waxed into an impressive set of handlebars. It was curled on the ends and extended well beyond the sides of his cheeks. Beyond his notable appearance, Tommy was a good pilot, a really nice guy, popular and justifiably respected.

After several laps along the trail, we finished dispensing leaflets and I saw in the mirror that Tommy was about to heave the empty box out the window. With considerable surprise at what I thought might be the result of such a move I said, "Hey, Tommy, don't throw it out the window! It may catch on the U-D anten--."

Too late! The box went out the window and just as I feared, impaled itself on the U-D antenna on the leading edge of the horizontal stabilizer.

Pilots old enough to remember the old navigation aid known as the Radio Range will appreciate the U-D antenna. The Radio Range transmitted four fan shaped signals, each a little larger than one quarter circle. The four quarter circles were the aural broadcast of alternately the letter A (dot-dash in Morse code) and the letter N (dash-dot in Morse code). The quarter circles were over-sized, so that they over-lapped on the edges. In the area of overlap, both signals were heard simultaneously by the pilot.

A pilot using the Radio Range and hearing the sound of the A or the N could tell on which side of "the beam" he was flying. If he heard a steady tone, this meant he was hearing both the A and N signals simultaneously, the dot-dash and the dash-dot overlapping, each filling the void of the other. In that case the pilot could tell that he was "on the beam" i.e., on course. Flying "on the beam" to stay on course was the intent of the complex navigation system. Compared to later systems, the old Radio Range was confusing and difficult for a novice to use.

Now, if the Radio Range wasn't bad enough, someone invented a modification of that system using the letters U and D in place of A and N. In Morse code, U is dot-dot-dash and D is dash-dash dot. Those two transmitted sounds had the same effect as using A and N. When they overlapped, they produced the steady tone and the pilot knew he was on the beam. The O-1 had a special antenna to receive the aural broadcast of the Morse code U and D signals. It was imaginatively called "the U-D antenna."

Since there was no radio station in our area transmitting such a signal, we had no idea whether the darned thing worked or not. The technological aspects of the operation of the U-D antenna were therefore meaningless. But aren't you glad you wondered about its purpose?

What we did learn on that particular day of dispensing leaflets was the sharp nosed bullet shaped U-D antenna located on the leading edge of the horizontal stabilizer, was perfect for spearing a cardboard box. There it was, both somewhat humorous and somewhat serious, a large box in residence on the tail assembly. It produced a lot of aerodynamic drag causing us to fly noticeably sideways. Airplanes don't land well when flying sideways.

Tommy looked it over and emphatically gave a complete technical assessment of the situation, "Well, shit!" I hesitated a moment and said, "I think I can probably shake it off."

I proceeded to jerk the airplane around in some vigorous moves considerably beyond normal maneuvers. The box didn't budge from its position. Tommy shook the control stick and said, "Let me try it." I shook the stick, confirming his control and said, "You got it."

Tommy put that poor airplane through a sequence of violent aerial maneuvers. I am sure that Cessna Aircraft, who built the O-1, would have said, "If you kick the airplane around that roughly, it may come apart in flight." It held together. The box, though, was so terrified that it released its death grip on the U-D antenna and fell harmlessly to the ground. Bye-bye, box. After we were back on the ground, we joked and laughed a lot about the unusual incident.

Sadly, this was not Tommy's last intimate experience with a large box. Like many of our FACs, he did not finish his year in Vietnam. Tommy came home in a larger box, draped by the flag of the country he served.

Chapter 23

Deadly Days Around Ducco

May 17-June 7, 1966 – The vicinity of Ducco Special Forces Camp

On May 17, 1966, the scouting patrol, Savoy Two Nine, made a safe escape (Chapter One) from their dangerous observation post back to Ducco Special Forces Camp. Dagger Three One, a flight of two A-1s, provided the immediate close air support for the highly successful surprise attack that sprang them loose from danger.

I was glad we got Savoy Two Nine out safely. It was a scary situation for them.

With the patrol safely back at Ducco, it sounded like the end of that story, but it was only the beginning. Immediately after their hasty retreat to the camp, I FAC-ed another flight of A-1s and three flights of F-4s into the area the patrol had been scouting. The additional air strikes beat things up pretty thoroughly. Later, Mervyn Unser relieved me and FAC-ed some more fighters into the same place. Collectively, we pounded the heck out of the area.

Everything around Ducco was becoming more hectic and more dangerous. Living conditions inside Ducco Special Forces Camp were tough, and outside the camp the fighting was becoming more intense and more widespread. Things only got worse.

23.1 – Ducco "municipal water system"

23.2 –A Ducco mother "in the kitchen".

23.3 – Ducco children care for younger Ducco children.

23.4 –Surprising refinement amidst Ducco's harshness

23.5 – Lighted arrow inside the camp, manually rotated to show overhead aircraft the location of the attacking enemy force

23.6 – The punji stake moat surrounding Ducco Special Forces Camp

23.7 – A youthful defender at Ducco Special Forces Camp

23.8 – In some of the jungle regions around Ducco, it was impossible to see anything below the canopy of the trees.

I got home to Pleiku pooped out on May 17th after the Savoy Two Nine rescue and everything that followed. I did Joe Everett's scheduling job early that morning and again late in the evening. In between, I sandwiched five hours ten minutes of intense flying. When the day was completed at 10:00 PM, I was ready for a shower. No such luck. No water. I settled for a wash rag job with half a helmet of water drained from the bottom pipe in the shower. Somewhere in the day, I learned Joe Everett was awarded the Purple Heart for a wound in the heel during a hairy adventure back in March.

The next day, May 18, 1966, a "Smokey Cub" C-123 was shot down about sixty miles northeast of Pleiku. Meanwhile, Capt George Engelmann, one of our FACs, was flying out of Kontum on a Tiger Hound Mission. He was hit in the left forearm by a small arms round at low altitude while FAC-ing over Southeast Laos. He was able to fly forty-five minutes back to Kontum and landed OK. I visited him at the Field Hospital in Pleiku. He had a shattered bone but didn't know yet how bad it was. His wrist watch, which partially deflected the slug, may have saved his life.

On May 20, 1966, the activity west of Ducco, near Cambodia, continued to build. I called for the scramble of two flights of A-1s from Pleiku and controlled them on a strike supporting the patrol Savoy Six One Alpha. They had just made contact with some VC and killed five with a grenade. The air strike turned out well.

There were reportedly 5,000 VC on the Cambodian border massing an attack to gain a major victory in the Central Highlands. There was cause for serious concern, and some people foretold the doom of Pleiku itself. I was more inclined to think Charlie would go after Ducco, Plei Djerang or Plei Me. The most current scare rumor predicted a VC attack launched against Pleiku on the 20th. It didn't happen.

On May 21st a reconnaissance team found fresh graves in the area of my strikes supporting Savoy Two Nine on May 17th. That confirmed our earlier belief the results were good. I also learned

Sgt O'Connor was the one in Six One Alpha patrol who killed the five VC with a grenade on the 20th. He took a rifle shot grazing his head during the fire fight but wasn't seriously hurt. That's kinda close.

On May 22nd I made two reconnaissance flights and then pursued a change of pace from the shooting war. I took a shipment of toothbrushes, toothpaste and other goods to Dr. Martin Newburgh, the Mennonite medical missionary establishing the Pleiku leprosarium. He was glad to receive the goods.

The boxes were from Nancy and others in Cheyenne. God bless her. She continued to do her part, and more, while I did mine. She helped our squadron's Civic Action Project chug along in the midst of the war.

The weather was bad on May 23, 1966. I flew visual reconnaissance at 1,500 feet above the ground and over lower clouds. The flight was of no value. It rained all afternoon and evening. I spent the night at the flight line on FAC standby alert with A-1 pilot Pete Franklin.

May 24th was tough. I tried to thank God daily for my preservation through the brief portion of eternity known as my life. Preservation, of late, had sometimes become a day to day question around Ducco.

On the 24th I was particularly grateful to be alive. Tommy McCloskey was shot down and crash-landed in a field south of Plei Djerang. He survived the landing and was observed moving around on the ground. Planes overhead lost sight of him and he was next seen two hours later 200 yards away from his plane. He had apparently been hiding, but the VC found him and shot him. I really felt bad about McCloskey. For some reason Tommy's death really hit me hard. He and I had grown closer during our ridiculous experience with the leaflet box impaled on the UD antenna. Tommy was a good guy and I liked him. Now, all of a sudden, Tommy was dead. **I hated it! I hated the war!**

Only a month earlier I finished the investigation of the accident that killed another friend, Otis Holmes. Holmes was a closer friend than McCloskey. I had more in common with him and knew him better than I knew McCloskey. Yet, somehow I kept my emotions from knocking me flat during the entire time I worked on the Holmes investigation.

The circumstances, however, were a lot different for the two situations. In Holmes' case, some people had judged him guilty of screwing up big time before the investigation even started. Pre-judging him was wrong and I was his only defense. I felt I had to maintain my focus and give him a "fair trial." Ultimately, the investigation neither acquitted nor condemned him, but I was satisfied I was faithful to Holmes and gave him the fair shake he deserved. I had to keep my emotions in check to get it done.

And now, Tommy was dead. I don't know why it hit me so hard, but it knocked me flat. I knew lots of guys who were killed. Usually, an assumed stoic façade seemed adequate to insulate me from the reality that I could be the next one. In our game as FACs, it was good to deny what could happen. But Tommy was still dead. Very dead.

Chaplain Brian Wesley conducted an adequate memorial service for McCloskey in the crappy room called the Chapel, between the bar and the mortar pit outside. The service was antiseptic. The Chaplain said all of the right words, but for me they were devoid of feeling. The service didn't assuage my grief. And I thought more people should have been present. Why hadn't they come? Maybe they couldn't afford to let the reality of Tommy's death get that close to them. It was threatening. It may have been too uncomfortable for them to endure. It got to me. **Damn the war! I really hated the war!**

In the area where McCloskey was shot on the ground after crash-landing, Sgt O'Connor and Sgt Elway and half a dozen Montagnards were also killed. Four days earlier, on May 20th, O'Connor got five VC with a grenade. On the 24th the VC got him.

I FAC-ed two flights of F-4s and one flight of A-1s there until after dark. I drew ground fire in that immediate area and about ten miles south of there. While I controlled those strikes the weather worsened. The cloud ceiling squeezed me lower to the ground and it got darker.

After 8:00 PM it was very dark and I was below the clouds at low altitude on the Cambodian border. That was bad news. I left the area very low on fuel and began climbing through the soup at night on flight instruments. Mountainous terrain between my location and home dictated the climb. At 11,500 feet I was still in the clouds, flying in what I hoped was the right direction and trying unsuccessfully to top the weather.

Of course, we were prohibited from flying in clouds. Yeah! OK. Give me another option!! There was another general rule, "Oxygen must be used over 10,000 feet." Really! This bird doesn't have oxygen. Don't bother me with rules that can't be followed. I just wanted to get this thing back on the ground.

The O-1's minimal flight instruments worked well enough to keep me right side up in the clouds. My estimated heading proved to be correct and enough breaks developed in the clouds for me to glimpse Pleiku. I was glad to catch sight of some lights on the ground because I had no workable Plan B. I dumped the aircraft down abruptly through little holes in the clouds, making a tight circling dive. Pleiku had never been so welcome.

While I was trying to get home in the dark, more than half of a reinforced company from Plei Djerang was wiped out. They were overrun and lost nearly two hundred men in the area where McCloskey was killed. Charlie also killed nearly fifty dependents with mortars in the village adjacent to Plei Djerang. The next morning, a battalion of the 3rd Brigade of the 25th Infantry Division moved into the area by helicopter to chase the VC. Charlie continued to get braver on the western border area.

On May 26th the 101st Airborne moved a battalion onto the west side of the road just across from the Pleiku compound. Things were pretty hot and their presence was a welcome sight. Those of us living in the Pleiku compound could sleep a little better. The 101st was a big unit with their own FAC. I asked him how it was to be an Air Force Officer assigned with an Army organization. He reminded me why I was glad I wasn't with an Army outfit.

On May 27th FAC Scott Jackson took two hits in his O-1 south of Plei Djerang. Charlie was still brave around there. The next day, Jackson was hit again flying in the same area. The 25th Division captured five weapons about the size of 20 mm cannon there. Charlie had some good sized stuff! Scary for O-1s.

The heavy responsibility of being a FAC was underscored dramatically on May 29th. Capt Vickers FAC-ed two A-1s, flown by Maj Yeomans and Capt Green, onto friendly forces of the 3rd Brigade of the 25th Infantry Division. Nine American soldiers were killed and approximately twenty more were wounded. I don't know if the mistake was Vickers' or if he was given incorrect target information. Napalm doesn't care who screwed up. It works on friendlies just like it does on bad guys.

I flew Jake Holton to Ducco on the 29th to deliver some radio gear and then covered a convoy for Maj Lynn Loomis, Stiff Brawl 36. They made it OK from Ducco to Plei Djerang. After the day should have been over, I had alert duty and slept at the flight line again. That got old.

May 30th was a bad day for two patrols working out of Ducco Special Forces Camp. Savoy Two Nine and Savoy Six Two Alpha ran into each other unexpectedly in the jungle northwest of Ducco. When the shooting between the two patrols stopped, Six Two Alpha had three dead and two wounded. I don't know who got into the wrong area, but someone made a serious mistake.

There was a good sized war going on mid-way between Plei Djerang and Ducco on May 31st. Three large US Army units were involved. The 1st Cav, the 101st Airborne and the 3rd of the 25th were working together trying to corner an estimated four to five thousand Viet Cong. Much artillery was available and the Army outfits had their own FACs. It was uncertain whether we in-country FACs were to be involved or not.

Instead, I flew some visual reconnaissance and made a big mail run for the Green Berets at Ducco. I delivered two mail sacks and five packages for them. The packages included one box of special ammunition, a 357 magnum Colt revolver, and a rifle scope. The first two were probably shipped illegally from the states.

I flew three hours ten minutes on June 2nd and accomplished nothing. I made a weather departure in the clouds (illegal, of course) all the way to Cambodia at 9,000 ft and still couldn't see the ground. I came back and flew visual reconnaissance but saw nothing. I might as well have stayed in bed.

The 3rd of the 25th, the 101st Airborne and 1st Cav combined to kill about 300 VC with a very favorable kill ratio in their continuing war west of Ducco. Someone in authority finally wised up and decreed that all Baron FACs should stay out of that area and leave the FAC-ing to the Army FACs assigned to the Army units. It was a practical decision.

The three combined outfits continued trying to corner two VC regiments and keep them from escaping back across the border into "sanctuary status" in Cambodia. It was always the same problem. When a superior force was after them, the VC just disappeared.

June 3, 1966, was a long day. I flew seven hours ten minutes searching for the second pilot of an F-4 shot down north of Kontum. The first pilot was recovered but the second one was still missing. I also FAC-ed two F-4s onto a ridge near Tu Marong, the location of the big guns which probably got the F-4. To end the day, I diverted from the search and flew cover for the last part of a helicopter lift of troops and equipment into a nearby landing zone. Fifteen seconds after the last helicopter, a big Chinook, lifted back off, Charlie dropped a mortar right where the chopper was sitting seconds earlier. That was close. Friendly artillery countered onto the source of the mortar launch. The whole place was zipping with tracers when I left for home. I wasn't even scheduled to be involved in any of that action. I refueled at Kontum on the way back and got home for a cold sandwich at 10:00 PM.

The <u>Stars and Stripes</u> newspaper on June 5, 1966, reported that Capt Don King was recently killed in action but didn't say where. Don King was my classmate in pilot training. Same guy? Don't know. Also on June 5th Maj Norm Dunn, an Air Force FAC attached to the Korean Marines, was killed when his O-1 crashed twenty miles south of An Khe. He appeared to be OK when he transmitted a May Day call on the way down. He was apparently killed either by the impact or the ensuing fire. FAC-ing was always recognized as unhealthy business.

On June 7th Capt Dave Urban, a local A-1 pilot, went into the ground with his bird thirty miles southwest of Pleiku, just north of Chu Pong mountain, on the Cambodian border. No explanation. FAC Marion Jordan and A-1 pilot Capt Dwyer watched him go straight in. There was no chance of survival.

Also on the 7th, I flew a back seat mission as part of Nick Ulrich's FAC check-out. He struggled with his maps in visual reconnaissance area C-7W. I let him fly beyond the west edge of C-7W and twenty miles into Cambodia before telling him he was lost. There were many instances where errors with maps ended up with someone dead. Lots of people had trouble acquiring the essential proficiency with the maps. What's new?

That was the period May 17 through June 7, 1966, around Ducco Special Forces Camp. It was a deadly three weeks. Lots of people didn't make it.

Chapter 24

Tape Recorders and Tennis

1965-66 – Pleiku and Ban Me Thuot

The military compound at Pleiku had many of the characteristics of a prison. The barbed wire that enclosed the area was meant to keep the bad guys <u>out</u> rather than keeping us "inmates" <u>in,</u> but living there still felt a bit like being in prison. The heavily armed guards and machine gun bunkers at the gates were there to protect against outside enemies, not restrain those who lived inside. While that meager protection felt good, the confinement was restrictive.

There was essentially no reason to want to be outside. There was little out there to attract interest and it was never really safe for "round eyes" outside of the compound. We lived where airplanes frequently drew ground fire in the traffic pattern on take off and landing. How safe could it be for an American or two outside on the ground?

So, what was there to do inside the compound during the time that remained after flying, eating and sleeping? Tape recorders and tennis. That was pretty much it. Tape recorders provided relaxing pursuit of music of one's individual taste. Tennis provided good exercise, a welcome change of pace in a regimen that included too little physical exertion. In addition to the game itself, tennis required the added exercise of pushing brooms across the court to remove either the accumulated dust or rainwater, depending on whether the current weather pattern was the dry monsoon or the wet monsoon.

The MWR (Morale, Welfare and Recreation) folks had the job of supporting the off-duty interests of military people. On a base "back home," that might include providing a boat and water skis or camping equipment for the military member and his family on a weekend. MWR might take a bus load of people to a ball game, a concert, the park or the zoo. They did a good job of supporting the morale, welfare and recreation interests of military personnel.

But in Pleiku? Ha! What could MWR do for the troops in Pleiku? There wasn't much MWR could offer inside the barbed wire. They did what they could. Tape recorders and tennis.

Tape recorders were good and bad. They provided the opportunity to engage in the hobby of building one's own little collection of music tapes of choice. MWR attempted to maintain a library of tapes to loan out to hobbyists. The lack of new tapes, wear and tear on the loaners and high demand made it difficult to find something good to check out and copy.

There were several requirements to copy a tape for one's personal collection. First was the acquisition of a tape recorder, probably from the Base Exchange at Tan San Nhut airbase in Saigon. They were heavy, bulky and expensive. The recorder had to be found, bought and transported back to Pleiku. Second, the copying process required another machine, presumably borrowed from a buddy who had also acquired a similar and compatible machine. Third, there had to be adequate space to set the two machines up side by side. Fourth, there had to be an available tape of reasonable quality to copy.

With all of these requirements met, the copying process could proceed. Electric connectors hooked the two large machines together. The six inch reels of tape turned simultaneously on both machines. Magnetic tape wound and unwound at seven and one half inches per second. The amateur sound studio experts watched and smiled their approval as the recording progressed. Then, without warning, the generators supplying electricity to the compound surged up and down a few times and ground to a halt.

24.1 – The crew chief relaxes with two Sony 500s in his high tech sound recording studio at the flight line.

"Damn those bastards! If those rotten Gooks would quit stealing the fuel and selling it on the Black Market there'd be enough to keep the generators running!" Anguished cries shattered the darkness. "That happened last night when I was trying to copy that same damned tape!"

There was also the factor of operator error. Many a master tape was ruined by improper threading and mangling of the magnetic tape itself. Tapes were ruined by accidentally erasing them or copying on top of the master. Frequently the operators were even less reliable than the generators. The entire process kept people occupied for quite a while.

Tapes did get copied, though, and played and played and played. One of our FACs, Leland Yates, put a face on the personality trait of inconsideration for others, "Oh, man, listen to that. Isn't that great!?" Some shared his musical taste, but many didn't. There was no privacy in the quarters, and when Yates cranked the volume up, everyone got blasted.

It became a sore point which LtCol Oliver had to resolve, "Either you turn the volume down and keep it down or I confiscate your tape recorder and you won't see it again until you leave

Pleiku." Yates understood that message and things got a lot quieter.

Tape recorders really did serve a worthwhile purpose. The diversion from the routine of flying injected welcome variety into the life of a FAC. On January 25, 1966, I flew a FAC cover mission for a Traildust operation (defoliation) at Chu Pong Mountain with three C-123s, two A-1s and one Huey chopper. When the spraying was completed I expended the A-1s' ordnance on a standby target. I came back to the compound for lunch and then recorded Beethoven's Third Symphony, Eroica. It came out well. Ah, yes. The incongruity of war.

Those large machines were the Sony 500 and the Teac recorders, the big monsters. A smaller recorder was used for another purpose. About the same time as my recording of Beethoven's Third, I bummed a ride to Saigon and back on a C-130 hauling fuel in large rubber bladders. I bought a pair of National RQ-116 recorders and some other stuff at the Base Exchange at Tan Son Nhut and returned with a lot less money. I kept one little recorder and sent the other home to Nancy. I hoped to surprise her with the transistorized recorder and tapes.

I surprised her, alright, but the surprise became a failure. The RQ-116 made voice tapes using a live microphone. Some people mailed the tapes back and forth instead of writing letters. It sounded like a good idea to let Nancy and the children hear my voice and I knew that I would thrill to hear their voices. I envisioned the exchange of tapes as an addition to letters, not as a replacement. It didn't work.

Nancy and the kids never became comfortable with creating one half of a conversation by speaking into a cold unresponsive microphone. I was disappointed with that failure, but soon learned I didn't do much better. I was never at ease making a personal tape in a public arena. I lived in a public arena. The cubicles we called "rooms" had walls that stopped a foot above the floors and doors consisting of strings of glass beads hanging vertically in the walk space. There were no ceilings. There was no such thing as privacy.

I couldn't help hearing while a guy in an adjacent cubicle made a voice tape to send home. "...I'm really disappointed with you boys for not helping Mom while I'm gone. You know that I can't do what I usually do around home and you have to be more cooperative when Mom tells you what to do.

"George, you have to get the papers on your route delivered on time and do a better job of your collecting and record keeping. I'm ashamed that you aren't more responsible. Joey, clean up your room when Mom tells you and don't talk back. Mom shouldn't have to tell you, anyway. And, both of you turn off that blasted TV and do your homework. All of it. I thought you were good students. And don't blame things on Mom. Grandma tells me that you're both causing Mom a lot of trouble."

What a discouraging message to hear from Daddy! That kind of "conversation" seemed to be worse than no conversation at all. I doubt those boys looked forward to the arrival of the next tape from Pleiku. For Nancy and me, letters worked very well. The recorders were an idea that initially sounded great but didn't work.

After I was transferred to Ban Me Thuot, Dan Preston and I shared an actual room with a little bit of privacy. Once when we worked into the wee hours of the morning copying tapes, we ruined one of the boss' good originals. The resulting cries of disgust at our own ineptness didn't disturb anyone else.

In Pleiku, MWR provided a special opportunity for recreation and exercise in the form of tennis. They did some advertising, promoted participation, organized the bracket and imaginatively called it "the big tennis tournament." I called it "The Pleiku International Open Tennis Tournament." After all, each and every entrant traveled 10,000 miles to play in the tournament. Well, it was true that every player had traveled 10,000 miles to get to Pleiku, but he sure as heck hadn't come to play tennis.

Vigorous athletic competition tends to create mutual respect and camaraderie among those who face each other in good contests. I came to admire Maj Jim Vincent as we played against each other prior to the tournament. In the tournament doubles competition my partner and I lost the championship match to Jim and his partner, Capt Herb Taylor.

Maj Vincent was a graduate of the United States Air Force Academy. He was a tall, handsome, well-built guy with wavy black hair and a quick friendly smile. His demeanor was always positive and cordial. I respected him and held him in high regard.

A few weeks later, I felt like I lost a really good friend when Jim bailed out of his burning A-1 just north of the Demilitarized Zone. The bail-out was successful but he was immediately taken prisoner on the ground. He was not heard from again.

The big tournament ran for several days to accommodate the many players' different schedules. The Pacific Stars and Stripes newspaper on June 2, 1966, reported the results of the final singles match.

Tennis Opponents Share Bunker after Match

Two men fully armed with M-16 rifles and tennis racquets spent forty-five minutes in a bunker at Pleiku AB recently during a practice alert. Capt. Dale N. Amend of Rocky Ford, Colo. and his opponent, Airman Second Class Richard A. Giffen of Milwaukee, Wis. had just finished the final set for the II Corps Tennis Championship when the alert sounded.

Each player had won three previous matches to get to the final match. The captain had just won the final match, which required two hours and twenty five minutes of running in the hot sun. The contest went five sets, 7-5, 1-6, 7-5, 2-6, 6-2. The match concluded only one minute before the practice alert was sounded etc, etc, etc.

24.2– The end of the singles Championship match of "The Pleiku International Open"

The article was about half fact and half hogwash. Some news writer was probably proud of conceiving the clever line about the "fully armed" stuff. FACs did indeed carry rifles to alerts, but Airman Giffen, like most support people, didn't have a weapon. And "armed with tennis racquets"? Come on, now! The paper also neglected to report that I faithfully wore my "piss pot" (steel helmet) which I used only for alerts and occasionally to dip water from the fire barrel for a bath when the water system wasn't working.

But, what the heck. Didn't your Mama teach you to believe only half of what you read in the newspaper? And the newspaper's comments about the final singles match were probably no more ridiculous than my own comments about traveling 10,000 miles to play in the tournament.

In Ban Me Thuot the tennis was different, notably of much higher caliber. The Army MACV commander, a Colonel, and his deputy, a Lieutenant Colonel, were both very good tennis players. I regularly joined up with an Army Captain of my own caliber and we played against the two "old guys." We played a lot of excellent doubles matches and all four of us enjoyed it greatly. Fortunately, the two senior officers were better than the two captains. We young guys did our best, but we beat them only about once in every three attempts. Everyone's honor was preserved and it was great fun. In Vietnam, brisk exercise and good fun were scarce commodities.

Three of the missionaries in Ban Me Thuot played good tennis. They played on the same court and frequently played with the military people. I played with them quite a lot and really enjoyed their company and the good competition. One late afternoon Ken Swayne (missionary) and I played doubles against the US Army Senior Advisor and the Vietnamese 23rd Division Commander, General Nguyen.

General Nguyen had the physical appearance of a boiled egg on tooth picks. Have you ever seen a boiled egg on tooth picks running around on a tennis court? And his facial features and all of his movements were like a fat weasel. However, for a general officer, he wasn't a bad tennis player.

The missionaries were not only good tennis players. They were also exceptionally fine people. Playing tennis with them was a particularly good and enjoyable part of a year I had not chosen or planned. I left Vietnam with pleasant memories of those wonderful people who so quickly became good friends. In particular, my friendship with Bob Ziemer developed easily and comfortably. I played more tennis with him than with the others.

I left Ban Me Thuot at the end of my one year tour and returned home. I didn't know that in less than a year and a half from my departure, the Communists would slaughter the Ban Me Thuot missionaries on January 29, 1968 during their Tet Offensive.

Chapter 25

I Got Five Kills! I'm An Ace!

May 1966 – Pleiku

"**H**ey! Help! Hey! Someone c'mere quick! Hey! Come gimme a hand! Hey! Help! Someone come! Help!"

It was the Flight Surgeon, Doc Pearson, across the small courtyard, yelling excitedly for no apparent reason. Pearson was normally an easy going guy, comfortable with the situation and his job in Vietnam. Only a few days earlier in this same area I had taken a good photo of him smiling for the camera as he held a large King Cobra in the striking position (yes, it was dead). Now it looked like Doc Pearson had flipped his lid.

Pearson was inside the building, pushing hard against the screen door, the only door, with one foot and both hands, apparently trying to get outside. The door opened to the <u>inside</u>. He had only to quit pushing the door to the <u>outside</u>, pull the door open to the <u>inside</u>, and walk out. When I got closer I could see his problem. Doc had been exiting

25.1 – Doc Monty Pearson and his cobra friend both smile for the camera.

the building when a large rat decided to take advantage of the open door and exit at the same time. Pearson reacted quickly and slammed the door on the rat, catching his tail and nothing else.

The rat was alive and well on the outside of the door while his captor pushed from the inside, holding the rat's tail tightly in the door. If Pearson opened the door to stomp on the rat, it would release the rat's tail and the rat would be long gone before Pearson could get it. The Doc was indeed in need of help when I arrived on the scene. I flattened the rat's head with the heel of my boot and we shared a good laugh at the rat's expense. I had just scored my first kill.

Rats for the most part were only a general nuisance which everybody disliked. However, they also posed a very real threat as carriers of serious disease.

In December 1965 there were a dozen fatalities from plague in a village nearby. Two of them were employees in the Pleiku compound, so I was glad to have the protection of shots. The medics poked people with needles as they went through the line for lunch. I'd already had my cholera and plague shots in Pleiku and the gamma globulin shot at nearby Camp Holloway.

Plague is extremely serious. Bubonic Plague is one of the worst epidemic diseases known to mankind. It is transmitted to human beings by fleas from infected rats. In Rome in A.D. 262, plague killed 5,000 persons per day. In the 1300s, a form of Bubonic Plague called the *Black Death* destroyed a fourth of the population of Europe.

In addition to the fact that most people really didn't like rats, there were compelling health reasons for fighting them. It's not likely that many of the military personnel in Pleiku knew or cared how many people died of plague in Rome in A.D. 262 or in all of Europe in the 1300s. However, they knew very well about the dozen or so who had died of the plague recently in the village next door. Compliance with scheduled immunizations against plague increased markedly.

Plague wasn't the only disease to worry about. Southeast Asia had plenty of serious diseases that didn't concern us at home. Although tuberculosis probably had nothing to do with rats, it was also a real concern. The MACV Mess Association had medics at the entry door giving the TB Schick test. The head waiter, a Montagnard named Mr. Nay, was laid off because he had TB. His wife and two children had died from the disease. I had previously received the TB test in October.

The rats didn't give a hoot about history or diseases affecting humans. They were concerned only with locating the next meal and making more rats. They were highly skilled at both tasks. Rats seemed to be everywhere.

In May 1966 there was a great abundance of rats in all sizes, including jumbo. The kitchen crew had to fight their way into the kitchen each morning, first expelling the rats and then starting breakfast. Army Maj Brent Caldwell cornered one in his room. He had a real room with a door and walls, not just partitions that stopped a foot short of the floor like ours. With the door closed, the rat made repeated laps around the room with Brent in hot pursuit. After several wild strikes with a big stick, Brent caught the rat between the eyes for a home run. I was really anxious for the arrival of the good traps that Nancy was going to send me so I could play too.

Frank Donahue opened his locker after work one day and was greeted by a large rat departing hastily. It ran under the partition and was last seen under my bed. In retrospect, it turns out that Frank left his locker door open the previous night and apparently the rat went in and spent the night taking inventory of the contents.

The next morning, with the rat still inside, Frank closed the locker door and left for the day. When Frank came back in the evening and opened the door, the rat was anxious to leave, having been imprisoned in the locker all day. I didn't blame the rat. I'd have left quickly, too, if I'd been shut in that locker all day.

On May 3, 1966, my room mate, Josh Ellis, and a rat had a stare down in our room. The rat eventually retreated under Josh's bed and then ran under the partition to the bed across the hall. Only a few nights earlier, a guy sleeping in that bed was bitten on the finger by a rat. Frank Donohue said a rat made several laps through the theater two nights earlier during the show. Frank said watching people jump up and down stomping at the rat was a lot better than the movie. Rats frequently ran past my feet while I wrote letters at night. It happened more commonly when the power was off and I was writing by the light of my big candle in the Coke can.

Rats were a fact of life and most people did nothing about them but call them a wide variety of bad names. A small minority of us were less complacent about the dirty rotten rodents. We were already in a war zone and the rats were another enemy, so we chose to fight. Unfortunately, the odds were in the rats' favor. The weapons at our disposal were sorely inadequate.

One particular "high tech" weapon attempt attracted quite a bit of attention but failed. Carl Jennings was a pretty good electronics whiz. That was why Collins Radio paid him a good salary to work on their equipment in Vietnam. He had an impressive large tool box full of "stuff that I picked up off the floor of the factory in Dallas." That was his modest reference to a carefully assembled inventory of parts and tools. He performed many minor miracles repairing tape recorders, radios and more.

Carl and another Collins technical representative decided to go after the rats with technology. They attempted to design and build an electronic device to attract and electrocute rats. An electric chair for rats! Hot stuff, huh? The first requirement was to make the big transformation from the unreliable local 120 volt power supply to the current and voltage necessary to electrocute rats. Even if that had worked, it would have been necessary to capture the rat and "make him sit in the electric chair." It was fun to talk about.

25.2– Carl Jennings, unsuccessful rat killer

Meanwhile, Josh Ellis and I agreed on a two-man contest to see which of us could score the first kill of a rat. The sum of the wager was 25¢. Big money! I was waiting anxiously for the arrival of the traps which Nancy was going to send. I wasn't worried about Ellis' possible success because I didn't think he had any weapons at his disposal.

Josh was excited by the delivery of three "catch 'em alive" traps he was secretly acquiring for our room. He hadn't told me about the traps. Airman Second Class Ingalls, "the trap expert," delivered them. He showed Ellis how the rat was to be attracted into the shoe box sized wire mesh trap, how the rat would take the bait and thereby release the trap door behind him. He would be a prisoner! Ellis was so pleased that he wanted an additional bet with me.

"OK, Dale, our 'first kill' bet is still on and I want another bet. I'll bet you another quarter I will catch a rat <u>tonight</u>."

I responded quickly, "I'll take that bet, Josh. You're on." Next morning there was no rat. It was the first easy quarter in my pocket.

Meanwhile, Frank Donahue acquired for me two traps of the "break their damned neck" variety. They were of the right design but had such weak springs they were worthless. Ellis knew I had gotten those traps but didn't realize they wouldn't work because of the weak springs. It was at this point in time Doc Pearson caught the rat by the tail in the screen door. What wonderful timing! The Doc conveniently provided me with a rat exactly when I needed it.

I put Pearson's "screen door catch" dead rat with the flattened head in one of the worthless weak spring traps and went looking for Ellis. I found him talking with some other people. I didn't lie to him. I didn't have to say a word. I just dangled the dead rat in the trap so he and several witnesses could see the evidence. Ellis paid up the agreed quarter for my success on the "first kill" bet. Never had fraud been so easy.

And then the good traps arrived from home. Thank you, Nancy! The playing field against the rats in our room became level. Watch out rats! The traps Nancy sent were of the same "break their damned neck" design, but much heavier and stronger than what Frank Donahue had gotten for me earlier. If I made a mistake with one of these babies, I could have a finger in a plaster cast for six weeks.

I refunded the fraudulent "first kill" quarter to Ellis and was ready to collect one legally using my good traps.

"Josh, I'll give you a chance to get your quarter back. The "first kill" bet is still on and I'll bet you another quarter that I will catch a rat under my bed tonight.

"OK, Dale, you're on."

Up to this point, another roommate, Greek, had been a spectator, but now he wanted in on the action.

"How's about letting me in, Dale? I'm with Josh. I'll bet a quarter you don't get one tonight." I agreed to Greek's quarter on the "this night" bet.

Greek had been innocently drawn into the rat business when it was found that Josh Ellis' wire mesh shoe box "catch 'em alive" trap really did catch something. It caught Greek's expensive transistor radio. The radio was found in the possession of "the rat trap expert," Airman Second Class Ingalls. The serial number on the radio convicted Ingalls of catching the wrong thing in our room and earned him a reduction in rank from Airman Second Class to Airman Third Class. The trapping of Greek's radio instead of a rat also captured Greek's fascination. Now he wanted to play the game too.

My strong new traps from home were excellent. The next morning I had a very dead 75¢ rat under my bed. I netted one "first kill" quarter from Ellis on the old bet and one quarter each from Ellis and Greek on the new "this night" bet. I was proud and rich.

After that, I caught three more under my bed in fairly quick succession. Including the one with his tail in the screen door, I had five kills. I triumphantly declared myself to be an "Ace." Rats provided a lot of good entertainment.

Rats, however, were still a real problem. A Pleiku Air Policeman had turned in all of his weapons and gear upon the end of his tour of duty. He was to fly to Saigon, thence home the next day. During the night a rat bit through his mosquito netting inflicting a wound on his stomach.

The next morning, Doc Pearson told the Air Policeman the bad news, "The rat gave you a pretty bad bite. Rats carry rabies and there is a real chance you can contract rabies from this bite. Rabies is bad stuff. You must have a fourteen day series of immunizations starting with the first one right now."

The Air Policeman's flight home was postponed for two weeks while he twiddled his thumbs in Pleiku with nothing to do but wait for his next daily painful immunization. He didn't find rats to be at all entertaining.

Chapter 26

The Amazing Medal of Honor Award

March 10, 1966 – As Hua Special Forces Camp

February 23, 1967 – Di Linh, near Dalat

The Medal of Honor is the highest U.S. military decoration. It is awarded in the name of Congress to members of the armed forces for gallantry and bravery beyond the call of duty in action against the enemy.

My desk dictionary presents the above definition on page 781. That page also has a picture of Maj Bernie Fisher wearing the Medal of Honor. Bernie was the first military member during the entire Vietnam War awarded the Medal of Honor. He also became the first <u>living</u> Air Force member awarded the Medal of Honor. Few survive the incident for which the award is made.

The second award of the Medal of Honor in the entire Vietnam War was to Capt Hilliard A. Wilbanks. Willie was one of our FACs, the only Bird Dog FAC to receive the Medal of Honor for the duration of the Vietnam War. Willie did not survive the incident for which the award was made.

It was my unique privilege to know both of those men personally. Bernie was a personal friend in Pleiku and Willie was one of our FACs in the 21st TASS.

26.1– Major Bernie Fisher

26.2 – The A-1 Skyraider

ALL SMILES after one of the most spectacular rescues of the Vietnam war are Majs. Bernard F. Fisher, left, and Stafford W. Myers. Myers crash-landed his A-1E on the North Vietnamese-held A Shau airstrip. Fisher also landed and, under heavy fire, picked Myers up in another Skyraider. The two pilots are shown just after arriving safely at Pleiku.

26.3 – Unbelievable rescue just completed

Bernie and I occasionally ate supper or lunch together and shared a mutual interest in amateur photography. Color film processing was not available in Vietnam. I sent film by mail to either Palo Alto, California or to Honolulu, Hawaii for processing. Those laboratories processed the film and returned the 35 mm color transparencies (color slides). The service was slow, but it worked. I also ordered copies for a few other amateur photographers, including Bernie. He and I went through boxes of slides together and I ordered copies for both of us.

Bernie was also interested in the Pleiku Killer and Choral Society. (See Chapter 27.) He didn't sing with us, but he appreciated our modest attempts at making music and supported our efforts.

On March 20, 1966, ten days after Bernie's dramatic rescue of Jump Myers at As Hua, I had lunch with Bernie Fisher and Denny Hague. We reviewed more color slides and Bernie selected those he wanted copied. After we finished with the slides, I asked Bernie and Denny to tell me about every thing that happened ten days earlier at As Hua.

I wrote their complete account in my letter home on that same day. My report is straight from the pilot who made the rescue and the pilot who led the strafing to cover him while he did it. I'm glad to note the great numbers of "news reports" of this amazing incident in many papers in the US were very close to what actually happened.

The following details relate to the heroics of only those particular six A-1 pilots directly involved in the rescue of Jump Myers. Many other people were involved in the conflict as As Hua was overrun, and I do not intend to slight them. Two other A-1s from Pleiku were lost. Maj Duncan, the Operations Officer of the Pleiku A-1 squadron, had one of those two A-1s shot out from under him. He bailed out successfully and was picked up by a chopper. There were also many who acted bravely on the ground and many who flew choppers. Five choppers were lost during the battle.

The drama began on Mar 9th, the day before the rescue. The As Hua Special Forces Camp, in I Corp north of Pleiku, came under heavy attack during bad weather. A great number (a newspaper article reported 141 sorties) of close air support missions were flown in defense of the camp. The air strikes were mostly ineffective because of the bad weather. Fisher was also involved on the 9th. He led two C-123 transports down through a small hole in the dense cloud cover which blanketed the mountainous area.

This enabled the C-123s to make their drops of ammunition to the outpost defenders.

On March 10, 1966, approximately three hundred native Montagnard strikers and a dozen Americans continued their attempt to hold the As Hua Special Forces Camp against large odds. Low clouds covered the hill tops leaving a ceiling of about 500 feet over the lowest ground. The A-1s could barely maneuver within the confines of the valley after coming down through a hole in the clouds a few kilometers away.

Jets were unable to operate within the small space between the mountains and under the clouds. Denny Hague told me that several times he listened on the radio to a flight of F4-Cs as they penetrated down through a hole in the clouds trying to find As Hau. The anxious next call from the flight leader was, "It's a box valley. Hit the burners!" With afterburners blazing the F4-Cs would make a quick pull up through the clouds to avoid the surrounding mountains. They ended up "on top" again with nothing accomplished.

The six A-1s involved in the drama were present in three two-ship formations. Maj Myers, the commander of the 602nd Air Commando Squadron in Qui Nhon, and his wing man, Capt King, came from Qui Nhon. Maj Fisher and his wing man, Capt Pacho Vasquez, were from the 1st Air Commando Squadron in Pleiku. Capt Denny Hague and his wingman, Capt John Lucas, were also from Pleiku.

The first two-ship formation arriving at As Hua came from Qui Nhon. They were greeted by a heavy barrage of ground fire. Both airplanes took many hits. Maj Myers managed to crash-land his burning plane on the pierced steel planking (PSP) runway adjacent to the camp. His airplane skidded to a stop at the side of the runway. He scrambled out of the cockpit with flames on his flying suit and dived for cover at the side of the runway.

As Myers crash-landed, the camp was under heavy attack from every side with all sorts of weapons. His wing man, Capt King, took a large hit in the center portion of his wind screen. The resulting wind blast into his face nearly blinded him. He was forced to abort the mission. He returned to Qui Nhon and landed safely.

Immediately after Jump Myers crash-landed, Bernie Fisher radioed the other three remaining A-1s, "I'm going to go get him. Cover me." He landed in the midst of extreme weapons fire.

At the beginning of Fisher's rescue attempt, a knowledgeable and well informed observer might have commented, "What an incredible display of selfless courage!" An equally perceptive and realistic comment could have been, "How senselessly foolhardy! It would be utterly insane to pursue such a suicidal attempt where the only possible conclusion was one more lost airplane and another dead pilot!" Either comment appeared to be one hundred percent correct.

As the rescue attempt began, Capt John Lucas had great difficulty maneuvering his A-1 because the hydraulic system in his plane had been shot out. With the aileron power boost inoperable, Lucas had to exert great force with both hands on the stick to roll the aircraft into and out of a bank. He had also just extinguished a fire inside his cockpit. Capt Pacho Vasquez, with less than twenty five "in country" missions of experience, was the relatively new pilot of the bunch. Vasquez had radio trouble and couldn't hear many of the calls, but he stayed in formation and made all of the strafing runs.

Maj Myers crash-landed on runway 15 and skidded to a point about two thirds of the way down its length. Fisher approached the same runway, but the smoke of battle obscured most of the runway from his view. When he acquired sight of the runway, he chopped power and touched down, but was too far down the runway to get the plane stopped. He rolled only about 200 feet, "poured the coal" to the engine and took off again.

He then made a 90-270 degree turn and landed on the same runway in the opposite direction, i.e. runway 33. This put him on the same runway, but rolling away from Myers' airplane. He rolled off the opposite end of the short runway into tall grass. He turned around quickly to go get Maj Myers, toppling several old rusty barrels he hadn't seen. During all of this, he was drawing fire from VC next to the runway.

The pierced steel planking runway was full of holes from bombs and mortars. Steel pieces jutted up, threatening to cut his tires or catch his propeller. Meanwhile, Hague, Lucas and Vasquez flew cover for Fisher on the runway. They made repeated strafing runs at low altitude along the edge of the runway to suppress ground fire against Fisher. After scattering the barrels while turning around in the grass, Bernie taxied nearly the length of the runway back to Myers' burning airplane. He stopped and set the parking brakes, kept the engine running, opened the canopy and unstrapped his harness. As he was climbing out of the cockpit to go get the downed pilot, Myers clambered onto the wing of the A-1 and jumped into the rear cockpit shouting, "Get this thing out of here!"

While Fisher and Myers were racing back to the end of the runway for takeoff, Hague, Lucas and Vasquez were making their seventh low level strafing pass along the runway. This strafing run was only for noise and show because they were out of ammunition. At the roll-in point, Lucas said, "I don't have any more ammo." Hague replied, "Neither have I, but they don't know that. Let's go."

Fisher got his A-1 to struggle up off the short runway with lots of new holes in his airplane and Jump Myers in the back cockpit. The miraculous rescue was completed against unbelievable odds and the intense drama was mostly over. However, they weren't done yet. They were still operating under a dangerously low weather ceiling in the mountainous area around As Hua. Pacho Vasquez joined up on Bernie Fisher's wing and the first two-ship formation climbed up through the low clouds for the return to Pleiku. Vasquez had little radio function, but he could fly on Fisher's wing.

Joining up and departing was more hazardous for Hague and Lucas. With no hydraulic aileron boost, Lucas had to arm wrestle the control stick with both hands to control the airplane. It was extremely difficult and dangerous for Lucas, the wingman, to accomplish that and maintain his airplane's position a constant "few feet" from Hague's airplane. Furthermore, Lucas' flight instruments were shot out. As soon as they pulled up into the clouds, his only spatial reference was the tight formation he held on Hague's wing. Hague flew as smoothly and steadily as he could to keep from shaking Lucas off. If Lucas had lost contact with Hague's wing, he would have been lost in the clouds without flight instruments.

The A-1 was an extremely durable airplane. The six aircraft involved in this incident at As Hua took a terrible pounding. Five of them survived.

Maj Myers' bird was shot out from under him. His burning A-1 crash-landed but he survived with minor burns. Myers' wingman, Capt King, had his wind screen shot out. He aborted the mission and landed safely back at Qui Nhon.

Maj Fisher's bird took nineteen hits when he landed at As Hua to rescue Jump Myers. The airplane got back into the air and made it home. His wingman, Capt Vasquez, took nine hits and experienced partial radio failure.

Surprisingly, Capt Hague's bird was not hit. His wingman, Capt Lucas, was hit twenty-two times. Lucas extinguished a fire in his cockpit. His hydraulic system was shot out, disabling his aileron boost. He flew home in the soupy clouds on his flight leader's wing with his own flight instruments shot out.

Surprisingly, the six A-1 pilots survived even better than the six airplanes. Five of the six pilots were unhurt and continued on the regular flying schedule without interruption. Myers was off the schedule briefly with minor burns.

This is the end of the dramatic story of Bernie Fisher, Jump Myers and the supporting cast of other A-1 pilots. Fisher's performance was heroic beyond description. The odds against successful accomplishment of the rescue defied reasonable definition. It's not surprising newspapers across the country gave the incident broad coverage. If any heroic act was worthy of the Medal of Honor, surely Bernie Fisher's rescue of Jump Myers was the one.

The second award of the Medal of Honor in the entire Vietnam War was to one of our FACs, Capt Hilliard A. Wilbanks. Willie's duty station was Dalat, under the control of our Ban Me Thuot boss, LtCol Olson. I had little contact with Willie because he was in Dalat and I was in Ban Me Thuot.

On September 18, 1966, I picked up aircraft #632 from periodic inspection in Nha Trang. It was my last trip to Nha Trang and nearly my last flight in Vietnam. The engine on #632 had reached the 800 hour maximum and had to be changed out. That made me late and I still had three stops to make delivering stuff for LtCol Olson on the way back to Ban Me Thuot.

My first planned stop was in Dalat to meet Capt Wilbanks. Because of rain in Dalat, Willie met me at Lien Khan, a small strip twenty miles south of Dalat. "Hey, Dale, what's up? LtCol Olson told me you were bringing some stuff for me. You got something that's important?"

"Naw, Willie. I have a big envelope full of junk for you. I'm driving the garbage truck today. And I'm not picking up garbage, I'm delivering it."

"I don't savvy. What's wrong with Olson?"

"It's not Olson. It's our favorite jackass idiot, Buster the Bastard."

"I should have guessed. What does that stupid SOB Buskirk have for us this time?"

"Another bunch of his stupid charts. More square filling to waste your time and keep him happy. I'm sorry to dump this on you."

26.4 – Capt Hilliard A. (Willie) Wilbanks

As we talked on that day, I had only a few days remaining in my year in Vietnam. Wilbanks was half way through his tour of duty. Neither of us knew he wouldn't live to see the end of his year.

Five months after I last saw Willie, the action for which he was awarded the Medal of Honor began. After a long march down the Ho Chi Minh Trail from North Vietnam, a battalion (four companies) of NVA (North Vietnamese regulars) arrived in the Dalat area. On February 22, 1967, under the cover of bad weather, they captured a major tea plantation. Overnight they dug fox holes and emplacements for guns, arranged camouflage and established an elaborate ambush site along the Saigon/Bao Loc/Dalat road.

On Feb 23rd, an ARVN (South Vietnamese) Company near Di Linh radioed their headquarters in Ban Me Thuot that they were beginning a sweep northward. They had heard rumors of an NVA unit and were looking for it. They found it. They walked into the ambush and were almost completely annihilated. All of their officers and NCOs were killed. The company commander's radio bearer, in compliance with the order, "Never let your radio be captured," tossed it into a well behind the plantation headquarters and jumped in after it, saving the radio and himself. All contact with the company was lost and the Ban Me Thuot headquarters became concerned.

Two 23rd Division Ranger companies were sent from the Dalat area to investigate and/or give assistance. Our FAC, Capt Bobby Young, was already in the area and LtCol Olson was on his way. They were both looking for the four well hidden NVA companies. Capt Young held two flights of four F-4s (eight birds) at altitude while Olson radioed Capt Wilbanks to come join the search. Wilbanks was already in the air near Dalat on his 488th mission. He quickly diverted to help. The loitering F-4s were nearly out of fuel and nothing had been found. Olson marked the most likely area of significance with a smoke rocket and cleared the eight F-4s to drop everything they had in one bombing run.

The timing was unfortunate. The F-4s blew up a lot of nothing in the wrong place and left before the NVA were located. Meanwhile, Wilbanks reported he was nearing the tea plantation. LtCol Olson flew over the area the F-4s had just hit, close to the plantation, to assess the results. The hidden battalion opened up on him as he flew over. He found them! Olson jinked for his life (took violent abrupt evasive maneuvers) and escaped with an elevator trim cable severed, but still flying.

Two more flights of fighters were on their way while the two ARVN Ranger companies from Dalat were unknowingly walking directly into the ambush.Wilbanks arrived and quickly jumped into the fray. He fired a marking rocket into the plantation just ahead of the Rangers as a diversionary tactic to protect them. He then dived and jinked low over the worst area of ground fire, firing his M-16 rifle out the window at the NVA companies. LtCol Olson called him twice to break it off and get some altitude, but got no response. Wilbanks continued jinking and firing at the NVA as they advanced to surround and overwhelm the Rangers.

Wilbanks bought time for the two encircled Ranger companies at great cost to himself. He was seriously injured by the intense ground fire and died soon after his airplane crashed.

More fighters soon arrived and the other two FACs directed F-100s, F-4s and A-1s onto the NVA battalion in the dusk and into the night. Under the pressure of continuing air strikes the NVA withdrew and eventually disappeared.

The Ranger Commanders reported they lost thirty-six men in the attack. They stated that had it not been for Capt Wilbanks' timely and heroic disruption of the NVA assault, their losses would have been at least two or three times as great. Olson was the only US Air Force eye-witness to the action. He agreed with the reports of the commanders on the ground and recommended Wilbanks be awarded the Medal of Honor.

After LtCol Olson's return to the United States, he maintained contact with the FACs who served under his command in the Ban

Me Thuot area. He made a serious effort to have all of his FACs included in the Medal of Honor presentation for Capt Wilbanks. I was instructing in Military Training at the United States Air Force Academy at the time and hoped to attend. I was disappointed the plans didn't work out and the rest of us FACs were not invited.

Capt Hilliard A. (Willie) Wilbanks posthumously received the second Medal of Honor awarded by the United States during the Vietnam War. He was the only Bird Dog FAC of the entire Vietnam War to be awarded the Medal of Honor. The award was accepted by his wife, Rosemary, on behalf of herself and their four children in a ceremony at Washington, DC. Willie never saw his two youngest children. The twins were born during his service to his country.

A memorial has been erected to honor Captain Wilbanks in Cornelia, Georgia, his hometown. He has been inducted into the Georgia Aviation Hall of Fame. His name is located at 15E 088 on the Vietnam Memorial in Washington D.C.

Chapter 27

The Pleiku Killer and Choral Society

Christmas 1965 and Easter 1966 – Pleiku

The Pleiku Killer and Choral Society sneaked unnoticed into existence under a different name, "The Southeast Asia Choral Society." Really! What presumptuous nonsense!

The local missionaries unwittingly helped it come into being. On November 7, 1965 Charlie Long, the lead missionary for the Christian & Missionary Alliance in Pleiku, captured four of us military guys at the Sunday afternoon hymn sing at their compound. Charlie christened us "a male quartette" and had us sing that evening at the Tin Lanh "church service" in "town." We enjoyed the pleasant surprise that we sounded a little bit musical. Soon the four of us and others were talking about the possibility of singing something for a Christmas Eve service at the chapel in the Pleiku compound.

The Chaplain, Capt Brian Wesley, quickly jumped at the idea, "There is a field organ available, and I know a lieutenant who can play it."

I said, "I have a good friend in Cheyenne, Wyoming who is active in music circles. I think if I ask him, he will probably send us some good Christmas music we can handle."

One of the other guys volunteered, "I know someone who will direct the singing."

The group urged me to write promptly to my friend and ask him to send us some music. Time was short before Christmas.

My Cheyenne friend, Travis Fenton, was an excellent high school history teacher and an excellent baritone in the First Presbyterian Church choir. On short notice Travis proved to also be an excellent supporter of our feeble efforts at making music far from Cheyenne. The music arrived in minimum time.

When we got together, I asked the others, "Who is this guy you know that will direct our group?"

They told me, "You're it!"

I couldn't believe how dumb I had been. I sang well, but knew nothing about directing. Having musical training, I did read music well, but for only my own single part of the score. My directing skills for choral music were zero. I was trapped and there was no escape. Indeed, I was it. It was "the blind leading the blind" all the way. The Southeast Asia Choral Society was off and stumbling.

At one of our "whoever can show up" practices, the Chaplain came to lend moral support. Lt Greg Phillips pumped vigorously on the foot pedals of the field organ. He had to compete with the clanking of glasses in the bar behind one wall and the banging of steel equipment against concrete in the mortar bunker behind the opposite wall. Midway between those noises, our motley crew made an attempt at singing.

After practice, Chaplain Wesley wrote a letter to Nancy including the comment, "Dale is organizing a Christmas chorus to sing two numbers for our service on Christmas Eve. It appears the music will fall somewhat short of Handel's great oratorio, The Messiah, but there will be a good spirit."

The Christmas Eve service went as planned in the "Chapel," the room between the bar and the mortar bunker. The Protestant Chaplain was a Methodist, the so-called Choir Director was a Presbyterian, the Organist was a Catholic, two of the singers were Catholic, one singer was Jewish and the other seven singers were of various unidentified lineage and pedigree. Who cared?

Somehow it was not bad enough to quench the guys' enthusiasm. They were already talking about Easter music.

They soon decided "The Southeast Asia Choral Society" was a bit broad in scope. The name Pleiku was more specific, and furthermore, we were in that part of the world because of our involvement in a war. The name evolved into "The Pleiku Killer and Choral Society." It was a nonsensical name used only as a joke within the group, but it stuck.

In musical schedules, Easter comes soon after Christmas. Once again I yelled for help from Travis Fenton in Cheyenne. He came through quickly again. The Pleiku Killer and Choral Society now had a larger and more ambitious task. Easter music! We cancelled more scheduled practices than we completed, all due to the unavailability of people. We seldom got a majority of the people together at the same time.

While we worked on the music, the Chaplain worked on the logistics of a sunrise service outside the Pleiku compound. The site for the service was Artillery Hill, known also as Monument Hill prior to the war. The hill, less than one mile from the Pleiku gate, was heavily protected by barbed wire. Inside were the 175 mm guns which could deliver ordnance onto targets 30 kilometers (18 miles) away with surprising accuracy. As a FAC, I controlled a couple of practice artillery strikes for these guns. It was impressive to radio a set of coordinates to the gunners and in a matter of seconds see a large explosion on the target. Wow! The big guns also provided a most unusual back-drop for the Easter Sunrise Service.

27.1 – A 175 mm gun on Artillery Hill

27.2 – An Air Force FAC is impressed by the 175mm gun's projectile.

27.3 – Routine gun maintenance.

27.4 – A gun crewman with bananas for his buddy

The "chapel" itself on Artillery Hill was a crude structure consisting of a roof supported by walls. Inside were stone benches on a dirt floor. There were openings available for doors and windows, but those luxuries had never been installed.

27.5 – The outdoor chapel on Artillery Hill (Monument Hill)

Col Warren DeWeese, the support group commander, helped the Chaplain with logistics. He arranged access into the restricted area for the crowd attending and provided buses to get them from the Pleiku compound to the hill. He encouraged others to attend the sunrise service and was present on Easter Sunday morning.

One can only guess about the lack of success for the Easter sunrise service had Col DeWeese's immediate predecessor still been the commander of the support group. Col Johnson disliked the Chaplain. He hampered everything Brian Wesley did up to the time he killed himself with alcohol. Johnson wasn't around anymore to harass the Chaplain, and Col DeWeese was excellent help.

The Pleiku Killer and Choral Society had a busy schedule on Easter Sunday. The "choir" sang well for the Sunrise service on Artillery Hill at 6:30 AM. Missionary wife, Irene Fleming, tromped vigorously on the foot bellows and played the field organ.

A surprisingly large crowd of 112 attended the service and many expressed their appreciation for the music.

Later in the morning, back in the Pleiku "chapel" between the bar and the mortar bunker, we did it all again with 91 in attendance. It was the largest crowd assembled there to date. At the end of "Christ the Lord is Risen" the choir built to a double forte climax and ended with a dramatic cut off. Following a few seconds of stunning silence, someone offered a quiet, but very audible comment, "Amen." It was most appropriate.

Weeks earlier, while we were preparing the Easter music, the Public Information Officer, Major Neumann, was busy pursuing his job. He learned of our efforts and told us he wanted to make a recording of our music when the time was right. He hoped to get it broadcast back in the states on The Armed Forces Radio Network. It didn't seem likely to happen, but it surely couldn't hurt to try.

On Friday, April 8, 1966, two days before Easter, we had our last practice. Carl Jennings, the Collins Radio technician who sang at the missionary hymn sing, came to make recordings for our guys. Major Neumann and his technician were also there to make the tape he wanted for Public Information purposes. Neumann was aggressive and knew what he was doing. He arranged for an A-1 and a pilot to take him and the tape from Pleiku to Tan San Nhut Airbase in Saigon the next morning.

Bernie Fisher took Neumann to Saigon on Saturday morning and was back in Pleiku on Sunday. Bernie returned with exciting news. All three major networks, ABC, NBC and Mutual, wanted the tape for stateside release on The Armed Forces Radio Network.

What?! The big networks really intended to use our recording back in the states?!

On Easter?! It was hard to believe!

I told Nancy a few weeks earlier what the Public Information Officer intended to do. I told her to find out which local station in Cheyenne carried The Armed Forces Radio Network. On Easter

Sunday morning, April 10, 1966, she heard the music we had recorded in Pleiku on Good Friday, two days earlier.

The Cheyenne station didn't give us a plug as "The Pleiku Killer and Choral Society." Shucks! But they <u>did</u> say, "And now we are glad to present Easter music sung by some of our military men at Pleiku Air Base in South Vietnam."

For just a short while the world became a little smaller.

Chapter 28

Meanwhile On the Home Front

October, 1965-September, 1966 – Cheyenne, Wyoming

Cheyenne, Wyoming was a good community. By the time I left Cheyenne for Southeast Asia, our family had three years of roots in the community. There were neighbors along our street who were good friends. Our two oldest sons attended an elementary school only two blocks from home. We had many good friends in our church a few miles away, close to the downtown area.

Francis E. Warren Air Force Base was adjacent to Cheyenne, on the west side of town. General facilities and official Air Force support were available for Nancy if she needed them. These can be important factors for the dependent family of an absent Air Force member. Nancy's mother and several other Garfield relatives lived in Fort Collins, Colorado only an hour south via Interstate 25. For all these reasons, we spent very little time pondering the question, "Where should Nancy and the children spend the year during my absence?"

Although it might have been desirable for her and the kids to live closer to extended family, a household move from Cheyenne to Fort Collins would have completely upset all of the other factors which were already stable. It was an easy decision. The best place for Nancy and the children was where they were.

The only change was there would be five family members, rather than six, in the same house. That, however, was an immense change for Nancy. She suddenly had both Mother's job and Daddy's job to do. It was a full-time task--for a year--twenty four and seven--no vacation--no breaks.

28.1 – Five family members and one empty space

It was very helpful to Nancy to load the four kids into the station wagon and make the quick trip to Grandma's house. She made the trip frequently and on a few occasions, Gram Garfield hopped onto the bus alone and came to Cheyenne for a visit. The children fared amazingly well while I was gone. To them, the year was merely the continuance of established routines. The credit goes to Nancy's loving and guiding presence.

During the year, Steve, number one son, had no significant bad physical experiences. Jim, number two, had some good stitches as marks of valor, from "taking it on the chin" while ice skating. Marshall, number three, broke a wrist when he crashed from the backyard swing set. He also made a trip to the hospital emergency room after encountering some wasps he found in Grandma's back yard. Elaine, the youngest, was minding her own business in her own front yard, when the neighbor's dog bit her in the face.

All of these events were things most kids normally experience. Commonly, they stick together and survive. Our kids stuck together quite well, so well, in fact, they all four had chicken pox at the same time. For that rather special occasion, Gram Garfield came and stayed for a week to help dispense lotion and sympathy.

Overall, the year went well for Nancy, if you can call full time around the clock every day for a year without any break "going well." For the entire year I longed for the ability to lighten her load, but I could do nothing directly to help with her unending responsibilities and duties. In my daily letters I tried to offer encouragement for her and the children. I wondered, however, if sometimes my writing about the things surrounding my life merely injected something more for her to worry about. In many ways, Nancy's job for that year was larger than my job. May God bless her always for the faithful and capable way in which she did her job so extremely well.

28.2 – By herself, Nancy kept the home fire burning.

Nancy also reached out into the community to give people some idea of what Vietnam looked like. She loaded our projector with a large bunch of thirty five millimeter photo transparencies I sent home and took her "slide show" on the road. Her first show was at Jessup Elementary School which our sons, Steve and Jim, attended. That initial effort was so successful a nearby elementary school heard about it and invited her to make the same presentation at their school.

The second outing prompted the following response:

Dear Mrs. Amend:

Thank you for coming to our school. We certainly enjoyed your presentation.

The letter from your husband, which you shared with us, and your visit have been of much educational value to our children. We certainly feel your fine visit has made it much easier for us to instruct our children in the American Way of Life.

Keep up the good work.

Sincerely,

Martin Youngman, Principal

Goins School

With her courage boosted by warm receptions at two elementary schools, she ventured farther afield. In Mitchell, Nebraska, where we had friends and extended family, she presented slides and a talk at the Mitchell Community Church. Also at our home church, First Presbyterian, in Cheyenne, she made the same presentation for our married couples group. At that gathering, a group letter to me made the rounds of everyone present. That letter, bearing a large number of signatures and greetings from so many friends, was very special to me.

The Presbyterian Church in Cheyenne was an important part of our family life during the three years I was there with the family. The following year, when I was in Vietnam, the church and many individual members continued to be supportive of me. Nancy and the children continued their regular activity in the church while I was gone. She was well known. It was hard to miss noticing a young woman regularly bringing four well scrubbed kids to church activities.

On Easter Sunday in 1966, our family's association with the church was particularly evident. A local Cheyenne radio station carried The Armed Forces Radio Network broadcast of the music we recorded in Pleiku only two days earlier. Some members of the church heard that radio program live.

Later, the whole congregation heard a re-run of the music. The USAF Home Town News Center sent to Nancy a copy of the tape we made in Pleiku. She loaned it to the church. Two weeks after Easter, on April 24, 1966, the church choir didn't make the usual presentation of anthems during morning worship. The Worship Bulletin for that service included an unusual announcement.

The two anthems for the second service today are from recordings made in Vietnam. Captain Dale Amend, a former member of our choir is now stationed in Pleiku. He is the director of a service men's choir. These two anthems were presented as part of the Easter Sunrise Service for the Army 1st Cavalry and also for the Easter service in the Air Force chapel in Pleiku. The organist is Mrs. Irene Fleming, the wife of an American Missionary. The organ used is a portable forty pound foot pedaled instrument. We think this music will bring our service men in Vietnam a little closer to us as we worship here today. Mrs. Dale Amend has made this music available to us. She is a regular worshiper with us each Sunday.

Nancy's life as a "widow for a year" was very difficult and stressful. Shepherding the activities of four kids and maintaining the household for everyone was a huge job. Sometimes it was nearly overwhelming. Friends would ask, "Don't you hate to see nighttime come?" She would respond, "Gosh, no! When it finally gets quiet around this house, I can relax. That's the time when I can re-read some of Dale's letters and write to him."

After the year became history, Nancy looked back and said, "The last few weeks of the year were agony because they passed so slowly. When that most special day of all days finally arrived, our reunion was glorious."

Chapter 29
Dalat--The Garden Spot

August 12, 1966 – Dalat

Dalat was known as the prettiest place in Vietnam. It was the highest "city" in Vietnam, 4,700 feet above sea level, situated among mountains that rose to 8,000 feet. Most of the population of Vietnam lived in the coastal regions and endured hot, humid weather. Because of its elevation, Dalat enjoyed a climate much cooler and dryer than the coastal regions. By comparison to the commonly miserable coastal regions, Dalat was delightful.

The population of the Southeast Asia region, known earlier as French Indo China, had long recognized the natural beauty of the area and its more pleasant climate. Dalat became a resort destination of sorts, complete with restaurants, shops and hotels. The facilities were of rather poor quality, but they did exist.

The climate was also agreeable for the production of fruits and vegetables not grown elsewhere in Vietnam. In Dalat you could buy strawberries in addition to rice and more rice. It was common to see a C-130 transport plane making a fruit and vegetable run from Dalat to supply military bases in other areas. Dalat was among the more pleasant and civilized places in Vietnam.

Although later political and military instability necessitated its relocation, the school for the children of missionaries serving in all of Southeast Asia was originally established in Dalat.

When the conflict between the government and the communist Viet Cong spread over all of South Vietnam in the early 1960s, a strange sort of quasi-truce prevailed in Dalat for an extended period. It seemed both sides enjoyed the benefits offered by Dalat, and neither side wanted to ruin a good thing. In Dalat proper, both sides honored the unspoken truce and refrained from military engagement with the other side. They shared the same shops, restaurants, bars and prostitutes. It was a strange arrangement, but relative calm prevailed inside the town.

On December 14, 1965, two of our FACs, Capts Mosley and Underwood, were shot down and killed near Dalat. On February 27, 1967, our FAC, Capt Wilbanks, operating from Dalat, was shot down and killed in the action for which he was posthumously awarded the Medal of Honor. Wilbanks was killed only about 30 miles south of Dalat. There was plenty of fighting near Dalat , but in the town proper, the de facto truce continued.

Dalat was one of our squadron's thirteen operating locations. Our Sector FAC in Dalat, Eric Jorgensen, rented a leftover French villa. It came complete with furniture and a live-in maid whose responsibilities included cooking, cleaning, laundry and keeping Eric warm in bed. Dalat was really different. For a FAC anywhere else to live like Eric did in the local community, without the protection of a military compound, would have been quick suicide.

Dalat was the destination for an unusual activity known as "In Country R&R." This had nothing to do with the Air Force R&R program under which most military members usually went to Bangkok, Hong Kong or Hawaii for a few days. Our FAC squadron conducted this improvised program in Dalat for the benefit of our sister squadron in Pleiku, the 1st Air Commando Squadron of A-1 fighter bomber pilots.

Occasionally one of our FACs would take an A-1 pilot from Pleiku to Dalat for a break in the action. Officially, there was no such program, but it did exist. It was a brief visit in Dalat, away from the usual grind in Pleiku, for some "stress relief" for the A-1 pilots.

Capt Kevin Joiner was an A-1 pilot in Pleiku who experienced more than his share of stressful military action and was selected for In Country R&R. I was assigned as his personal pilot/taxi driver.

On August 12, 1966, I flew from Ban Me Thuot to Pleiku, ostensibly for some radio maintenance and other minor repairs. The real purpose of the flight was to pick up Kevin Joiner and take him to Dalat for In Country R&R.

I squeezed the O-1 into Dalat under poor weather, and Eric Jorgensen picked us up in his personal jeep. Jorgensen had somehow wrangled/stolen/permanently borrowed the jeep from the Army in Dalat. Initially that sounded like a pretty good deal, but the Army hadn't given up very much. The jeep was old and tired and operated only in second gear.

If you were content with starting in second gear and operating only in second gear, it wasn't too bad. The jeep also had no reverse gear. A discreet operator quickly learned to park clear of obstacles or to park where he could roll backwards downhill, away from a tree or building before resuming second gear operation. Overall, it was a lot better than nothing.

Jorgensen loaned me the jeep, a sweater and some pants, his size, not mine. Because of last minute schedule changes, my bag got left behind. We took the jeep around town to shop in real shops and Joiner bought several things for himself and for buddies in Pleiku. My purchases were limited to a belt to hold Jorgensen's pants up above my ankles and a beautiful elephant hide purse as a birthday present for Nancy. We had dinner in a real restaurant, ordering from a real menu. Dalat was really different from life inside the military compound in Pleiku or in Ban Me Thuot.

After dinner we adjourned to the local bar for more stress relief for Joiner. Kevin began some rather serious consumption of local beer and I worked on seeing how long I could make a bottle of orange carbonated drink last. The orange "pop" was similar to the stateside beverage and was considered safe to drink. The bar hostesses quickly befriended us to let us know how welcome we were and a smooth fourteen year old business man, who spoke functional English, was always ready "to help us." His business was pimping for the hostesses.

The amiable teenager introduced himself as Nguyen Gao and identified a particularly comely young lady who caught Joiner's eye as Co Min. "You like Co Min? Co Min pretty girl. Co Min very nice girl. I get Co Min for you. OK?"

Nguyen Gao's cordial conversation continued, Co Min smiled prettily and Joiner had another beer. I continued to stretch my bottle of orange pop.

Nguyen Gao was a very personable youth. Even if Kevin Joiner had been sober, he probably would have liked the boy. Their conversation flowed smoothly as the young entrepreneur pursued his next sale and Joiner pursued another beer.

"Nguyen Gao, you really are a fine young man. I like you. I'm going to adopt you, take you home to the states and get you a good education."

"Yeah, OK. I get Co Min for you. OK?"

"I'm still thinking. Get me another beer."

Numerous repetitions of the same conversation followed and Co Min continued to pass by, pausing to flash her provocative friendly smile for Joiner. Eventually, Kevin's decision making capabilities became adequately lubricated by beer and he called his new friend, "Hey, Nguyen Gao. Get Co Min for me. I want Co Min."

To Joiner's surprise, Nguyen Gao ignored him and didn't respond. This happened twice more and it became evident that Nguyen Gao was avoiding Joiner. Joiner repeated his request more forcefully, "Nguyen Gao, where's Co Min? Get Co Min for me! I want Co Min!"

It was obvious that Nguyen Gao could not dodge Joiner any more. He gave a succinct status report of the business proceedings in the bar, "She fuck now. Back pretty soon."

Another patron in the bar had an eye for Co Min and purchased twenty or thirty minutes of her charming affection. Joiner had to wait his turn.

Nguyen Gao's forecast proved to be accurate. Soon Co Min returned, as fresh as a new daisy in May. Her hair was neatly combed, her make up was fresh, and her provocative smile was just as appealing as it was before she disappeared with the previous customer. Nguyen Gao quickly completed the business transaction with Joiner for Co Min's services. Kevin, Co Min and I left the bar.

Jorgensen's second-gear-only jeep performed faithfully and I hauled my two passengers to our overnight accommodations. The "hotel" was "modern" with running water. In fact, in my room, the running water was all over the floor. They went to their room and I went to the bad smelling bed in mine. In the U.S., these lodgings would have been terrible. In Vietnam, this was a nice place.

In the morning I knocked on Joiner's door, "Hey, Kevin, it's time for us to go."

He was quickly dressed and ready to leave. I asked, "Where's the girl?"

"She's still asleep."

I asked, "Well, how was it last night?"

"Would you believe I don't remember?"

That was the end of all conversation about the previous evening.

We returned Jorgensen's second-gear-only jeep and his clothes that didn't fit me. I flew Joiner back to Pleiku and returned to Ban Me Thuot. This concluded the August 12, 1966, episode of "In Country R&R."

When I got back to Ban Me Thuot, there were no reports to be completed on the mission. Officially, none of this ever happened.

Chapter 30

The Oldest Profession--Prostitution

Time immemorial – Vietnam and everywhere else

Prostitution has been a booming business for all of recorded history. It has flourished especially in times of war, where large numbers of males have been displaced from their previous general populations.

In Pleiku, Vietnam, things were not any different. My roommate, Greek, came back from downtown all aglow, "You should have seen the sweet little doll that I laid this afternoon. What a sweetheart! And it cost just 300 piasters. That's only about three dollars, and ya know what? She's in love with me."

I said, "Greek, you're crazy. She isn't in love with you. She's in love with your wallet and she knows how to get into it. Where did you find her?"

"At the Vietnamese government whorehouse over toward Camp Holloway."

"How old was she?"

"I don't know. I'd guess about nineteen or twenty. She was really good."

"How much English could she speak?"

"None, but that didn't matter. We both knew what we were there for and we didn't need any conversation. I liked her a lot. I'm going to go back for her again. I took a couple of rubbers along, but I got so excited I forgot to use one."

I never knew what Greek believed or didn't believe. I did know he was anxious to return to his three dollar sweetheart.

On a broader scale, I talked with an Army officer who had just returned from the big First Cavalry base forty five miles east of Pleiku. He told me, "I met an Army doctor at An Khe yesterday. His sole job is keeping four hundred prostitutes in the Vietnamese government whore house healthy. The obvious intent is to minimize the incidence of venereal disease among US troops who patronize the place. The commander of the base decided that rather than have a lot of his people down with VD, he'd rather have the prostitutes his men patronize be free of disease. Many of his men visit the whores. The commander is responsible for thousands of troops and decided to do what he can to keep them as healthy as possible."

It was quite a sociological phenomenon. The US Army doctor didn't see Army personnel to treat them. He spent all of his time attending to the health of hundreds of Vietnamese whores.

The disease problem wasn't limited to the huge Army base in An Khe. The first Flight Surgeon I knew in Pleiku, Doc Walt Rivers, told me about an incident he observed. "We were at Lake Bien Ho checking on the water supply for the Pleiku compound. It was a pleasant afternoon and a local prostitute was doing business under a tree at the edge of the lake. I watched from a distance and counted as fifteen GIs in sequence copulated with her. Not long after that, four of those GIs were in to see me with VD."

The new Flight Surgeon, Doc Pearson, showed me his Air Force record book of Pleiku personnel who had VD. Pearson said, "There are one hundred ten cases broken down in rank order in this book. Most of them are airmen or junior Non Commissioned Officers. The patients listed have all sorts of venereal diseases, and some of them are really bad."

On one occasion, the inflated price of prostitutes in Pleiku became a problem between American GIs and Vietnamese soldiers. For some reason, the price for whores skyrocketed. The

American GIs were able to pay the higher prices, but the Vietnamese soldiers were being hurt financially. That caused bad feelings toward the Americans. Eventually the price for whores came back down and the tension eased.

In Saigon the business of prostitution was better organized and usually took the GI for quite a bundle of cash buying liquor for himself and "Saigon Tea" for his hostess. Saigon Tea was a watered down drink with nearly no alcohol. This practice kept the hostess sober and spent the GI's money. She kept smiling sweetly and he kept shelling out about 160 piasters (about $1.60) for each cup of Saigon Tea. The GI was usually half drunk and half broke before he got the sexual encounter he came for. Although the business of prostitution was better organized in the big city, the law of supply and demand still governed. As the time for national elections in Vietnam approached, towns everywhere close to military installations were declared "Off Limits" to keep American military personnel away from anticipated trouble. The lack of the dollar turning over put a crimp in local businesses.

The Pacific Stars & Stripes newspaper reported the story on September 8, 1966.

Saigon is getting a taste of what life would be like without a lot of American troops around. Because of the strict curfew that will last until after the national elections on Sunday, the normally busy streets in the downtown area are all but deserted after dark. Most of the bars have declared a holiday for the thousands of hostesses who make their living drinking "Saigon Tea" with servicemen.

Until the curfew, a soldier had to almost throw himself under the wheels of a taxi to get one to stop during the early evening. This week empty taxis have been available on every corner and the cabbies haven't been able to gouge for double and triple fares. Most of the restaurants are remaining open and the few dining customers are enjoying unusually good service.

Downtown traffic is light and moving smoothly. The street vendors who normally block the sidewalks are gone by nightfall. Military Policemen are keeping a close check on the downtown area, and even the civilian employees connected with the government have been told to stay off the streets until the national elections are over.

The national elections came and went peacefully. The general curfew was lifted. The girls with smiles and pretty make up were back on the streets and prostitution again thundered along at full speed. It seems likely the business will always flourish.

Chapter 31
R&R on the Thai Railroad

April 27-May 1, 1966 – Bangkok, Thailand

R&R was "Rest and Recuperation," a very welcome break in the 24/7 routine of fighting the war in Vietnam. Three of us who lived close together came to know each other reasonably well. We made plans to go to Bangkok, Thailand together on R&R. We seemed to have similar interests regarding what we might do for a few days of leisure in a strange and fascinating place. In particular, none of us planned to ride the Thai Railroad. The other two were Lieutenant Jim O'Riley of the II DASC radar site and Lieutenant Frank Donohue of Civil Engineering.

When we boarded the four engine C-118 transport in Pleiku on April 27, 1966, I saw a familiar smiling face. The pilot was Major Nathano Eliopolous. He and I had gone through "Snake School" (Jungle Survival Training School) together in the Philippines en route to Vietnam. Nathano and I talked in October about our respective assignments in Vietnam. As we went our separate ways after landing in Saigon, he said, "When you're ready to go on R&R, I'll take you there. I'll be flying the C-118 around Vietnam and to other places." Sure enough, he took us to the thriving, modern, bustling city of Bangkok, Thailand. Thanks, Nathano!

Arriving in Bangkok, we quickly confirmed the Thai Railroad was a booming business. The common expression was, "All of Bangkok works on the Thai Railroad. Everyone's laying ties (laying Thais)." Many people who did not provide the actual service for customers in the bedroom helped to facilitate the business. The pimps were always busy arranging the sale of girls. Taxi drivers took clients to restaurants, bars and hotels. Others sold the drinks and served the food. A large staff managed the hotels and provided the many services to guests. The Thai Railroad ran quite efficiently.

We hadn't finished checking into our modern, clean, three person suite when a polite, well dressed and well spoken young man approached us, "I'll get you a very nice pretty girl." Everything about the Century Hotel was classy and well presented, including the marketing of "nice pretty girls." We declined politely.

Frank Donohue had a good friend, Air Force Lt Jeff Dillon, who was assigned in Bangkok. Jeff was the US Mail Service Officer for all of Southeast Asia. Since his assignment was an "accompanied tour," his wife, Pat, was also there. The Dillons had a nice modern second floor apartment with an outside patio overlooking the swimming pool. A Thai maid did all of their house work, including preparation of all meals. The Dillons were gracious and generous in hosting us for supper. The maid did all the work. It was all very nice.

After supper, we jumped from the Dillons' second floor patio into the ground level swimming pool just for the heck of it. Frank documented it with my camera to prove it happened. We philosophized about the tremendous differences between these two "rice bowl" countries, their respective economies and cultures. Thailand and Vietnam were two nearly contiguous countries in the same region of the world. Otherwise, they were worlds apart.

Frank, Jim and I were real tourists. We took more pictures of Buddhist Temples than you could believe. The beautiful, colorful temples were a dream for an amateur photographer. We swam at the Century Hotel and dined at the Crown Club atop the Firestone Building. The environment in Bangkok seemed to be forever removed from the way we lived in Pleiku. We toured the famous floating market and the Kings Royal Barges on the huge slow Chao Phraya River. Laughing children swam nude from their house boat homes and waved to us tourists. What became of the war?

31.1 – From the dining room to the patio and then into the pool.

31.2 – Some of Bangkok's colorful, lavish, ornate, Buddhist temples

31.3 – The floating market along the river's edge did a thriving business.

31.4 – Bangkok had an unlimited supply of spectacular temples for photographers

31.5 – A fierce guard stands watch in front of another temple.

31.6 – Banana boats, part of the bustling river freight business

On each of our many trips through the Century Hotel lobby the same polite young pimp cordially offered, "I'll get you a nice girl. A pretty girl." He was so amiable it was impossible to become irritated by his persistence. Eventually, though, it did get a little old. Once again he said, "I'll get you a nice girl. A pretty girl." On the spur of the moment, I thought we should have some fun with him. I decided to play with his head.

I said, "OK! We want a girl." His face lit up at the prospect of a sale. I held up one finger and said, "We want a girl. One girl. We'll take turns and save money. We want one girl." His face fell in disbelief and he said, "No, no! No can do!" I repeated my request for one girl and he walked away shaking his head. He couldn't believe I insisted on only one girl for the three of us.

Jeff Dillon's wife, Pat, was gracious in hosting her husband's friend and two more buddies for dinner in their apartment. She was also the perfect guide to show the three of us around Bangkok. She had time on her hands, a car at her disposal and she knew the city. Pat took us on several shopping trips. She took us to a silk factory where I bought five lots of gorgeous Thai silk which Nancy later sewed into five beautiful outfits for herself. Pat also took us to a bronze ware factory where I bought a large table service of dinner ware.

For one of our later shopping trips, the three of us were waiting in the lobby of the Century Hotel for Pat Dillon. Our friendly pimp was also there and obviously saw us. Since the occasion when I insisted he get one girl for the three of us, he kept his distance. Pat walked into the lobby to take us shopping. The three of us stood and talked with her for a short while. We then walked across the lobby toward her car. She led the way followed by Frank and Jim. I came along last, walking behind the others.

31.7 – A Thai silk factory

31.8 – Nancy sewed gorgeous outfits from this Thai silk.

I turned to wave and smile across the lobby at our friendly pimp. I pointed first to Pat and held up one finger. Then I made a sweeping inclusive gesture of my arm for the three of us guys and held up three fingers. It clearly presented the appearance of being the one girl I told him we wanted for three guys. One for three! He couldn't believe we arranged it ourselves. One girl for three guys!

Crazy cheap Americans! It was all wrong. The Thai Railroad was a respectable classy operation. It wasn't supposed to work that way. He was still shaking his head when we went out the door. I didn't have the courage to try to explain it to Pat Dillon.

Chapter 32

Ban Me Thuot and The Best FAC

Summer 1966 – BanMe Thuot

After nine months in Pleiku, I was transferred to Ban Me Thuot for my last three months in Vietnam. It was a simple matter of utilizing FACs where they were needed. It was good personnel management.

The job did not change significantly. I was still a FAC in Vietnam in the same squadron. I was still flying the O-1, controlling air strikes and doing my part in running the air war. My call sign, however, did change. I became Baron Four Two instead of Baron One Zero. The call sign identified both my operating base and me personally. Our operating procedures for flying were the same and Buster the Bastard screwed things up at every opportunity in Ban Me Thuot just like he did in Pleiku. The good part was Ban Me Thuot was a little farther away from BTB.

The terrain and the inhabitants around Ban Me Thuot were almost the same as in Pleiku. We were still in the Central Highlands, just ninety miles down the road. The large population of native Montagnards who lived around Ban Me Thuot were of the same Jarai and Raday tribes. Their living styles were the same.

The women walked along barefoot, wearing the customary single wrap of cloth which covered the body from the ankles to just above the waist. Many of the women carried naked babies in cloth slings. When the women stopped to urinate in public, they stood where they were, lifted the bottom of the cloth wrap up to just below the knees and continued the chatter with companions. When the stream finished splashing the sidewalk, they dropped the bottom edge of the cloth wrap and continued on their way. No one looked twice. Just like Pleiku? Well, not quite. In Pleiku, they peed in the dirt because there were no sidewalks.

Not only were the sanitary and clothing styles of the Montagnards different from ours, so were their dietary habits. On a warm July evening, insects like dragonflies besieged me while I wrote a letter. The critters were slower and smaller than dragon flies, and were harmless. But they swarmed to the light in large numbers at night and were quite bothersome. The natives swept them up by the bucketful, pulled off their wings and ate them with great relish. I didn't try them.

Overall, the move to Ban Me Thuot was a change in location without changing anything else. Montagnards were still Montagnards and FACs were still FACs. My life hadn't changed much. It was mostly "fly the airplane and do the job." Back in the compound after a day of flying, the free movies after supper were similar to those in Pleiku. They were all bad. At the start of the last (fourth) reel on September 4, 1966, the projector suffered a stroke and was no longer able to make any sound to accompany the picture. Shortly thereafter, it suffered spasms of the picture and stopped completely. I didn't learn if the minimally pulchritudinous heroine chose the Cavalry Capt or the trail scout. And the Cavalry never did get any Indians before the projector died.

The next evening, the theater continued with the fourth reel of the Cavalry and Indians movie. I ambled over and watched Geronimo and Cochise and a whole mess of their Indians annihilate a rather large part of the US Cavalry. They never did show who got the heroine. Maybe the Indians got her. She wasn't worth much anyway. The scheduled movie followed and was supposed to be better, but I abandoned the flick to write a letter.

I wrote home every day and Nancy wrote nearly that often. In addition to letters from her, occasionally something else arrived, forwarded through Pleiku to Ban Me Thuot. One such item prompted me to request a favor of Nancy, "Please call Mrs. J. D.

Tabor, 115 E. 35th St for me. I hope you can find her number in the phone book. Ask her to thank the ladies of the Desmond Circle, Daughters of Adriella, for their continued interest in my assignment. Tell her I am scheduled to be home later this month. They sent me another card and another package of Kool-Aid that arrived today."

Who in the heck were the kindly old grandmothers in the Desmond Circle, Daughters of Adriella who sent Kool-Aid? I had no clue who they were or how they knew my name and address. It was the stuff from which jokes were commonly made, but I wasn't joking. Sometimes it was easy to feel like no one knew and no one cared about what we were doing 10,000 miles from home. I appreciated the fact they cared about me. I wanted to be sure Nancy expressed my thanks to them.

The mail did reach us satisfactorily in Ban Me Thuot, but it was difficult to acquire other things vitally needed for continued operation. We were a small outfit with limited resources. Those conditions were typical of the thirteen FAC squadron operating locations. Ingenuity and persistence were the substitutes for abundance of parts, equipment and various supplies. We made many trips to Pleiku for parts and service on our airplanes. Whatever couldn't get done in Pleiku probably had to be corrected in Nha Trang. Periodic inspections and major maintenance for the O-1 were done in Nha Trang.

A bit farther south down the coast from Nha Trang was the big new F-4 base at Cam Ranh Bay. If we had business in Nha Trang, it was rather easy to also drop in at Cam Ranh. Cam Ranh was situated on a large isolated peninsula of sand and sand and more sand, jutting into the ocean. The F-4s flew from a new runway constructed of large inter-locking blocks of aluminum laid on sand. The F-4 was a new airplane, the entire support facility was new and all of the people there were "round-eyes," Americans. Practically no Vietnamese people were present.

The base itself looked like it had been plopped down onto a brand new empty sandy peninsula that magically appeared and protruded into the ocean from the coast of southern California or Florida. Within the confines of the base, things didn't look like Vietnam. This big, new base had lots of people and lots of equipment and facilities - - lots of "things" and "stuff" we didn't have in Ban Me Thuot. Visiting Cam Ranh made me feel like a kid from the "far back" country shopping at Wal Mart or Home Depot. What I wanted was probably there, if only I could find it.

Soon after my move to Ban Me Thuot, I was at the big new Cam Ranh base on business. That is, I was "on business" if locating something I needed could be called business. When I returned to Ban Me Thuot with my new acquisition in the rear cockpit, our crew chief, Sgt Joe Bronson, met me as I taxied in.

"Hey, Captain, what in the Hell you got in the back of your airplane? And how did you get it in there anyway?"

"Hi, Bronco. I made a "midnight requisition" in broad daylight at Cam Ranh. C'mon and help me get it out of the airplane."

It took Bronco and me several minutes of pulling and twisting to extricate my newly acquired mattress from the rear cockpit. I marveled that I had successfully stuffed the thing into the airplane by myself. I told Sgt Bronson, "The mattress was in one of the living quarters at Cam Ranh and no one was guarding it with a gun. I figured I needed it more than anyone there did, so I borrowed it. Permanently. Carrying it from the quarters to my airplane on the flight line was pretty easy. Cramming it into the rear cockpit was a lot harder."

Bronco was duly impressed. "I can't believe you got that thing in there alone. I guess the fact that you got back proves the mattress didn't block the movement of the control stick in the rear cockpit, but I can't see how."

I threw my "new" mattress on top of the derelict pile of material that preceded it. It provided a better place to sleep and served as a symbol of the practice of acquiring what we needed by whatever means were necessary to get it.

While Ban Me Thuot was very similar to Pleiku, there were significant differences. Prior to the 1960s, Pleiku was only a small village. Only after the increase of Vietnam military forces in the early 1960s and the American "Big Build Up" in 1965, did Pleiku mushroom to about 20,000 people by 1966.

Ban Me Thuot, by contrast, was larger and older than Pleiku. It was the capital "city" of Darlac Province. There was more agriculture, especially tea plantations, in the area. The tea plantations prospered under French management and Ban Me Thuot itself had a few shops and some paved streets and sidewalks.

However, after the French were kicked out in 1954, the infrastructure of the city deteriorated. A frequent comment was the Vietnamese lacked the technological capability to maintain flush toilets and traffic lights. That sounded harsh, but it was true. All management capability departed with the French and the city struggled to survive. While Ban Me Thuot was a lot more "city" than Pleiku, it still wasn't much.

In the city of Ban Me Thuot, the Grand Bungalow was the outstanding edifice. It was built in 1954 as a hunting lodge for the emperor, Bao Dai. Its general appearance was reminiscent of the YMCA camp in Estes Park, Colorado, in the Rocky Mountains. The ceilings in the main building were thirteen or fourteen feet high. The plumbing included running water which fed poor showers over old porcelain tubs. The walls were varnished wood and the floors were heavy wooden planks.

The grounds around the Grand Bungalow looked surprisingly nice. There was a small area of grass mowed with the only lawn mower I saw operated by Vietnamese. There were a few cultivated trees and shrubs.

32.1 – The Grand Bungalow.

Dan Preston and I lived in a small room in one of the several ancillary buildings around the Grand Bungalow. Compared to the conditions in which most military personnel lived "in the field," things were quite comfortable and nice. Of course, the facilities were nothing like the facilities of a modern city like Bangkok or even Saigon. This was still Ban Me Thout in the Central Highlands with its tribespeople and its lack of development.

The days when the emperor used the Grand Bungalow as a hunting lodge were long gone and the Vietnamese military appropriated the facilities. The United States Military Assistance Command Vietnam (MACV) used the facilities jointly with the Vietnamese. In that arrangement the term "assistance" alluded to a

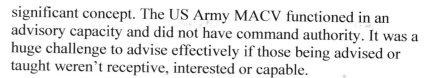
significant concept. The US Army MACV functioned in an advisory capacity and did not have command authority. It was a huge challenge to advise effectively if those being advised or taught weren't receptive, interested or capable.

The large military force in Ban Me Thuot was the 45th Regiment of ARVN (Army of the Republic of Vietnam). They were large in numbers and apparently small in initiative, ambition and bravery. The MACV boys, in their <u>advisory</u> capacity, were constantly frustrated by their inability to inspire, direct, instruct and motivate the Vietnamese troops. It was difficult for MACV to accomplish anything.

In the midst of this conglomeration were three Air Force FACs. Major Doc Dawkins was the Dar Lac Province Air Liaison Officer. He was responsible for BanMe Thuot and other FAC operating locations. Captain Dan Preston was the Sector FAC for Ban Me Thuot and I was the number three FAC. Later on, Capt Dick Overgaard, a former B-52 pilot, became our fourth FAC. Later also, Lt Col George Olson replaced Doc Dawkins. About thirty five Air Force enlisted men served as crew chiefs, radio operators and controllers at the radar station.

32.2 – The Ban Me Thuot Barons in a lighter moment

32.3 – Baron Four One, Dan Preston.

32.4 – Baron Four Two, the author.

The Air Force crew in Ban Me Thuot functioned in an atmosphere of camaraderie, cooperation and mutual support. Much credit for this good operation was due to the boss, first to Maj Doc

Dawkins and then to LtCol George Olson. They were both good bosses.

However, a bigger factor in the success of the Ban Me Thuot operation was the one I call The Best FAC. That was Capt Dan Preston. Preston had been there longer than the others and was extremely capable and effective.

Dan was a very interesting person with and for whom to work. He was very dedicated, hard working and had great initiative and ambition in pursuing what he felt needed to be done. He offended people with his blunt honesty and occasional lack of tact. He had a temper that flared and was intolerant of those who he thought were incompetent or goofing off. To him, everything related to the job was vital and <u>had</u> to be done. He had both positive and negative dealings with the MACV advisors. Those interactions proved my observations to be accurate. Dan and I got along well. I had considerable admiration for his zeal and persistence.

Preston had the appealing looks of a movie star and a glowing smile that obscured the intensity that surfaced when things got serious. He carried a special 30 caliber automatic with a long banana clip for extra rounds. His "air strike" demeanor was accurately portrayed when he sat in the cockpit of an O-1 with that weapon lying over the left canopy rail, pointed at the action.

Preston encouraged everyone to do more and be better. He pushed himself the most. FACs were limited to a maximum of 85 hours of flying time per calendar month. That limit could be waived to 100 hours by the Squadron Commander and, with special permission, could be further waived to 125 hours. When I arrived in Ban Me Thuot, Dan had flown over 100 hours for each of the previous five consecutive months. Dan said, "Well, I'm going to get the job done. Sometimes it takes more than 125 hours in one month, so I just keep flying and quit logging time after I hit 125 hours."

32.5 – Dan Preston with the looks and style you'd expect to see in the movies   *32.6 – Preston strikes a dramatic pose for the camera.*

Dan was always eager to do more and be more effective. When I returned from Pleiku with aircraft #851, the only O-1G aircraft I ever saw in a year in Vietnam, Dan was rubbing his hands together. Nearly all of the O-1s we flew were E models, with an occasional F model. The G model was expected to have a little more power for better performance. Dan was excited.

FACs were regularly admonished that our job was to control air strikes. We were <u>not</u> to attempt to be a weapons delivery platform. That was a dilemma for FACs. Several FACs had needlessly died from trying to fight the war themselves, usually with complete lack of success. Much to the contrary, one of our FACs, Willie Wilbanks, was credited with saving many lives and was posthumously awarded the Medal of Honor for taking on a vastly superior enemy force by himself.

32.7 – Preston, the author and the crew chief relax at the flight line.

Dan's excitement was prompted by the hope the G model O-1 could do what our E models couldn't do. Initially I wasn't aware of what he was trying to cook up with the new bird.

A few days after we acquired the G model, he said, "C'mon, Roomie, we're going to have some fun. I got the Army helicopter guys to mount a pair of rocket pods on our new G model. Each pod holds seven rockets, but fourteen rockets might be too heavy for the bird. I told them to load only five rockets in each pod. Now we have ten rockets instead of four. We can load some white phosphorus rockets for marking targets and some rockets with high explosive heads for attack. That way if we're covering a convoy that comes under attack, we can retaliate immediately with the HE heads. The way it is now, the bastards can ambush the convoy and run before we can get any fighters there to hit 'em.

32.8 – The author, Capt Dan Preston and the "G" model with the forbidden rocket pods

"I'm going to test fly the bird and fire ten rockets. You're going to fly chase plane on my wing and observe the test. We'll land, load more rockets and switch places. You can see how the airplane flies and fire another ten rockets while I watch from the other plane. When we finish the test, I'm going to call Harv Turner (our Squadron Commander) and ask him to come to Ban Me Thuot and see what we have."

FACs always wished for the weapons capability to make immediate retaliation. That's why the OV-10 was developed and put into service. But that was still years in the future. In the '65-'66 time frame, the O-1 was already overloaded every time we took off. Could it be feasible to demand even more from an overloaded airplane?

We made the test flights according to Dan's plan. On the first flight, I was impressed watching Dan fire the rockets. It was something I would not have imagined our little airplane could do. When it was my turn, I gave the engine full power on the runway and waited as the aircraft rolled and rolled before getting into the air. It flew like a lead sled. Really heavy. I fired a salvo of four rockets simultaneously and it felt like I had opened a drag chute. It seemed like the airplane had stopped and backed up. Later I fired one high explosive rocket at a few large water birds around a water hole. To my surprise, I hit the target and killed four of the large birds. I actually had my very own 4 KBA (four killed by air). Well, immediate strike capability was what Dan wanted!!

Dan's enthusiastic call to LtCol Harv Turner, in Pleiku, was not met with the same degree of delight. "You what?! You put two of those heavy pods and ten rockets on the plane?! The damned thing shouldn't have even gotten off the ground. You get those God Damned pods off that airplane now and don't even think of doing any thing like that any more. The only thing accomplished by that kind of crappy nonsense is getting more FACs killed. Dammit, Dan, how many times have you been told that you guys are FACs, Forward Air Controllers? You are not flying fighters. You are not delivering ordnance. We're already expecting too much from the O-1. And, no, I am not going to come see your new toy. Sheesh, Dan, I have enough to worry about without any more of your crazy ideas."

Preston was always in the middle of everything that happened militarily in Ban Me Thuot. On July 13, 1966, MACV held their usual "Post Operation Critique" of an operation near Buon Ho two days earlier. MACV assisted in the planning phase, but the operation was conducted solely by the ARVN without American participation. It was unbelievably disastrous. They bombed their own command post, called artillery fire on each other and lost six men crossing a river, four by drowning and two by accidental friendly fire.

The Post Operation Critique was a regular MACV practice to refine their own procedures and train the Vietnamese forces. The critique this time was conducted by the Deputy Commander of the Ban Me Thuot MACV, LtCol Silverman. Since Air Force FACs were not part of the MACV chain of command, we were only observers at the critique. Dan Preston, however, was not highly proficient at being a quiet non-participating observer. In the part of the critique called "Lessons Learned," he interrupted the proceedings, "Colonel Silverman, why is it the lessons learned two days ago sound just like the lessons learned in the critique after the operation last month? If the mistakes two days ago are the same as the mistakes we made last month, it sounds like we didn't learn a damned thing from the lessons learned last time."

Preston commanded such a high degree of respect he could say that without offending LtCol Silverman or getting himself thrown out of the critique. Silverman said, "Dan, you're right and we have to correct that." Dan was indeed completely correct on the matter. Furthermore, neither Silverman nor Preston dared touch the real issue and say, "The big problem is the incompetent gooks can't do anything right." The question of Vietnamese competence was a political hot potato. It was a very serious issue that was beyond the ability of Americans to remedy.

Meanwhile, back in Pleiku, Buster the Bastard heard about the political problem related to Vietnamese competence. He decided to jump into the middle of the matter. As usual, he made things worse. He latched onto a rumor that Preston refused to accept some A-1s flown by Vietnamese pilots for an air strike he was conducting. BTB alleged Preston's rejection of Vietnamese pilots had caused embarrassment for the Air Force with the Vietnamese. He directed Maj Dawkins and Dan Preston to appear before him in Pleiku with a written report of the matter.

Buskirk miscalculated on the supposed issue of embarrassment. Much to the contrary, General Nguyen, who commanded the ARVN 23rd Division in Ban Me Thuot, knew Preston and held him in high esteem. He heard about BTB's allegations against Preston and was concerned Preston might be removed from the position of Sector FAC for Darlac Province. General Nguyen didn't like that idea at all. He fired a salvo to Pleiku supporting Preston and blasting BTB. The General's influence caused the whole thing to blow over quickly. Dan Preston came back to Ban Me Thuot with a slight smile on his face. Everyone concerned observed once again that Bosworth T. Buskirk really was the north end of a south bound horse.

Dan Preston always completed his excellent job performance by accomplishing the necessary paper work. Frequently, after I stretched out for the night on my permanently borrowed Cam Ranh mattress, Dan would hammer away on his old mechanical typewriter. "Roomie, are you sure the typewriter doesn't bother you? I have to finish this report and get the next schedule done."

"The typewriter doesn't bother me at all, Dan. So long as the lamp shade keeps the direct light out of my eyes I'm just fine."

That was the status of things in our room one night when the field phone rang. It was the Squadron Commander, LtCol Turner, in Pleiku. "Dan, Lt Binkley is finalizing plans for tomorrow morning and told me something about your not being here."

"Yeah, Colonel, I can't make it. I have to fly."

"Can't make it!? Have to fly!? What in Hell are you talking about?"

"The Green Beret grunts at Duc Lap Special Forces Camp have an operation going out in the morning. It's called Operation Wildcat. I have to cover them."

"Preston, that's absolute bullshit! Do you know who's coming and why you have to be here?"

"Well, yes, sir. Binkley told me. But that doesn't change the fact that I have to fly cover for the guys at Duc Lap in the morning."

"Captain Preston, I don't know exactly what Lt Binkley told you, but I'm informing you that you have to be here tomorrow morning."

"Colonel Turner, you sound like you're really serious. I wish I could make it."

"God Damn it, Preston! I'm not negotiating and I'm not discussing the matter. I am telling you. You are going to make it tomorrow morning. If you aren't in your place in line at ten o'clock tomorrow, I guarantee your ass is hamburger. And I promise you I will personally turn the handle on the meat grinder. If there are any details you don't know, you'd better be talking to Lt Binkley pretty damned early tomorrow morning."

Turner hung up. Dan was quiet for just a moment and then said, "Roomie, I think he means it. I gotta go to Pleiku early in the morning. You'll have to take my place and cover Operation Wildcat for the guys at Duc Lap."

"I think we both knew that before Turner called, didn't we?"

"Yeah, I suppose we did." He paused. "And now I have another problem. The Air Force insignia and wings on my fatigues really look crappy. I got the new stuff last week, but I haven't had time to get to the tailor shop and have them sewn on."

I said, "I can fix that. You already have the tags that say "Preston" and "Baron 41" and they're OK. I have the other things on my fatigues and they look pretty good. I'll just take those tags off my fatigues and put them on yours."

It took some careful work with a razor blade, but I got the insignia, wings and rank off my fatigues. I found enough old rough safety pins to secure the tags in place on Dan's fatigues. Some of the safety pins were too big, rusty and badly bent, but that didn't matter. The pins were on the inside of his fatigue jacket where they didn't show. The transplanted insignia, wings and captain bars looked good enough. Barely good enough.

Dan was in his proper place on Pleiku Airbase at ten o'clock the next morning. On August 3, 1966, when Lt Binkley read, "Captain Daniel Preston," Dan took one step forward, rendered a crisp salute and stood at attention. President Lyndon Baines Johnson pinned the Silver Star for valor in combat on his chest.

Dan knew two days before the ceremony the President of the United States, the Commander in Chief, was coming to Pleiku. He knew the President was to make the formal presentation of the Silver Star to one Captain Preston, the recipient of that high honor. As the time for the presentation drew near, he quietly told Lt Binkley, "No, I can't make it. I have to do my job. They're depending on me."

Most people probably can't even imagine a man being that dedicated to the performance of his duty. Most people never met the US Air Force FAC, Captain Dan Preston.

When Dan retuned from Pleiku after the ceremony, his first words to me were, "How did it go for Operation Wildcat? Did all of the Duc Lap guys get back safely?"

I said, "Yeah, they're all fine. Everything went smoothly. How was the presentation ceremony?"

"It was OK. I'd rather have been flying. Man, I gotta get this damned thing off." He peeled off his fatigue jacket, revealing several prominent red scratches on his chest.

"Hey, those are some pretty good scratches. Did LBJ poke you when he fastened the medal on your chest?"

"Well, in fact, he did jab me. Twice! He was having some trouble with his bi-focals and the clasp on the back of that thing was tricky. But that wasn't the problem. The real problem was all of your damned oversize bent scratchy safety pins you used to fasten the insignia on my fatigues jacket. Those damned pins scratched the Hell out of me."

"My damned oversize bent scratchy safety pins indeed! You should be thanking me for bailing you out and making you look presentable to meet the Prez. Did you flinch and yell "Ouch!" when LBJ stabbed you?"

"Hell no! What do you think I am? A wimp?"

No, Dan Preston certainly was not a wimp. He was, in fact, The Best FAC I ever knew.

Chapter 33

Huckleberry Finn--the Ugly American

July 1966 – Ban Me Thuot

The story of Huckleberry Finn, Ban Me Thuot style, is funny and sad at the same time. To understand the story you must get to know Jay Kunzman. Jay was a highly skilled FAC. He performed extremely well under stress in dangerous situations. That's what being a FAC was all about. There were few FACs, if any, who were better than Jay Kunzman. Perhaps that was why some of the unusual things he did were overlooked.

FACs in general broke a lot of rules and regulations. Frequently the situations in which we operated left us no choice. We broke the rules to get the job done or to survive under unusual circumstances. Usually it was a good decision to break the rule for a justifiable reason. Accordingly, no one complained or second-guessed what we did.

Jay Kunzman was willing to smash a rule to fit his personal desires. He didn't talk about it or try to justify it. He just did it. Jay was missing for two weeks with no explanation. It was tough to disappear from Ban Me Thout. Only after he reappeared, the cat got out of the bag. He somehow managed to get onto an airplane to California and spent a vacation at home with his wife. It was all strictly unauthorized and illegal, but he got away with it. Although Jay could have been subjected to serious disciplinary action, people in authority chose to not notice what happened.

As Jay's one year tour in Ban Me Thuot was coming to an end in late June 1966 I was reassigned from Pleiku to replace him. I arrived before Jay left and there wasn't room for both of us in the room he shared with Dan Preston.

Jay had already checked out psychologically. He was doing nothing but taking up space while waiting for the calendar to turn over during his last few days in Vietnam. While Jay did nothing, I flew his missions and lived out of a bag of stuff on the floor of the crowded transient bay. He stayed half drunk most of the time and mostly drunk half of the time. I saw little future in that pursuit, but his business was his, and my business was mine. I was anxious for him to leave for Saigon, en route home, so I'd have a bed. Jay was amiable and likeable, but there was a lot about his lifestyle I didn't approve or admire. Meanwhile, I lived in the crowded transient room. The intended capacity of the transient room was two. The population was seven.

On July 5, 1966, Dan and I took Jay to the Ban Me Thuot East airstrip. We expected to congratulate him on the completion of his tour and bid him farewell. The C-47 shuttle plane expected to stop for him en route from Pleiku to Saigon never showed up, and neither did the replacement aircraft. Jay had to catch his return flight to the US, so I took him to Tan San Nhut Air Base in an O-1.

The Saigon trip was the most successful Saigon trip I made in a year in Vietnam. I measured the success of a trip to Saigon in inverse proportion to the amount of time I was on the ground there. I was on the ground for a total of only ten minutes, so I called it a great trip. Furthermore, I hauled away the body occupying the bed I was supposed to be sleeping in. I had my own bed. Yea!

Kunzman departed Saigon on July 7th and, thanks to the International Date Line, arrived in San Francisco on the same calendar day. Wow! I would have been thrilled to change places with him. In Ban Me Thout, I did change places with him. I had my own half of a small room with Dan Preston and my own bed.

Jay was gone, but he left behind a legacy. It was the story of Huckleberry Finn.

Jay was a personable, cordial guy who made friends quickly and comfortably. In the dining hall a Vietnamese girl of about 18 or 19, named Co My, was employed as a table server. Jay struck up a casual friendly relationship with her and "helped" her as she tried to improve her minimal command of the English language. He taught her just about every vulgar, profane and obscene word used in the war. Under his tutelage, she acquired considerable proficiency in using all of them. Jay also taught her there was one thing which was so very nasty and foul that she should <u>never</u> say it. He taught her she should <u>never</u> say, "Huckleberry Finn."

It became popular entertainment to make the most of her newly learned language skills. One evening at dinner, a transient pilot was at the table. Jay struck up a conversation with the guy passing through. After a while Jay led the visitor into the trap, "The serving girl's name is Co My. When she comes back by the table, ask her to bring you a glass of iced tea."

When Co My came back past the table, the visitor held up his glass, gestured to the girl and said, "Co My, would you please bring me some iced tea."

While she was gone to fetch the tea, Jay told the unsuspecting visitor, "When she comes back with the tea, ask her to say "Huckleberry Finn."

When she returned with the tea, the innocent visitor said, "Co My, say Huckleberry Finn."

She stiffened and glared indignantly at the new guy, "No good God damned fuckin' sum bitch ass hole!!!" She took a step back, paused and then defiantly declared, "I no say!!"

She then turned and stalked away, satisfied she had defended her honor against something nasty by refusing to say those horrible words, "Huckleberry Finn." The shocked visitor sat with his mouth hanging open while all those who knew Jay Kunzman and Co My nearly doubled over with laughter.

The scene was complete utter nonsense. It was ridiculously funny, but quite sad at the same time. The Ugly American was seated among us. I didn't assign that title to the unsuspecting guy who had been suckered into playing the part of the straight man. I put that label on Jay Kunzman, the one who was "helping the serving girl, Co My, learn the English language."

Chapter 34

The Last Survivor--Temporarily

July-September 1966 – Ban Me Thuot and Saigon

January 1967 – Florida.

Maj Karl (Doc) Dawkins, the ALO (Air Liaison Officer) for the 23rd Vietnamese Division, was our FAC boss in Ban Me Thuot. I met Doc prior to my move from Pleiku to Ban Me Thuot. We both flew temporary support for the 3rd Brigade of the 25th Infantry Division. The 25th had just arrived in Vietnam and was conducting an operation near Ban Me Thuot. Doc was flying out of Ban Me Thuot and I was flying out of Pleiku.

I stayed with Dawkins during the time we supported the operation conducted by the 25th. He was a very decent sort of guy and a strong family man. We enjoyed talking about our families instead of going to the bar to get drunk. Doc and I had a total of two wives and nine kids waiting for our return. We shared similar values about home and family. Our FAC assignments in Ban Me Thuot overlapped by only six weeks, but during that brief acquaintance I appreciated how much we had in common. He was a <u>good</u> boss. Everyone liked and respected him.

Prior to becoming a FAC, Doc flew the F-105 over North Vietnam. He was the sole living survivor of his original F-105 squadron. The other twenty four pilots were all dead. F-105 losses over North Vietnam were horrendously large. Dawkins would likely have been number twenty-five out of twenty-five dead had he not been transferred from his F-105 squadron to become a FAC.

34.1 – Doc Dawkins inspects an M-60 Machine gun mounted on an Army O-1.

I had another pilot friend, Rex Dunivent, who flew the F-105 over North Vietnam. Doc's squadron and Dunivent'squadron were sister squadrons. Dunivent's squadron lost two thirds of its pilots.

Yes, there were worse jobs than being a FAC.

Soon after my arrival in Ban Me Thuot, Doc developed lower back muscle spasms that continued for five days. It appeared likely to be sciatica. The pain was so severe that it put him completely out of commission. Over his protestations, Dan Preston and I ganged up on him and <u>informed</u> our boss, "You <u>must</u> have medical help. There is none here and you <u>are</u> going to see a doctor." We packed a bag for him and I took him in an O-1 to Nha Trang to see the flight surgeon.

On the trip down, he writhed around in the back cockpit. He disconnected his shoulder harness and safety belt trying to get comfortable. For about fifteen minutes he was passed out from the pain. The flight surgeon in Nha Trang said Doc had to get to the hospital. With help, I got him back into the O-1, took him to Cam Ranh and checked him into the hospital.

I returned to Ban Me Thuot, hoping that drugs and bed rest in the hospital would cure his ills. We were concerned for his welfare and wanted him back on the job. A few days later Doc was back at work, a welcome presence. All was well.

All was well, at least for a while. On August 4, 1966, he received notification he was due in Saigon on the 6th to take over the job of directing "out of country strike operations." It was a prestigious job with a lot of visibility and great opportunity for advancement.

He had been hand picked by General Overland for the job. He didn't like leaving the job in Ban Me Thuot, but the new one looked particularly good for his future. We congratulated him on his selection and wished him the best, hating to see him leave. He would be hard to replace.

Doc was doing well at his new job at Tan San Nhut Airbase in Saigon when I spent my last night in Vietnam. I had contacted him ahead of time and he offered me a place to sleep over night. His little ten foot by ten foot room had a set of bunk beds and an air conditioner. I was glad to visit with Doc Dawkins one last time, and most appreciative for a good place to sleep. I caught my flight home and Doc continued the grind in Saigon.

Maj Karl (Doc) Dawkins was the sole living survivor of his original squadron of twenty-five F-105 pilots. From F-105s, he received orders to be a FAC, the Air Liaison Officer in Ban Me Thuot in the Central Highlands. He survived in the FAC business until a higher priority job took him away. He was chosen by name for a job in a career fishbowl environment in Saigon. He worked under intense high level oversight without going crazy. Doc's overall story was an impressive account of being a survivor.

After Vietnam, Doc returned to the States in January, 1967. His assignment was flying jets for the Armament and Development Test Center at Eglin Air Force Base in Florida. It was a prime assignment. Many pilots would have rated the job as their number one choice for assignment.

After all of his experiences in Vietnam, Doc was back home, re-united with his family and performing a great job. It sounded like "and everyone lived happily ever after."

Unfortunately, that was not to be. Doc was making a test flight over the Gulf of Mexico when radar and radio contact with his plane were suddenly lost. He disappeared and was never seen again.

Chapter 35

Ban Don and the Big Black Birds

August 1966 – Near Ban Don Special Forces Camp

There were many big black birds around Ban Don Special Forces Camp. I don't mean "Blackbirds," the ones with the pretty red patches on the wings, perched on reeds and cattails, singing nice songs in swampy areas. I mean really <u>big black birds</u>. Buzzards. They frequently flew over the area, circling at both high and low altitude. They were big. Really big.

On an August afternoon, I was flying a particularly dull, uninteresting, visual reconnaissance mission and saw several of them making lazy circles in the sky. I idly mused, "I wonder if I can fly formation with one of those big feathered critters? After all, here they are, cruising in <u>my airspace</u>. Of course, it's pointless and stupid. It's of no practical value and it'll be impossible anyway. Good. I'll try it."

I selected one making big wide circles and matched his altitude. I flew a wider concentric circle on his outside wing and edged closer to join up with him. My 75 knots was much too fast to stay on his wing in formation. I over-shot him by quite a bit. In pilot training, so poor an attempt at joining up on my leader's wing for formation flying would have merited a pink slip (failure) for the ride.

On my next try I put down full flaps and flew on the edge of a stall, using high power to maintain slower level flight. I gradually tightened the circle to fly closer to the buzzard. Since my airspeed was still greater than the bird's, I kept flying slower and slower until my airplane stalled and fell, somewhat like a rock. No big deal. I just recovered from the stall, climbed back up to the bird's altitude and tried again.

On the next few tries the only question was which predictable result would be the first to occur. The surprised bird might get irritated at me for invading his airspace, become excited, fold his wings and dive to get away from me. If that didn't happen, my little airplane might again stall out and fall from the sky. Both results were repeated on the next few attempts. I concluded that even with my slow airplane, formation flying on the wing of one of the big black birds was not possible. Of course, I knew that before starting the experiment, but it was an interesting interlude during a dull day.

Things more serious than flying formation with buzzards were happening at the same time. I chanced to see an old friend, Herb Jacobs, one of our FACs, when I was in Nha Trang. His bird had just taken a 30 caliber slug through the fire wall by his right foot. It went through the battery cable and the tachometer and cut a line into the fuel gauge. It spilled fuel into the cockpit and went out through the roof. He was cut slightly in the face by metal fragments and landed O.K. at Nha Trang. It was the last mission of his tour. I guess it was nice to make the last mission worth remembering.

On the same day, LtCol Turner told me we had lost forty five Air Force O-1s in Vietnam so far in 1966. That was forty-five birds in only seven months. That's a lot! Our losses were large.

On August 7, 1966, I flew three times, a total of seven hours ten minutes. It was a long day. It included pounding approximately fifty uniformed Viet Cong northwest of the Ban Don Special Forces Camp. I put four sets of fighters on them. FAC Dick Overgaard and his fighters attacked the same bunch of VC before I did and probably accounted for most of the reported twenty-one KBA (killed by air). I'm pretty sure my fighters got some of them.

The fourth flight of fighters I controlled was Dagger Two Six, two A-1s out of Pleiku. Their ordnance was nearly expended, meaning the air strike was almost done, when I was surprised to feel a sharp impact on my airplane. I was working right on the tree tops and my first reaction was surprise at the possibility I'd become so focused on the ground target I failed to clear the top of one of the tallest trees. I pulled up and checked my engine instruments. Everything looked O.K.

"Hey, Dagger! I just hit something or something hit me. Look me over. Can you see anything wrong?"

The A-1s were also flying at rather low altitude nearby and quickly gave me a response, "Can't see anything, Baron. You look alright. There are several of those big black birds flying around the area. Maybe you hit one of them."

I checked the left wing. Everything looked O.K. Just as I looked at the right wing a large black feather came loose and fell away. Sure enough! One of the big black birds had just paid me retribution for invading his airspace. He bent up my airplane!

Dagger Two Six checked on me, "Baron, are you O.K.? Can you tell what happened?"

"You were right, Dagger. I did hit one of those big black guys. The impact caved in the leading edge of the right wing. I can't tell yet how serious the damage is, but I'm not going back down on the deck for the rest of the strike. Can you dump the rest of your ordnance in one more pass? If you can, we'll call it a day."

"Affirmative, Baron. We'll make the last run and be dry. Are you sure you're able to get home all right?"

"I'm not sure, but I think I'm O.K. I'll do a stall series on the way back to Ban Me Thuot just to be sure my plane can make a safe final approach and landing. Thanks for checking me out. I'll see you guys next time."

The leading edge of the right wing was crumpled enough to affect the aerodynamics of the wing. If the wing lost enough lift, it could stall out during final approach to landing and drop that wing onto the ground. The plane could cartwheel. Not good.

I climbed to a safe altitude and reduced my airspeed and simulated a normal final approach to landing. Sure enough, the airplane began to stall and roll to the right while flying at normal final approach airspeed. I repeated the test a few times to define the extra airspeed required to make a safe approach and landing. I landed safely at the higher than normal final approach airspeed. Any good experienced pilot would have done what I did. A novice pilot would quite likely have made a dent in the ground.

I was glad the big bird hadn't hit the propeller, which was only a few feet inboard from the actual point of impact on the airplane. That amount of force inflicted on the prop of the O-1 would have caused engine failure. If that happened on the tree tops where I was operating, I would have had very little time to successfully miss all of the trees and put the plane down in one piece with a dead engine. If I got it down in an open space, if there was one, the two A-1s were there to call a chopper to retrieve me.

Even if I accomplished all of that and made it down O.K., there was another concern. There were certain folks of different political persuasion already on the ground nearby, and we had just been hammering them with an air strike. They may have been unhappy with me. Would they have found me before the helicopter found me? We'll never know because I didn't have to put the airplane down there. I liked it better the way it actually concluded.

The next day, on August 8th, Dick Overgaard and I took two planes and alternated on the high-low procedure, one above flying cover and one below looking. We looked all over the area we hammered heavily on the 7th. There were no VC to be found. We saw nothing.

On August 10th, Dick Overgaard flew cover for a chopper-borne ground party that checked on the area we hit three days earlier. In only one part of the area they counted fourteen bodies. Their count didn't contradict Sunday's initial report of twenty-one, since they searched only a part of the area and counted only a portion of the dead. Apparently the strikes were very successful.

They also brought back a captive who waved a white flag and surrendered. He was a North Vietnamese Regular sergeant. We had thought, mistakenly, the bunch we hit on Sunday were Viet Cong from somewhere in the local area. They were not.

The prisoner's battalion left Hanoi on March 12th. That was five months earlier! His was the second of three battalions of seven hundred eighty men each. That battalion had already been hit by air three times before our strike on Sunday, August 7th. The battalion had about five hundred men remaining. They were headed for IV Corps in the Delta.

They buried sixty seven men by the small river after our Sunday strikes. These were in addition to the fourteen counted on August 9th, making a total of eighty-one. The original report of the results of the air strikes was greatly in error. The target was far more significant than thought and the air strikes were far more successful than reported. The ground search party also found a Chinese radio, a Chinese assault rifle and the seat of a 12.7 millimeter anti aircraft gun (50 caliber). We were glad they didn't have that big one set up to use on us. It would have quickly blown us out of the sky.

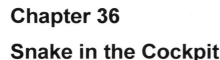

Chapter 36

Snake in the Cockpit

1945-1966 – Flashback

1966-67 – Ban Me Thout, Bao Loc and Gia Nhia.

George Olson was an interesting guy with an intense lifelong passion for flying airplanes. At the age of eighteen he gained admission into the cadet pilot training program of the US Army Air Corps. Unfortunately for George, the Army Air Corps did not need pilots but did need navigators. Over his vehement protests, he was squeezed out of pilot training and into navigator training.

During navigator training, he spent all of his spare time and money on private flying lessons on weekends. At the end of the Army Air Corps program he had navigator wings, a commission as a second lieutenant and a private pilot license.

World War II had been over for a year and George was a twenty-one year old navigator on a B-29. They flew out of Tokyo making practice bombing runs on a small Pacific island. George befriended the aircraft commander and finagled some flying time for himself at the controls of the B-29. He even made two take-offs and two landings, most unusual for a navigator.

World War II was over and many people just wanted to go home. Not everyone in the B-29 outfit was happy and some of the enlisted men didn't like flyboy officers. A disgruntled cook mixed strong GI soap into the dehydrated potatoes served for dinner in the officers' dining facility. The result was disastrous. During their mission on the following day, first the co-pilot and then the pilot of George's crew became violently nauseated and then passed out. Other crew members dragged those two men from the cockpit and

George, the navigator, assumed the controls. The flight engineer acted as co-pilot.

Olson declared an emergency on the radio, aborted the mission, jettisoned the bomb load into the ocean and successfully landed the airplane back in Tokyo. Other aircrews had similar but less severe problems.

Fortunately, George's food poisoning symptoms developed slowly. Had he become violently ill during the aborted mission, the B-29 and its crew most likely would have been lost. After their dramatic safe return, he spent the night unconscious on the floor of the latrine and nearly died.

The cook was court-martialed, dishonorably discharged and committed to Leavenworth Prison. Olson was commended for his actions in saving the airplane and its crew and was offered the choice of entering the US Military Academy or entering US Air Force Pilot Training. He jumped at the chance to realize his lifelong dream and became a full-fledged US Air Force pilot.

It was nineteen years later in Ban Me Thuot when I came to know George Olson. He was an old Lieutenant Colonel and I was a Captain. Olson replaced Maj Doc Dawkins as the Air Liaison Officer of Darlac Province and became our new FAC boss. He was far past being a spring chicken, but hadn't lost his flair for doing things in a dramatic manner.

Soon after Olson arrived, I went along in his back seat as he flew a visual reconnaissance mission. He approached a wooded ridge at low altitude and said, "I want to have a good look at something." He extended full wing flaps and pulled the throttle back to idle as we crossed the top of the ridge and plunged like a rock down the other side. The ridge was steeper on the other side and he pushed the nose down to follow the contour of the land, just clearing the trees.

36.1 – LtCol George Olson, new Ban Me Thuot FAC boss

As we flew over a small village he said, "I wanted to see what was going on in that village before they knew I was coming. I wanted to maintain the element of surprise."

I <u>had</u> to tell him, "Well, Sir, you're the boss and I'm working for you, but I've been here almost a year flying this airplane. I'd suggest you don't do that again. This engine has a penchant for quitting when the throttle is pulled back to idle. With full flaps, idle power and low airspeed, we were going down like a rock. If the engine had even hesitated when you brought the throttle back up from idle, we'd have met all those folks on the ground up close and in person. You'd have surprised them all right. You'd have surprised the Hell out of them <u>and</u> us. We'd have been <u>in</u> the trees right by their shacks."

Olson wasn't offended by my comments. He knew he was "the new kid on the job" and had sense enough to listen to one of his pilots with nearly a year of experience in the FAC business.

We quickly recognized he was a good boss who cared for people, especially those who worked for him. Although he arrived in Ban Me Thuot only seven weeks before I left for home, I developed a lot of respect for him. A few months after I left Vietnam, he was instrumental in obtaining the approval of the Medal of Honor for Capt Wilbanks.

George Olson's good follow-on communications with his former FACs enabled me to find him later. I was visiting Hurlburt

Field in Florida on a business trip from the US Air Force Academy. He lived nearby and I gave him a call. In his usual manner of caring for people, he and his wife graciously invited me to their home for dinner.

After dinner we sat in the living room visiting. I said, "I saw the big article in Airman Magazine (an official Air Force publication). That was a great picture. I was somewhat surprised no one gave you any trouble over hauling that critter in your airplane. What ever became of your big snake?"

George remained seated and casually reached down to the floor at the side of his chair and picked something up. With a long gentle swinging motion of his arm he unrolled it clear across the living room floor. There it was! Twelve feet of beautiful cured skin previously wrapped around a forty pound python.

"Hey, that's spectacular! Tell me the whole story."

"I found it in a village outside of Bao Loc. A Montagnard there had the snake in a large basket and wanted to sell it. I gave him four US dollars for the snake and tried very hard to buy the basket. For some reason he refused to part with the basket and that left me with a problem. How was I going to get my new pet back to Ban Me Thout?

"With help I finally got the snake stuffed into a big strong fiber glass sand bag. I tied the top securely and set my big bag full of snake on the back seat of the O-1. I took off and headed for Gia Nhia. I had to make a stop there to see one of my FACs on the way back to Ban Me Thuot.

"Half-way to Gia Nhia I felt something against my left foot. Hey! Here came the snake! How could he possibly have gotten out of that bag? Well, he had gotten out of the bag. He was crawling forward along the left side of the airplane from the rear cockpit into the front cockpit. A real problem was developing. A twelve foot python is extremely strong. He was a lot stronger than I could control, even if I didn't have to fly the airplane while wrestling with him.

"He reached the left rudder pedal and turned to the right, approaching the right rudder pedal. If he jammed the rudder pedals I might be able to continue flying, but I probably couldn't land the plane safely. I considered my options. I did have my M-16 rifle, my 38 caliber pistol and a good knife, but I didn't want a dead snake even if I was able to kill him. And I really didn't want metal fragments from a bullet or a part of the airplane flying around inside the cockpit. I didn't know what damage I might cause to the airplane and I might hurt myself more than I hurt the snake.

"By the time I got to Gia Nhia, he was wrapped around both rudder pedals and around both of my feet. I could scarcely move my feet, much less the rudder pedals. Fortunately there was no surface wind when I landed and I didn't need the rudders for directional control. I got the plane down safely. On the ground, I still couldn't move the rudder pedals and therefore couldn't turn the airplane to get off the runway. I shut the engine down on the runway and waited for Capt Zimmerman and the crew chief to come help me.

"By the time they got there to see what was wrong, the snake had wrapped himself around the rudder pedals in both the front and rear cockpits. The three of us finally peeled the big snake loose from the little airplane and got him into a duffel bag. I hoped the duffel bag would prove to be stronger than the failed sand bag.

"Back in Ban Me Thuot I had him in a cage near the flight line. He quickly became a star, attracting many visitors, but he wouldn't eat. We tried the usual python menu of chicken, but he wasn't interested in chicken. He also refused our offering of ducklings, small chicks and dead rats. We enlisted about a dozen people to hold his body down in a straight line and inserted a plastic tube down his throat. We put two pounds of wieners down the tube. He expelled them. We put the wieners inside him again and he expelled them again.

"Finally we got him a live rat from a 'live trap'. We dropped the wiggling rat into the cage. The snake grabbed it as soon as it hit the ground and swallowed it. Success! We discovered his preferred menu! We had to catch more live rats!

"Later the snake died. I had the skin preserved and brought it home. I keep it here by my favorite chair. It never fails to start a good conversation."

I was satisfied to finally learn the rest of the amazing story about George Olson's big snake. Before me on the floor was the convincing evidence this had been one heck of a big powerful snake. I wouldn't want it tangled around the flight controls of that little airplane when I was flying it.

Chapter 37

The First Air Cavalry Grocery

August 1966 – Buon Blech Special Forces Camp

Dick Overgaard flew back to Ban Me Thuot from Buon Blech Special Forces Camp with sixty pounds of sugar, thirty pounds of lunch meat in six-pound cans and a case of canned corn. He said, "Look at all of this stuff. I don't know what I'm going to do with it. Ralph Horner (the Senior Advisor) urged me to take it, so I brought it back. Got any ideas ?"

My eyes lit up at the sight of Dick's bonanza. I didn't hesitate, "I know exactly what to do with it. C'mon and I'll show you."

We unloaded Dick's loot from the O-1 into the jeep and went to the Ban Me Thout missionary compound. I introduced Dick to the Swaynes and we gave them the food. Mrs. Swayne divided the food into smaller portions and shared it with several other American missionaries. I was glad Dick had discovered a gold mine of food at Buon Blech. I was anxious to do some of my own hauling.

The small mountain of food came into existence courtesy of the First Air Cavalry Division. They assembled a large force in the Buon Blech area and launched a major sweep to the west. They sought a major engagement with Viet Cong and North Vietnamese forces in the area. Unfortunately, it didn't work out that way. The usual problem that plagued American forces for the entire ground war in Vietnam prevailed. The bad guys weren't to be found. They were smart enough to disappear whenever a superior force threatened them.

As a result, the First Air Cav swept quickly through the area from the starting point near Buon Blech all the way to the Cambodian border. They met essentially no resistance and the operation took far less time than was expected. A huge supply of food provided to support the troops on that operation was left behind at the starting point. With all those abandoned groceries underfoot, Ralph Horner, by default, became what I called "The Proprietor of the First Air Cavalry Grocery."

In terms of supply and demand, a great imbalance of food had been created. There was a huge supply and no beneficial use for perfectly good food. The Special Forces Camp was a small isolated outfit and couldn't begin to use all of that food. Ralph wanted us to take all we could and I was glad to oblige. The American missionaries in Ban Me Thuot commonly had trouble getting food other than rice and more rice. They were glad to accept it.

The day after Dick's discovery, I had some air strikes near Buon Blech. I stopped at the Special Forces Camp and picked up more food left by the First Air Cav. I planned to really load up, but they had a man with a large suitcase who needed to go to Ban Me Thuot and I couldn't refuse him. I loaded the unplanned passenger, his suitcase and about two hundred pounds of food into the rear cockpit. His fare for the trip to Ban Me Thuot was holding all the baggage in place. I told the Green Berets at the camp I was taking the food to American missionaries in Ban Me Thuot. They liked the idea and told me to come back and get all I could haul.

Two days later I took a sergeant from Lac Thien Special Forces Camp to drop some leaflets. When I finished the day's scheduled flights, I returned to the grocery business. At Ban Me Thuot, I loaded four cases of pop, four cases of beer, some mail, a hand-turned grinding wheel and some electrical connections for the guys at Buon Blech.

In exchange for those goodies I got a free lunch and an estimated five to six hundred pounds of various canned goods from their big pile. The entire rear section of the airplane was filled from floor to ceiling.

In addition to the concern about excess weight, the bulk of all that stuff posed another hazard. If some of the unsecured load should jiggle around and fall, it might obstruct the movement of the control stick or the rudders. The controls in the rear cockpit were interconnected with the controls in the front cockpit. If a big heavy box fell against the stick and jammed its movement in the rear cockpit, it would also jam the stick in the front cockpit.

It was a serious overload for the old girl to get it all off the ground from the short runway at Boun Blech. She made it and cleared the trees at the end of the runway. Back at Ban Me Thuot I landed carefully.

Two of our enlisted men went with me to deliver the groceries. I gave the food to Mrs. Swayne to distribute among all of the American missionaries. There were six families and several single nurses in the compound, so the six-pound tins of canned meat, the ten-pound cans of peas, etc., were divided and used economically. The missionaries appreciated the help with variety for their menu and the supplement to their budget. For some variety of our own, we kept a few cans of grapefruit juice for ourselves.

The grocery business continued anytime I was able to fit it into my work schedule. The next day, I landed at Buon Blech to haul some radios for the Green Berets to Ban Me Thuot for maintenance and repairs. I had enough room to haul more grub from the First Cav food pile. I didn't open the cases and load the plane as heavily as I did on the previous trip. There were two cases of carrots, two cases of dehydrated pea soup mix, a case of tomatoes, a case of corn, a case of grapefruit juice and a twenty-five pound tin of dehydrated milk. It was still a pretty good load.

The First Air Cavalry Grocery was an unusual situation. I was glad to take part in salvaging a lot of good food. It would have sat in the weather until the cans rusted and the food spoiled. Capt Ralph Horner and his men helped me a lot to make it happen.

Cooperation between FACs and the Green Beret Special Forces guys was a standard arrangement, so you might say, "What's new?"

Cooperation was nothing new, but the existence of The First Air Cavalry Grocery itself was truly unique. The American missionaries and I were the beneficiaries of the food bank. Of course, we FACs routinely supported the Green Berets, but I wished for a particular way to say thank you for all the groceries. I had no way to do it.

But the opportunity to repay my debt did arrive. It developed abruptly on August 29, 1966. I was controlling an air strike about twenty five kilometers from Buon Blech when my boss, LtCol George Olson, broke in on the radio, "Baron Four Two, this is Four Zero."

I responded, "Four Zero, this is Four Two. Standby. I'm in the middle of an air strike. I'll get back to you as soon as I'm finished."

Four Zero persisted, "Negative, Four Two. Break off your air strike now. Patrol Three Eight Alpha out of Buon Blech is under attack southwest of the camp. Take your fighters over there and see if you can help."

"Roger, Four Zero. I'm on my way now. My fighters have already expended everything but their guns (20 millimeter cannon). I'll see what I can do."

The three F-100s I was controlling were on the same radio frequency and heard all of the exchange between Olson and me. They anticipated my next instructions, "Foxfire flight, pull up, maintain a tally ho on me (keep me in sight) and stand by. How much fuel do you have left?"

"Roger, Baron Four Two, we have twenty five minutes before bingo fuel (minimum fuel, requiring them to depart for their home base).

"I think that may be enough. It will take me eight or ten minutes to get to the camp and a little more to locate the patrol and develop a plan of attack. I hope to have you on target within fifteen minutes. Hold above and follow me while I contact the patrol."

Then on my FM radio, "Three Eight Alpha, this is Baron Four Two."

"Baron Four Two, this is Three Eight Alpha. We need some help quick." It was the leader of the patrol, Ralph Horner, on the radio.

"Three Eight Alpha, say your location."

"We are on the trail that heads two three zero degrees from the camp. We are about three klicks southwest of camp."

"I'm not quite there yet. Are you drawing fire and can you tell where it's coming from?"

"Affirmative, we're drawing machine gun fire from only about thirty to fifty meters farther southwest on the trail. We're also getting mortar fire. I think the mortar is set up on the trail less than one klick away."

"Roger. I'm close enough now I should be able to find you if you throw a can of smoke (smoke grenade). Can you throw it <u>on the trail southwest</u> of your position?

"Affirmative, Baron. I'm throwing yellow smoke <u>southwest</u> - - <u>now</u>."

"I have your smoke. I'm going to put my rocket (white phosphorus) on your yellow smoke to give my fighters a better target. Smoke rocket - - <u>now</u>. (Pause) Confirm your location from my smoke rocket."

"Roger, Baron. That was a good hit. Your smoke rocket is right on my yellow smoke."

"OK, Partner, I have three F-100s coming in with their guns. That's all they have left. Keep your heads down."

I still hadn't seen the patrol. They were flattened out as low as possible to avoid incoming machine gun fire and the shrapnel from mortar fire being lobbed onto them.

Our communication using their yellow smoke grenade and my smoke rocket <u>had</u> to be accurate.

Back on my UHF radio, "Foxfire, do you have my smoke?"

"Affirmative, Baron."

"Foxfire, your strafing target is the trail running <u>from</u> the northeast <u>to</u> the southwest on a heading of about two three zero degrees. <u>Begin strafing *at* my smoke. Do *not* hit short of my smoke</u>. Friendly troops are near by. Foxfire Leader, strafe the center of the trail beginning at my smoke. Strafe the trail southwest for one klick. Number Two, strafe parallel to your leader, but offset ten meters to the right. Number Three, strafe parallel to your leader, but offset ten meters to the left. Three One Leader, you're cleared in hot. Number Two and Three, you're cleared to follow."

The three F-100s of Foxfire Flight did exactly what I instructed. I had them make a second run exactly like the first. They saturated the area very skillfully. Twenty millimeter cannon fire with high explosive shells is quite lethal.

"We're Winchester (out of ammunition), Baron Four Two. How did we do?"

"I can't give you a good BDA (Bomb Damage Assessment), Foxfire. The friendlies were pinned down flat and I never could see any of them. And I never saw any of the VC. If the communication and smoke markings by the friendly patrol were accurate, it should have been good. You guys did exactly what I called for. It was excellent work. See you another day."

F-100s were the most effective jet aircraft we controlled for ground support in South Vietnam. In 1965-66 many of the F-100 pilots had spent their last ten years flying that airplane. They were experienced and they were good.

Back to my FM radio, "Three Eight Alpha, Baron Four Two. My fighters used all they had left. Are you OK now?"

"I think so, Baron. I don't think we have any casualties. We'll stay down for a couple of minutes and then make it for camp. I think all the VC that are still mobile took off down the trail to the southwest."

Circumstances on that day were fortunate. The air strike we aborted was a low priority "tree splitting" mission. Nothing was lost in leaving it. Although the F-100s had already expended everything they had except for their twenty millimeter cannon, the guns were exactly what we needed to support the patrol on the ground.

The F-100s and I just happened to be in the right place at the right time. Sometimes everything works out well. Supporting the patrol from the Boun Blech Special Forces Camp was a perfect way to pay my grocery bill at the First Air Cavalry Grocery.

Later I learned the payment had been more effective than I had known at the time. I thought I'd done a good job and I knew the F-100s had done exactly what I instructed. I couldn't tell just how good it was.

It was twelve more days before I talked again with Ralph Horner. On September 10th, I landed at Boun Blech to talk to him and make another grocery run. It was our first meeting since August 29th when I put the F-100s onto the source of machine gun fire and mortars to support his patrol out in the weeds.

I said, "Ralph, I was really concerned because I thought the 20 millimeter cannon fire was awfully close to your position. How close was it?"

"They hit about ten meters from my position. Your rocket was right on my yellow smoke. The jets started strafing right on your smoke and ran southwest on the trail. You can damn well believe we kept our heads down."

"Ten meters! That's too damned close, Ralph! We could have killed you guys!"

"Yeah, it was extremely close, but we needed it that close. You put it exactly where we needed it."

"That still scares me. I thought we had more clearance than that. I asked you if you could throw smoke southwest down the trail. Can't you throw a smoke grenade farther than ten meters?"

"Why, Hell yes, I can. If I'm standing in the open with no one bothering me, I can throw one thirty or forty meters. This was different. Have <u>you</u> ever tried to throw one of those things when you're lying flat on the ground with people shooting at you?"

"Well, I'm glad you threw it at least as far as you did. I told the F-100s to start their strafing *at my smoke and *not* hit short. I'm glad they were accurate."

After we talked some more, the Proprietor of the First Air Cavalry Grocery helped me load nine more cases of food for the missionaries into my little airplane.

Chapter 38
Of Heroes, Traitors and Cowards

During the Vietnam War – In the United States and Vietnam

The topic of heroism prompts more of a discussion than you might expect. Where there are heroes there are also likely to be non-performers, detractors and even an occasional traitor.

Let's consider two specific cases which portray the antithesis of hero.

Jane Fonda was born into a wealthy, famous and privileged family. She enjoyed a large material head start in life from the beginning. Hollywood easily promoted her physical beauty and considerable acting talent into movie stardom. From that position of popularity, she launched her personal campaign against the Vietnam War and against the country which had given her fame and fortune.

She even traveled to North Vietnam to speak out against the United States. The summit of her campaign was clearly portrayed by the widely publicized photo of her sitting at the controls of a North Vietnamese gun. During that visit to North Vietnam, she participated in a staged mockery of a visit to a few American Prisoners of War.

As part of that travesty, she engaged in a "friendly handshake" with several American POWs. Certain POWs ingeniously placed tiny slips of paper bearing a name and serial number into her palm. This minimal communication enabled Fonda to inform certain dependents in the United States that their husband, father, brother, or son was alive. She refused that opportunity to be decent. Instead, she chose to personally betray those POWs face to face.

She gave the slips of paper to the camp commander, subjecting those POWs to further torture. "Hanoi Jane," as she was known, was universally disrespected and hated by all who served in the US military in the Vietnam War.

The Constitution of the United States (Article III, Section 3) states that giving aid and comfort to the enemy is treason. Hanoi Jane was the personification of treason. Jane Fonda was definitely a traitor.

Other less serious incidents of shameful conduct are not treasonous, but fall far short of faithful and honorable discharge of duty. Consider the case of Captain Jed Williamson. As a young man, Williamson won an appointment to the US Air Force Academy where he received a fine college education at taxpayer expense. Upon graduation, he was commissioned a Second Lieutenant in the Air Force. In accepting his officer's commission, he raised his right hand and swore to defend the United States and its Constitution against all enemies, foreign and domestic.

He went to pilot training and earned his wings, again at taxpayer expense. In a few years he advanced to the rank of Captain and was flying the F-100 from Clovis Air Force Base in New Mexico. When his squadron received orders and was deployed to Vietnam, Captain Williamson refused to comply with his orders. He wouldn't go. His country had supported and trained him at great expense for several years. He had sworn to defend his country, but he reneged on that promise. He turned out to be a coward.

Most folks would probably hold cowardice to be less despicable than treason. However, in a discussion of war and the people who took part in it, the label "coward" is still a very undesirable title to have hung around one's neck.

Changing from the negative to the positive, consider the word hero. The dictionary defines "hero" as "A man noted for feats of courage or nobility of purpose, esp. one who has risked or sacrificed his life: *a war hero.*" Commonly, heroes are proclaimed as such by others, not by themselves.

Chapter 26, Amazing Medal of Honor Award, describes the first two recipients of "The Highest U.S.Military Decoration" in all of the Vietnam War. The first of those two was an A-1 pilot in Pleiku, a personal friend of mine. He survived and came home to well-deserved recognition. The other was a fellow FAC in our squadron. He flew from another operating location and I saw him only occasionally. He died in the action for which he was decorated. The medal was presented posthumously to his wife. These two men were certainly war heroes. There were few other recipients of the Medal of Honor in the Vietnam War.

Our squadron of FACs, the 21st Tactical Air Support Squadron, was awarded the Presidential Unit Citation "for extraordinary gallantry in connection with military operations against an opposing armed force during the period 1 Aug 1965 to 1 Feb 1966." That was standard terminology that blanketed everyone in the squadron. It didn't single out any individuals and didn't specifically identify any heroes. It did allude to the reality that Forward Air Controllers were regularly in the middle of whatever was going on involving airplanes, air strikes and close air support of people on the ground.

The job of being a FAC was a high profile assignment, regularly fraught with great risk. The "risk of life" per the earlier definition of hero, was a routine occurrence for FACs. It was not possible to discharge the duties of controlling air strikes without accepting the risk involved. Most people who knew what FACs were and what they did felt that any FAC who performed his duties faithfully for a year and survived was a hero. Because of the nature of our job and the conditions in which we operated, Bird Dog FACs were among the most highly decorated men in the Vietnam War. Our loss rate was also high. I was a Bird Dog FAC and I was happy to come home in one piece, still of sound mind and body.

There were 58,479 men who either came home in a box under the flag of the country they served, or who were never found. Was I more of a hero than they? And how about those who did come home, but with a body or mind damaged beyond normal use? Yes, it is true, I did come home more generously decorated than most who served in Vietnam, but I just did what was my job. I am satisfied I performed my job faithfully and fully, and I am proud to have served my country well. I do proudly cherish the awards I received. I believe they were justly deserved.

This book reports many large and small acts of heroism. Do I care if you think I am a hero? No, I don't care. I have already told you, I am not.

Do I care what you think of me as a man? Yes, I care immensely.

What you think of me depends on the values and basic beliefs which govern your life. My beliefs and values are grounded in the traditional Christian and moral teachings on which this country was founded. That's what I believe and that's how I try to live. It is my sincere hope that those who know me understand what I believe. I will be honored if they report that Dale lives according to what he believes. That will make me feel I have done some things right in my lifetime.

Chapter 39
Various Viet Vignettes

Killed By His Own Airplane

The Vietnamese Air Force (VNAF) had a limited number of airplanes which they operated mostly on their own. Their questionable competence in flying and their shaky judgment in decision making were frequently evident.

Maj Nguyen Phuong Vinh, thirty-three, was a VNAF Squadron Commander with fourteen decorations including a Presidential Unit Citation from the U.S. Following a bombing mission, he had "hung ordnance" (bombs that would not properly release) on his aircraft. He landed his B-57 Canberra twin-engine jet bomber at Pleiku to have the three malfunctioning bombs removed from the airplane. After the bombs had been safely taken from the plane, he attempted to start the engines to taxi to a parking location.

The engines refused to start and the major recruited some men to push the plane. On a downhill slope, the plane rolled too fast and Vinh attempted to use the brakes. The hydraulic pressure failed and the brakes would not hold. Vinh jumped out of the plane in the dark. He apparently slipped and fell. The wheel of the plane ran over him and crushed him.

This incident was more than an unfortunate accident. It was the result of an extremely foolish decision. Immediately prior to the accident, Major Vinh refused the offer by a U.S. Air Force ground crew to move the plane using a tug. He said he didn't want any help and that <u>he</u> would have the plane moved. He paid with his life for that very bad decision.

Major Vinh was run over twice. First, he was run over by his own ego. Second, he was run over by his own airplane.

*****

F-4 Air to Ground Attack Accuracy

The F-4 was a new and expensive airplane in Vietnam in 1965-66. By a higher level directive, the F-4 pilots on their bombing runs pickled (released) their ordnance at an altitude so high it was unlikely they were going to hit the target.

That prompted FACs to sarcastically say, "The F-4 kills more VC in South Vietnam than any other airplane. When the VC see a FAC overhead, they know an air attack is imminent. They quickly run a quarter of a mile away from the target area and sit down to watch the show. A quarter of a mile from the target is where the F-4s drop their bombs. So, the F-4 kills more VC than any other airplane."

That often repeated story usually prompted a smile on the face of a FAC because it alluded to the truth regarding F-4 bombing accuracy. However, it would be grossly unfair to the F-4, and to the pilots who flew it, to let the story end there. Air-to-ground support was not the forte of the F-4. Remember, the F-4 flew air-to-air combat missions with different results.

Colonel Robin Olds, the Commander of the celebrated "Wolf Pack," was the most decorated pilot in all of the Vietnam War. He led his fighter planes in air-to-air combat against the MIGs over North Vietnam and received multiple awards of every high military decoration except the Medal of Honor. He was a famous Ace. What did he fly?

Robin Olds flew the F-4.

*****

Where Did All of That Money Go?

Hong Kong sounded like an exotic place for a man to pursue a few days of R&R. It was a modern city with everything to see and everything to do. Hong Kong was as different from Pleiku as night was from day. The city had essentially unlimited shopping opportunities to buy anything imaginable for a buddy in Vietnam or for someone important back home.

It was the potential for wonderful shopping that led to the downfall of Captain Timothy O'Donnell. "Odie" O'Donnell was an A-1 pilot headed for R&R in Hong Kong. Many of his buddies wished they could have arranged a trip to Hong Kong. They asked Odie to do some shopping for them while he was there. They loaded him up with impressive shopping lists and over three thousand dollars in cash for their purchases.

Captain O'Donnell went on R&R as scheduled and came back as scheduled. However, when he returned he had none of the merchandise on the shopping lists and no cash. Things were tense around the A-1 squadron.

On his first mission following his return from R&R, Odie rolled into a dive on the first pass of his bombing run. He continued the dive lower than normal toward the target. He went lower and lower - - too low! His wing man, following at a normal safe distance, making his own bombing run, called on the radio, "Odie, pull up." There was no response. The wing man shouted over the radio, "Pull up! Pull up!"

Odie and his A-1 went straight into the ground. It was evident Odie intended that to happen. The A-1 and the entire full load of ordnance blew up and left a large hole in the ground.

What happened to all of the money Capt O'Donnell took to Hong Kong? No one remaining in the A-1 squadron knew. Odie knew, but Odie wasn't talking.

*****

Five Thousand Combat Missions in One Picture

The Pacific Stars and Stripes newspaper had some staff people visiting Pleiku in April 1966 looking for news to put in their paper. They helped cook up a particular gathering in the Officers Club and wrote the article about it. The photo in question documented the occasion.

Meet Some Truly High-Flying Guys
By Maj Ed Swinney
Pacific Stars and Stripes Executive Officer

One night in Pleiku, a bunch of the boys were celebrating the end of the day when one of them suddenly wondered just how many combat missions had been flown by those present during the dinner hour.

He began going from guy to guy, adding up the number of missions they had flown. At first it was just an informal thing prompted by curiosity. As the total mounted, a sense of pride in accomplishment became an additional incentive to count further.

The number grew so large different guys made checks and double checks to verify the accuracy of the count. The Information Officer, LtCol Edwin Derryberry, got into the act to lend credibility to the count. He wanted to make sure no one moved around to be counted twice during the final survey.

One of the guys counting said, "You'd better check my addition, Colonel. According to my count, these twenty five guys have flown almost 5,000 missions." Derryberry checked and found the addition to be accurate. Suddenly 5,000 missions became an attainable goal.

One of the FACs said, "Somebody go get Urbanik. You'll probably have to drag him out of bed, but I think that he can put us over the 5,000 mark."

A couple of the guys went and rousted Capt Frank Urbanik out of the rack. He had an early A-1E mission the next day and was already asleep. They peeled him out of bed, poured him into a flying suit and hauled him into the bar to pose in the group photo.

The twenty six pilots together from five outfits represented a grand total of 5,032 missions. The pilots were from the 1st Air Commando Sq., the 4th ACS, the 5th ACS, the 21st Tactical Air Support Squadron and the 633rd Combat Support Group. *(I was seven months through my one year tour and contributed my current count of two hundred forty-six missions to the group's grand total.)*

39.1 Twenty six pilots and 5,032 missions in one picture. (The boss's secretary, at right, didn't count.)

The average tally was one hundred ninety-four missions per man. In a few cases, two pilots flew in the same plane on one mission. That was counted as two "pilot missions." Each pilot counted the mission. That was, however, the exception rather than the rule. Most of the missions had one pilot in one aircraft.

There was a wide spread in the number of missions flown per pilot. Capt Jim Norris flew his first combat mission on the day the photo was taken. He was in the right-hand seat of an A-1 Skyraider. Maj Bob Winger, an "old head," West Point '52, was in the left (pilot's) seat. Also on the day the photo was taken, Capt Mel Orwig, a Bird Dog FAC flying the tiny O-1E, flew his four hundred forty-ninth mission.

As luck would have it, we news folks were glad to be present when the great 5,000 mission count in Pleiku was accomplished. It was our privilege to write the story and provide the photo documentation for this assembly of warriors from the sky. We dragged our camera gear through the monsoon rains and got everyone ready to say "cheese." As we snapped the shutter, someone yelled, "Let's hear it for The Pacific Stars and Stripes."

We heard it, all right. A very loud "Booooo!" The shutter snapped, but there was no flash and, therefore, no picture. Our fancy Japanese electronic flash gun had crapped out.

But everything turned out okay.

We borrowed an old-fashioned $2 flash gun and bulb from Medal of Honor nominee, Maj Bernie Fisher. Then we successfully recorded the scene for posterity.

Posterity? Well, at least the picture filled a bare spot on the wall of the Officers Club in Pleiku.

How Bad Was Colonialism?

French control of Vietnam came to a dramatic conclusion when many of the remaining French military forces were slaughtered in the battle of Dien Bien Phu in 1953. Prior to that time, the area comprising Cambodia, Laos, North Vietnam and South Vietnam had been known as Indo China. It had been a French colony for about sixty years. French influence lasted for a long time after the battle of Dien Bien Phu, but French authority, control and management abilities were gone.

During the French colonial period, rubber and tea plantations thrived in South Vietnam, supplementing the basic rice economy. The French made money, the world markets had rubber and tea, and the local populace had jobs where there had been no jobs. Was that good or bad? Were the French helping or hurting?

By the middle 1960s, little that required "the know how to make it work" was working anymore. When the French left Vietnam, all of the knowledge about how to make things work departed with them. The Vietnamese didn't know how to do it, whatever "it" was. The tea and rubber plantations weren't adequately managed and were scarcely productive.

Was South Vietnam better off under French supervision? Was it better when workers on tea and rubber plantations were being paid and someone was maintaining flush toilets, traffic lights and other things? Or was it better now since "the damned French" had been kicked out? How bad was colonialism?

My War Injuries

Not many pilots walk into an airplane propeller and live to tell about it. I did that, and I'm still alive.

However, it didn't happen the way you might think. Late one evening, I realized I'd left my two 35 millimeter cameras hanging on a knob on the instrument panel of the O-1 I flew that afternoon. I drove a pickup truck back to the flight line to retrieve them. They were where I left them. I took them from the knob and headed back to the truck parked on the other side of the airplane. I walked briskly in the dark and made the turn around the front of the airplane.

Smash! I hit the propeller right across the top of my nose. The propeller wasn't hurt and a large band aid covered the cut on the top of my nose. The result was semi-spectacular. The colorful contrast of the bright red merthiolate against the purple bruise background on my nose was a wonderful conversation piece.

Malaria pills never caused cuts or broken bones, but they did produce other effects worthy of careful attention. There was a common saying, "There's only one thing different about Sunday in Vietnam. That's the day when my watch turns red and I take my malaria pill." Taking the malaria pill on Sunday, usually meant diarrhea on Monday. Failing to plan ahead didn't cause injury, but it could result in an unhappy memory about Monday.

There were always dangers associated with combat flying, but with respect to personal health, the year in Vietnam treated me well. One notable threat to physical welfare was the "game" of volleyball. I say "game" in quotes because those competitive contests were regularly pursued with great enthusiasm, if not reckless abandon. A particular hazard in the game of volleyball in Pleiku was the six inch drop-off at the back of the concrete slab which comprised the court.

In one game, I made a good save in the back court just as I stepped on/off the edge of the slab and sprained an ankle rather painfully. X-rays showed no fracture to the ankle, and the pulled thigh muscle and bruised butt were of only temporary significance. I got around so well on crutches that I strained the un-injured leg. I had to get some muscle relaxant for the good leg in order to sleep at night. Without flying, the four walls soon began to close in. After eight days, I was glad to get back in the air, even with a tightly wrapped sore ankle.

Not everyone was that fortunate in the volleyball battles. When I hurt my ankle, two of the spectators on the sidelines were former players. One had a plaster cast on his broken ankle and the other had a plaster cast on his broken wrist. But, what the heck! It all counted towards completion of the 365 day tour, and the calendar kept rolling with or without a cast. Who cared about a broken arm or leg?

Stronger Marriages?

A popular adage states, "Absence makes the heart grow fonder."

Does that adage allude to only the relationship between a man and a woman where a firm commitment exists? Does it relate to the fact that when large numbers of men are displaced from their previous society, prostitution sprouts en masse and flourishes at their new location?

My Pleiku roommate, Greek, a single man, couldn't wait to re-visit his new-found three dollar "sweetheart" in the government whorehouse. Meanwhile, my friend, Chaplain Brian Wesley, a married man, was presumably responsible to influence the moral character of the men he served. Did either one of those two men influence the other? Is it possible to draw a meaningful comparison between those two men in a discussion of marriage?

What effect did prolonged separation have on most marriages?

In one week in April 1966 I talked with two men who felt their marital bonds were strengthened by the forced separation of their tours in Vietnam. One of them was the A-1 intelligence officer, Cliff Taylor, who held down the back seat of my O-1 as an observer. The other one was a Gooney Bird pilot.

The weak ones re-wrote the book when it became easy to "get away with things." However, you can't escape the fact that you always have to live with yourself and with your God. You can never fool God and you can never fool yourself, no matter what you are doing or when or where you are doing it. I didn't write about it much, but it made me feel good to talk with men who had solid Christian and moral beliefs and stood by what they believed.

No Oil? - - - It'll Quit

I returned to Ban Me Thuot after a mission and stopped at our Air Force combined office and radio station. Just as I walked in the door, a call came in, "Mayday, Mayday! This is Baron Five Zero. I am about thirty five miles southwest of Ban Me Thuot. My engine is failing. I'm going to try to put it down on the highway." I rushed back to the airfield, scrambled into the air and flew to his location.

By the time I got there, an Army chopper had picked him up and was just leaving to take him to Gia Nghia, his operating location. Baron Five Zero was Maj Dave Wiley. He had just dead-sticked his O-1 onto Highway 14. He got it down without any damage about three miles on the Vietnamese side of the Cambodian border. Considering the very large trees that covered the whole area, and almost covered the highway, he did a great job.

I stayed and flew FAC cover with some fighters while the army tried to get a heliborne lift of troops into the area to secure things around the plane. Eventually, because of low fuel, I had to leave. An Army O-1, Headhunter Six Seven, attempted to coordinate the effort but couldn't handle the job. I think if I had been able to stay, I could have gotten the heliborne troops in OK. Everything was finally aborted due to weather and darkness. I ended up with eight hours five minutes flying time for the day. Five hours twenty minutes of that flying time was after 5:00 PM. That was a <u>long</u> day.

The next morning Dan Preston covered the heliborne lift of about one hundred ten troops into the area while some Army pilot fool prepared to make an attempt to fly the bird out of there. Fortunately, before he tried it, the actual condition of the engine was discovered. The engine had thrown a rod through a cylinder. He never would have made it.

Initially, Maj Wiley was the hero for making a rather amazing landing under nearly impossible conditions. He later became the goat when it was discovered the engine failure was due to the loss of all engine oil. The oil filler cap had been left off. The oil apparently siphoned out in flight causing the engine to fail. An inadequate preflight inspection was the cause of the problem. A good preflight inspection would have secured the filler cap. The oil would not have siphoned out and the engine would not have failed. All of this would never have happened. The whole thing was a fiasco that ultimately blew over rather gently. It could have ended up much worse.

Dan and I took turns covering the rest of the operation to retrieve the O-1. A Huey chopper carefully lifted it from the highway through the trees to the nearby Duc Lap outpost. A big Chinook chopper picked it up at Duc Lap and brought it to Ban Me Thuot. It had nearly no other damage and sat at Ban Me Thuot awaiting an engine change. Such things kept a FAC's life from becoming boring.

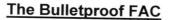

The Bulletproof FAC

How do you explain fate? Could you explain it better if it was called predestination? Would you prefer to say "it wasn't his time"? You might choose to say Captain Rod Fortner was bulletproof and let it go at that.

Rod was one of our FACs, an amiable, quiet guy. I knew him rather well. He was long and lanky and barely fit into the cockpit of the O-1. When he sat up erect, his helmet rubbed against the roof of the airplane.

One day Rod landed with two holes in his airplane. It was evident a thirty caliber round had entered through the windshield and exited through the roof of the O-1. Rod received a minor wound inflicted by plexiglass fragments from the windshield. The wound was of no real consequence. Most pilots would have thought it was "kinda neat" to have the Purple Heart awarded to Rod for a little bit of blood following the incident.

Rod's crew chief didn't let it go at that. He stretched a string between the entry hole and the exit hole in the cockpit and called Rod. "Hey, Captain, come sit in the cockpit." The crew chief's point was obvious. With Rod seated in the cockpit, the string showed the bullet should have gone through the middle of his head. "What in the Hell did you do, Captain? Did you see that round coming and duck?"

"No, I was leaning hard against the left window and looking at something on the ground when I heard the pop on the windshield and felt a sting on my face."

If Rod had been sitting upright at that moment, he would not have come home to explain what happened.

On another occasion, Rod was flying out of Kontum. He took off to the west over town in the O-1 and had engine failure. He turned around and almost made it back to the runway. He crashed beside the runway and flipped upside down. The airplane instantly became a pile of junk. Rod crawled out and walked away with bruises, still amiable, quiet and unperturbed.

One evening Fortner and I were standing on the porch of the Grand Bungalow in Ban Me Thuot shooting the breeze. I said, "Joe Milton told me you got pretty upset at some guy who ruined your maps. I wasn't sure of all the details. What happened?"

"I was flying over the Chu Pong Mountain area. The VC had some bigger guns around there and I got hit by one of them. We think it was a 12.7 millimeter (50 caliber) weapon. The bullet came up through the floor and hit my map case. It went edgewise through the slack end of my seat belt and cut it off. It shattered the stock off my 38 caliber pistol on my belt, went through my flak vest, through my survival vest and out through the roof."

"Did you feel anything?"

"Oh, I felt the bump, but that was all. It didn't touch me. And, yes, Joe told you right about my maps. The round went through the middle of my map case and ruined every damned one of my good maps. That really pissed me off. You know a FAC can't live without his maps. It took me a long time and a mile of scotch tape to make a complete new set."

Too Dangerous For A FAC

Five days of leave. Yea! Away from Vietnam for five days. Yea! My good friend, Tom Peterson, was flying C-130s out of Okinawa, and my plans to visit him and his family were confirmed.

On August 19, 1966, LtCol Olson took me from Ban Me Thuot to Cam Ranh Bay, where C-130s regularly departed for Okinawa. I checked my weapons and other FAC gear at the personal equipment section and went to the aerial port to get on a C-130 for Okinawa as a passenger.

The sergeant at the aerial port desk greeted me, "No, Captain. Passengers aren't allowed on the C-130s going to Okinawa today. It's too dangerous." He continued to inspect my leave slip which I had laid on the counter. "And even if this was a flight that took passengers, I couldn't let you on. This leave slip isn't properly completed."

His official negative reception got my goat big time. "No shit, Sarge! I'm not terribly concerned about the danger. I fly on the treetops and get shot at regularly for a living and you're telling me your blinkin' C-130 flying to Okinawa is too dangerous?! Four engines turning at 10,000 feet sounds pretty damned comfortable to me. And I really don't care a Hell of a lot about your stupid leave slip business either."

It was quickly obvious our exchange of ideas lacked mutual accord. He went to lunch, which was evidently his principal interest, and I picked up my bag and walked to the flight line where the C-130s were parked.

It didn't take me long to find a C-130 that appeared to be preparing for departure. I greeted the pilot standing in front of it. "Howdy. Your bird?"

He looked at the bag on my shoulder, "Yes, it is. You lookin' for a ride?"

"Yeah. I need to get to Okinawa to visit friends."

He looked at the pilot wings on my fatigues, "What are you flying over here?"

"The O-1."

"Bird Dog FAC?"

"Yeah. Busy job."

"I know about you guys. You do a lot of good work. I wish I could give you a lift. I'm leaving in about twenty minutes for Okinawa, but it's illegal for me to take you. Of course, if you were to walk up those stairs when I wasn't looking and find yourself a seat in the back of my plane, I wouldn't even know you were on board. I'll be looking over in this other direction for a few minutes."

We understood each other perfectly. He appreciated me and I appreciated him.

On Okinawa, it was great to spend time with Tom and Rachel and their kids. It was good to have a taste of something a lot more like home than anything in Vietnam.

After my visit with the Petersons, I found a C-130 going from Okinawa back to Cam Ranh. Once again, I stowed myself away as an illegal passenger.

Dangerous? It didn't seem like it to me. I slept soundly all the way home.

Chapter 40
Happy Homecoming

September 24, 1966 – Saigon and the United States of America.

$\mathbf{M}$y last mission in Vietnam was to haul myself and my bags from Ban Me Thuot to Tan Son Nhut airbase in Saigon. I flew O-1 #632 one way and left it for Dan Preston, returning from R&R in Hawaii. Dan would fly it back to Ban Me Thuot.

Farewell, FAC business! Farewell Vietnam! I was done!

Doc Dawkins, my old boss, had an extra bunk in his 10ft x10ft room. It even had air conditioning! It was good to see Doc and nice to have a good place to sleep.

As the year drew near its close, Nancy and I were two freight trains of love and anticipation running at full steam toward each other on a single track. We were both eager for the head on crash. My letters told how anxious I was to see her. It was nearly my last letter from Vietnam that said, in part …

My Dearest of all Things,

Nine days, Sweetheart! It seems it will never pass! I love you indescribably. I'm extremely anxious just to be in your presence and experience the nearness of you.

I'm looking forward to the many things we can do in Denver for several days, but even more so, I'm looking forward to how many of those things never get done because we're busy loving up a storm all by ourselves for sooo long!! Only <u>you</u> produce in me that "nothing in the whole world could possibly be wrong right now" feeling.

Sometimes I feel I <u>cannot</u> wait another nine days to have you in my arms; but I must. There is no alternative. I can't believe how wonderful it will be just to <u>see</u> you, to have you run into my arms and kiss me in such a manner there is no doubt in the minds of spectators how we feel about each other. Let them stare. They will be jealous, or at least admiring, as they watch.

I want to kiss you and hug you close to me in front of the crowd. I may jump up on my suitcase in the Denver airport and shout, "Look, everyone! This is the most wonderful woman in the whole world, and she's <u>mine</u>, all mine! You may watch while I taste her sweet lips again. And I'm the luckiest and happiest man in the world, because she cares, and because she loves me!"

And then I will take you away--all alone--to myself!

I love you, Nancy. Dale.

Flight 244 departed at 6:00 A.M on September 24, 1966. I was on a Flying Tiger Airlines DC 8 on my way home to the most wonderful woman on the face of God's green earth.

Our flight spent two hours on the ground at Yokota, Japan for fuel and then continued to Travis Air Force Base in California. We arrived at 7:30 AM, about fourteen and one half hours after departing Saigon. When the wheels touched the runway at Travis, cheers erupted from the military members returning from Vietnam to the United States. "This is my own, my native land." Yes, it was <u>good</u> to be back in my own country.

Due to crossing the International Date Line, we arrived only shortly after we left Saigon. It made for "quick travel" and a long day for travelers. A bus took me to San Francisco and a Boeing 727 brought me to Stapleton airport in Denver, where Nancy met me. The year's separation was over!

We spent two days pleasure riding through familiar places in the Denver area. We visited a few old friends and enjoyed dinner at a favorite place from college days. We bought tickets for our four children and their Grandma Garfield to fly from Cheyenne to Denver. We met them for a special day at the zoo and then drove back home to Cheyenne.

Our family was all together again. I was back in the country that I loved. It was time to look forward to my next US Air Force assignment.

40.1 – Medals are nice to have. My real prize stands beside me.

40.2 – A good family is more valuable than the Distinguished Flying Cross any day.

Epilogue

After spending a year controlling air strikes as a Forward Air Controller, my personal "hands on" involvement in the Vietnam War was over. The war, however, was roaring along at full speed when I returned home. The United States continued to be deeply involved.

The United States Air Force Academy needed recently returned pilots who had "been there and done it" in Vietnam to instruct cadets. I taught Military Training to outstanding future officers at the Academy for four years. It was a privilege to work with the cream of the crop. The classroom work was good. Additional volunteer duty with the cadets outside the classroom was better.

I was the Officer Representative (Super Housemother) for the USAF Academy intercollegiate pistol team. For "away" matches I also flew the airplane to take the team to West Point (Army), Annapolis (Navy) and other competing colleges. It was good training for the cadets and wonderful experience for me. During the time I was their "Officer Rep," not coach, the pistol team was the national NCAA champion for three straight years.

The William H. Hickox Memorial DeMolay Club at the Academy provided continued leadership and character development for cadets who were DeMolay chapter members prior to coming to the Academy. I was the Officer Representative for the club. We traveled Colorado and New Mexico for the cadets to perform public installation ceremonies of officers in local DeMolay chapters. The precise formal ceremonies and subsequent demeanor of the cadets in local communities gave a marvelous presentation of the Academy to the general public.

The club members frequently overloaded our family living quarters on the Academy grounds for casual social occasions. The cadets loved "Mom Amend," and our children benefitted from the informal association with the cadets. We developed lasting friendships with the DeMolay cadets.

I completed my Air Force career at Kirtland Air Force Base in Albuquerque, New Mexico. My job assignments at Kirtland were back in engineering. I worked in the Plans and Programs Office of the Air Force Special Weapons Center and later in the Directorate of Aerospace Studies. In 1979, after twenty four years in the blue uniform, I retired from the United States Air Force as a Lieutenant Colonel.

When I retired from the Air Force, our four children were established in schools. Moving the household would have been disruptive for them and we liked where we were. We stayed in Albuquerque.

My Air Force pension was adequate to "buy the beans and pay the rent" if we sat in one place and did nothing else. We had greater ambitions. For additional money to educate the kids and travel the country in our "slow boat to somewhere" motor home, we pursued many small independent real estate ventures. We bought, painted up, fixed up and re-sold many houses. It was hard work, but it accomplished what we needed.

Our family is the most important part of our lives. All four of our children, their spouses and our eight grandchildren live within thirty minutes of our home. We see them each Sunday in church and on many other occasions. We are most fortunate.

Much of my life revolves around five "G"s: Grandkids, Gardening, Glads, Golf and General Good fitness.

One of our Grandkids is always doing something we are invited to attend. We try to be there. It's a privilege.

I am an avid Gardener. I define a good neighbor as one who says "yes" when I ask if she can use another bunch of the latest produce in season.

Following my father's legacy, I grow Gladioli for our church. The bouquets of flowers are delivered to those in hospitals and shut-ins.

I love the game of Golf, pounding the ground with expensive sticks.

I am a strong advocate for maintaining General Good physical fitness. On my seventy-fifth birthday, Nancy followed my bicycle and drove the "tail gunner" vehicle, protecting me from going home on some Minnesota flatlander's front bumper. We posed together at the top of Independence Pass in Colorado at 12,095 feet.

There's one more G. I believe in God. I am humbled by His Greatness, His Goodness and His Generosity.

I am Grateful.

Made it to the top.

The partnership endures.

Glossary

A-1	Douglas A-1 Skyraider. Korean War vintage prop fighter bomber capable of carrying large ordnance loads with long loiter time. Considered obsolete by 1950, it was favored by FACs as the best strike aircraft for missions in South Vietnam.
A-4	Skyhawk. A single seat light attack jet aircraft flown over South Vietnam from Navy carriers.
Abort	To suddenly stop or cancel a flight or mission.
AK-47	The standard automatic assault weapon used by North Vietnamese and Viet Cong soldiers. It fired a 7.62 mm bullet and was easy to maintain and use.
ALO	Air Liaison Officer. Responsible for air operations within his Corps area. II Corps FACs were operationally responsible to the II Corps ALO.
ARVN	Army of the Republic of Vietnam. (South Vietnam). Pronounced ar-vun.
B-57	Canberra. Twin engine jet bomber.
Baron	The call sign of all II Corps FACs. The name Baron used with a number identified a particular FAC. No one else used that call sign.
BDA	Bomb damage assessment. The reported results of air strikes as assessed by the FAC or ground troops.
Bingo fuel	Minimum fuel required for safe return to base.

C-47	Old twin engine prop driven transport with many names. Gooney Bird. Spooky.
C-130	Hercules. Four engine turbo-prop transport.
C&MA	Christian and Missionary Alliance. The U.S. denomination sponsoring missionaries in Pleiku and Ban Me Thuot.
Call sign	The identifying words and numbers assigned to an aircraft for the purpose of radio communications.
Charlie	Viet Cong, VC.
Corps	One of four geographical sub-divisions of South Vietnam, numbered from north to south, I, II, III, and IV. II Corps was spoken Two Corps.
DASC	Direct Air Support Center. II DASC, pronounced two dask, was the center for II Corps.
F-100	Super Saber. 1950s jet fighter.
F-105	Thunderchief. Jet fighter bomber. Known as the Thud for extreme losses bombing North Vietnam.
F-4	Phantom. Jet fighter bomber. New in Vietnam in 1965-66.
FAC	Forward Air Controller. Pronounced fack. The pilot who controls attacking strike aircraft engaged in close air support of friendly troops or against other targets.
FM	Frequency modulation. The radio band used by Army units and by FACs when talking to ground troops.
FNG	Fuckin' New Guy. Derogatory reference for a new military arrival in Vietnam.

Gook   Vietnamese soldier.

Green Beret   US Army Special Forces soldier.

HE   High explosive.

Ho Chi
Minh Trail   Trails used by the North Vietnamese to move men and supplies down through Laos and Cambodia into South Vietnam.

Jarai   The largest Montagnard tribe.

KBA   Killed by air. By either fixed-wing aircraft or helicopter.

KIA   Killed in action.

Klick   Kilometer, one thousand meters. Approximately 0.62 statute miles. A standard unit of measurement on tactical maps.

Knot   One nautical mile per hour. Used to measure airspeed of airplanes. Equal to 1.15 statute miles per hour.

LZ   Landing zone for helicopters.

MACV   Military Assistance Command Vietnam. Pronounced mack-vee.

May Day   International distress signal calling for help.

Montagnard Indigenous ethnic minority of the Central Highlands. Pronounced mon-tan-yard.

Napalm   Incendiary weapon made of jellied gasoline. Usually air-delivered against personnel.

NVA   North Vietnamese Army. Communist. Also PAVN, Peoples Army of Vietnam.

O-1	Small, slow, light aircraft flown by FACs. A modified Cessna. Known as the L-19 in the Korean War.
PAVN	Peoples Army of Vietnam. Communist. Also NVA, North Vietnamese Army. Pronounced pav-en.
POW	Prisoner of war.
PSP	Pierced steel planking. Interconnecting metal planks which can be used to quickly construct a runway.
Punji stake	Sharpened stakes of bamboo placed in the ground by the thousands around Special Forces Camps to protect against enemy attack on foot.
R&R	Rest and recreation away from the war.
Raday	The second largest Montagnard tribe.
Round-eye	American.
Slope	Vietnamese person.
U-10	Helio Super Courier. Bullshit Bomber.
UHF	Ultra high frequency . The radio band used by most military aircraft.
VC	Viet Cong. Communist South Vietnamese forces. VC could be fulltime or sometime soldiers. Distinguishable from the fulltime soldiers of the NVA.
VHF	Very high frequency. The radio band used by some military aircraft.
VNAF	Vietnamese Air Force. Pronounced vee-naf.

VR   Visual reconnaissance. FACs spent a major part of their time in aerial VR to locate or confirm targets.

WIA   Wounded in action.

Yard   Montagnard.

3507465

Made in the USA